Key Words in Religion,

M000205250

'From *The Passion of the Christ* to the presumed "clash of civilizations", religion's role in culture is increasingly contested and mediated. *Key Words in Religion, Media, and Culture* is a welcome and interdisciplinary contribution that maps the territory for those who aim to make sense of it all. Highlighting the important concepts guiding state-of-the-art research into religion, media, and culture, this book is bound to become an important and frequently consulted resource among scholars both seasoned and new to the field.'

> **Lynn Schofield Clark**, author of *From Angels to Aliens: Teenagers, the Media, and the Supernatural* and editor of *Religion, Media, and the Marketplace*

'David Morgan has assembled here a fine team of scholars to prove beyond a doubt that the intersections of religion, media, and culture constitute one of the most stimulating fields of inquiry around today. Definitions of religion and culture require renewed and robust readings in light of newer forms of (mass) mediation, and the contributors deliver the goods. This highly useful and theoretically sophisticated text will likely assume "ritual" status in this emergent field.'

> **Rosalind I. J. Hackett**, Distinguished Professor in the Humanities and Professor of Religious Studies, University of Tennessee, USA

'This volume is a major intervention in the literature on religion, media and culture. Drawing together leading international scholars, it offers a conceptual map of the field to which students, teachers and researchers will refer for many years to come. The publication of *Key Words in Religion, Media and Culture* is a significant moment in the formation of this area of study, and sets a standard for cross-disciplinary collaboration and theoretical and methodological sophistication for future work in this area to follow.'

> **Gordon Lynch**, Professor in the Sociology of Religion, Birkbeck College, University of London, UK

'This book offers a range of refreshing essays on the relationships between media and religion. Its selected key words open doors to understanding contemporary society. The cultural perspectives on mediation and religious practices give some illuminating and surprising analyses.'

> **Knut Lundby**, University of Oslo, Norway

David Morgan is Professor of Religion at Duke University, USA. Author of several books, including *Visual Piety* (1998) and *The Lure of Images* (Routledge, 2007), he is also co-editor of the journal *Material Religion*.

Key Words in Religion, Media and Culture

Edited by

David Morgan

Routledge
Taylor & Francis Group

NEW YORK AND LONDON

First published in the USA and Canada 2008
by Routledge
270 Madison Ave, New York, NY 10016

Simultaneously published in the UK
by Routledge
2 Park Square, Milton Park, Abingdon, Oxon OX14 4RN

*Routledge is an imprint of the Taylor & Francis Group,
an informa business*

Typeset in Sabon by
HWA Text and Data Management, Tunbridge Wells
Printed and bound in Great Britain by
TJ International Ltd, Padstow, Cornwall

British Library Cataloguing in Publication Data
A catalogue record for this book is available from the British
Library

Library of Congress Cataloging-in-Publication Data
Key words in religion, media, and culture / edited by
David Morgan.
p. cm.
Includes bibliographical references and index.
1. Religion and culture. 2. Mass media in religion.
3. Mass media–Religious aspects. I. Morgan, David, 1957–
BL65.C8K49 2008
201'.7–dc22   2008002209

ISBN10: 0–415–44862–X (hbk)
ISBN10: 0–415–44863–8 (pbk)
ISBN10: 0–203–89407–3 (ebk)

ISBN13: 978–0–415–44862–8 (hbk)
ISBN13: 978–0–415–44863–5 (pbk)
ISBN13: 978–0–203–89407–1 (ebk)

Contents

Contributors

Editor

David Morgan is Professor of religion at Duke University and author of several books, including *Visual Piety* (1998), *The Sacred Gaze* (2005), and *The Lure of Images* (2007). He was a member and chairperson of the International Study Commission on Religion, Media, and Culture. Morgan currently coedits the Routledge book series "Media, Religion, and Culture" and is cofounder and coeditor of the journal *Material Religion*.

Contributors

J. Kwabena Asamoah-Gyadu is Associate Professor of contemporary African Christianity and religion and media at the Trinity Theological Seminary, Legon, Accra, Ghana. He was a member of the International Study Commission on Media, Religion, and Culture, has been a visiting scholar at Harvard University, and currently edits the *Trinity Journal of Church and Theology*. In addition to having written his book *African Charismatics* (2005), he has published widely on Christianity and media in contemporary Africa.

David Chidester is Professor of religious studies and director of the Institute for Comparative Religion in Southern Africa at the University of Cape Town. His books include *Salvation and Suicide: Jim Jones, the People's Temple, and Jonestown* (1988; revised edition, 2003); *Savage Systems: Colonialism and Comparative Religion in Southern Africa* (1996); *Christianity: A Global History* (2000); *Nelson Mandela: In His Own Words* (2004); and *Authentic Fakes: Religion and American Popular Culture* (2005).

Isabel Hofmeyr is Professor of African literature at the University of the Witwatersrand in Johannesburg, South Africa. She has published widely on South African literature, postcolonial studies, and transnationalism. Her award-winning book, *The Portable Bunyan: A Transnational History of The Pilgrim's Progress*, appeared in 2004.

Stewart M. Hoover is an internationally known scholar of media and religion and media audiences. He is a Professor of media studies and religious studies at the University of Colorado in the United States and directs the Center for Media, Religion, and Culture there. He is coeditor of a book series on media and religion published by Routledge and is author, coauthor, or editor of eight books, most recently *Religion in the Media Age* (2006).

Peter Horsfield is Associate Professor and director of Learning and Teaching at the School of Applied Communication at RMIT University in Melbourne. He was a member of the International Study Commission on Media Religion and Culture and is Chair of the Porticus Fellowship Program for Research in Media Religion and Culture. He has published widely in media and religion and most recently was coeditor of *Belief in Media: Cultural Perspectives on Media and Christianity* (2005).

Pamela E. Klassen is Associate Professor in the Department and Centre for the Study of Religion at the University of Toronto, where she also directs the Religion and the Public Sphere Initiative. She is the author of *Blessed Events: Religion and Home Birth in America* (2001) and is completing a book on Christianity, medicine, and practices of "mediation" entitled *Healing Christians*, which is forthcoming from University of California Press.

Birgit Meyer is Professor of cultural anthropology at the Department of Social and Cultural Anthropology at the Vrije Universiteit, Amsterdam. Her publications include *Translating the Devil: Religion and Modernity Among the Ewe in Ghana* (1999); *Globalization and Identity: Dialectics of Flow and Closure* (edited with Peter Geschiere, 1999); *Magic and Modernity: Interfaces of Revelation and Concealment* (edited with Peter Pels 2003); and *Religion, Media and the Public Sphere* (edited with Annelies Moors, 2006). She is coeditor of *Material Religion*.

Jolyon Mitchell is Senior Lecturer at New College, Edinburgh University and a former BBC World Service producer. He helped to create such programs as "Garrison Keillor's Radio Preachers" (1994) and an Omnibus documentary on West African video film (2002). He is author of *Visually Speaking* (1999) and *Media Violence and Christian Ethics* (2007); coeditor of *Mediating*

Religion (2003) and *The Religion and Film Reader* (2007); and coeditor of the Routledge book series on Media, Religion, and Culture.

Sarah M. Pike is Professor of religious studies at California State University, Chico, where she teaches courses on American religions. Pike is the author of *Earthly Bodies, Magical Selves: Contemporary Pagans and the Search for Community* (2001) and *New Age and Neopagan Religions in America* (2004) and is currently writing a book about religion and youth culture. She chairs the Committee for the Public Understanding of Religion of the American Academy of Religion and is on the Academy's board of directors.

Dorothea E. Schulz teaches in the department of religious studies, Indiana University. She received her Ph.D. in sociocultural anthropology from Yale University and her *Habilitation* from the Free University, Berlin. Her publications center on Islam in Africa, the anthropology of religion, gender studies, media studies, and the anthropology of the state. Her recent work is on Islamic revivalist movements in Mali that rely on various media technologies to promote a relatively new conception of publicly enacted religiosity.

Joyce Smith is Associate Professor in Ryerson University's School of Journalism, where she directs the online journalism program. In addition to studying the representation of religion in Canadian, South African, and American news sources, she has written on religion in popular media, including a study of American Christian leaders (*The Ministry and the Message*, 2003). She was an editor with the globeandmail.com and a founding member of the Centre for Faith and the Media.

Jeremy Stolow teaches media history in the Department of Communication Studies, Concordia University, Montreal, Canada, and is also an associate member of the Center for Religion and Media (New York University) and the Centre de recherche sur l'intermedialité (Université de Montréal). His forthcoming book, *Orthodox By Design*, deals with contemporary Orthodox Jewish print culture in transnational perspective. He is currently researching the relationship between spiritualism and the advent of electrically mediated technologies in the nineteenth-century Atlantic world.

Johanna Sumiala is Research Fellow at the Academy of Finland/University of Helsinki and holds a Ph.D. in media studies. Author of numerous articles, she is also a coeditor of and contributor to such books as *Implications of the Sacred* (2006) and *Images and Communities* (2007). She is currently a national cocoordinator of the Nordic Research Network on the Mediatization of Religion and Culture.

Jojada Verrips is Emeritus Professor of European anthropology at the University of Amsterdam. He has written and edited a number of books in the Dutch language and is currently working on a book entitled *The Wild (in the) West*. His main interests are anthropology and religion, anthropology and (abject) art, aisthesis or aesthetics as an embodied and embedded phenomenon, anthropology of the senses, blasphemy, cannibalism in the Western world, maritime anthropology, vandalism, and violence.

Angela Zito, Associate Professor of anthropology and religious studies at New York University, cofounded and codirects the Center for Religion and Media there. She specializes in Chinese culture and history, especially issues of embodiment and practice. She has written *Of Body and Brush: Grand Sacrifice as Text/Performance in 18th-century China* (1997) and coedited *Body, Subject and Power in China* (1994). She is currently making a documentary film on calligraphy as self-cultivation in public in Beijing.

Preface

All books describing themselves as lexicons of key words must trace their origins back to Raymond Williams's exceptional book, *Keywords: A Vocabulary of Culture and Society*, the first edition of which appeared in 1976. This book is no exception, for at least two reasons. First, key words are words that do important cultural work. Not every word has done so. One of these forms of work is to limn and organize a new structure of consciousness, a pervasive and shared way of thinking and feeling. Williams was drawn to a growing number of words that captured pivotal changes in English following the Second World War. For him, compiling a vocabulary of keywords was not a philological exercise akin to the production and raison d'être of the *Oxford English Dictionary*. It was the purpose of certain old words and new in his own historical moment that mattered to Williams. *Key Words in Religion, Media and Culture* seeks to capture an important and recent turn in the social analysis, historical study, and humanistic interpretation of religion as media.

Second, Williams's approach to the problem is also echoed here. He began by assembling a list of words that adhered in a cluster from which his project gradually expanded to a much larger group of words. In the present case, that core cluster consists of three words: religion, media, and culture. But the rest of the words were anything but an afterthought. Saying what religion, media, and culture have come to mean in the last two or three decades among scholars deeply engaged in studying the religious significance of media as practices, artifacts, and the product of various audiences, publics, and institutions has not only been the impulse behind this book but—more important—the dominant activity of a worldwide number of writers, scholars, and media practitioners. In other words, the rest of the terms considered here have served scholars as a primary means of defining the core terminology of media, religion, and culture.

A number of volumes have been inspired by Williams's *Keywords*. They may be said to form a genre that consists of assembling critical terms that serve as the primary conceptual tools of an entire discourse. Key words are the nomenclature that comprise a field of inquiry, which is significant both because it is what draws scholars together into an extended community of interpretation and because it helps thematize what it is that draws them together. Key words communalize knowledge making and direct inquiry by freeing up thought from older discursive formations in order to pursue new lines of investigation that respond to new social conditions. That is not all key words do. They also inform the most basic structures of study absorbed by students and they serve as the medium in which writers and teachers may strive for a degree of reflexivity that will endow their work with critical engagement in the entire history of thought and practice that constitutes the knowledge of their particular field.

A look at the cover of this book will signal yet another aspect of key words as tools. When made the object of critical and historically minded reflection, a field's defining nomenclature draws it beyond the rarefied precinct of words uttered in academic halls into the much livelier spaces of the worlds of things that scholarship endeavors to study. One place that words go is the past, largely because a word is the intersection of present need and inherited use. Words may be described as the collision between what people have thought and done long ago and what they are struggling to accomplish or enjoy in the present. This means that words are much more than the technical instruments of scholarly discourse. They are densely storied, heavily freighted semantic habits that make the universe as familiar, small and short-lived as we are. Words are social events, institutional devices, among the most powerful media of social life. Words are also inextricably entangled with things, bodies, feelings, and public practices and rituals. The key words assembled and explicated here are no exception. More than merely ideas, and never Platonic essences located in the mind of a philosopher's god, words emerge from and return to the dense avenues of human sociality, the dark histories of power, the shattered places of lost hopes. One of the most important developments in the recent study of religion has been the compelling assumption that religion is productively understood as a robustly embodied, diversely mediated set of practices. Moreover, these practices are never stable and they are always contested. The study of the key words gathered here should be measured against these fundamental insights, which have been vigorously pressed over the last two or three decades by anthropologists, sociologists, historians, and scholars of material and visual culture.

The list of critical terms selected and explicated in this book will signal many things to readers. It will certainly indicate that the study of media and religion is broadly interdisciplinary. Before the 1980s, the field, if it even was one, was largely the domain of historians of Christianity, Christian communicators, and seminary professors, geared toward the improvement of church communication policy and practice, education, evangelism, and preaching. Matters have changed since then. Though religious organizations are even more engaged by the study of media, a wide range of academic scholarship has explored the subject. Anthropology, cultural studies, media studies, visual and material culture, film studies, and religious studies are among the next generation of disciplines drawn to the study of media and religion. The new paradigm that this book articulates has described itself under a triad of terms: religion, media, and culture. What the third term means will be considered in detail in the Introduction here and in several of the Key Word essays. For the time being, it is important to say that the religion, media, and culture approach is not limited to the tendency to focus on journalism and communication policy, which is the legacy of the older practice. The aim here is not to dismiss or ignore them but to expand the remit and to change some key assumptions about what "religion" and "media" are in academic study. The difference turns on the third term, *culture*. The dominant approach taken here is constructivist in nature.

The Culturalist turn that began in the 1970s has led scholars to frame the study of religion and media in terms that decenter religion and media from traditional, institutionally dominated definitions, refocusing on the intersection of institutions, authorities, and production with popular practices, circulation, and reception. The intent has been to bring the study of religion and media into productive conversation with the study of culture—indeed, to see both religion and media as culture, or even religion as mediation. This has meant questioning the uniform treatment of media as technologies controlled by cultural producers. In that paradigm, media are instruments for converting ideas or intentions into mass-produced forms for mass dissemination. This assumption regards media as forms of representation, ways of coding or symbolizing aims for the purpose of broadcasting them. It is patterned on an anachronistic view of the human person as a soul or anima generating ideas, a self-moving force that instrumentalizes the world around it for the sake of communicating its will or intentions. The result is a dualist split between form and content, soul and body that regards culture as a symbol system manipulated by producers or communicators. The direction of communication is fundamentally unilateral, a transmission from sender to receiver. Culture is the set of symbols that register concepts, ideas or feelings generating from the interior of human beings.

Such a conceptualization of culture fails to grasp its dynamic, dialectical character, the host of discontinuities, multiplicities, impurities, paradoxes, and contradictions that actually comprise the life-worlds of everyday existence. Moreover, culture is not simply the apparatus that builds people's worlds for them, as the expression of their desires, or the desires of the technocratic state or the military-industrial complex or global corporate capitalism. Culture is people constructing their lives from what these larger entities provide but also resisting them, changing them, hating, regulating, and abetting them all at once. Media are not simply information delivery or the representation or misrepresentation of reality, that is, the tools for consumers and believers to acquire or believe what they want. Media of all kinds—newspapers and the evening news but also toys, advertisements, food, clothing, photographs, houses, and music—are constitutive ingredients in the social construction of reality. People build their worlds, and their worlds build them. It is this dialectical world-and-self-construction that the Culturalist paradigm, described by the key words assembled here, means by the term *mediation*. To get at this elusive, even magical power of human activity, scholars of media need to wrestle with culture. But that is not all. One of the principal and most widely influential cultural activities of human beings may be designated by the term *religion*. Belief, understood in the broadest manner—as a domain of practice no less than creed—is a powerful glue holding together the worlds in which people live, which they build and maintain in order that it may bolster and nurture them. How that happens, how religion is mediation, constitutes the guiding question of the study of religion, media, and culture.

Not everyone is likely to be content with this formulation because it marks the place where one discipline trails off into another, where communication studies becomes anthropology or religious studies or the investigation of visual culture. But the liminal character of the interdisciplinary study of religion, media, and culture at work in the essays of this book is not intended as normative. It is aimed instead at defining an intersection of inquiry that has something vital to offer a more robust understanding of religion and media, from whatever direction scholars conduct their work.

* * * * *

One striking difference between this book and Williams's *Keywords* is that what he was able to do by himself, this book undertakes only as a collaborative effort among fifteen accomplished scholars. It was a communal effort and one that I intend will document by its very nature the community of interpretation that has given rise to the turn in thinking that occasions the book. In addition to the authors represented here by their fine work, I acknowledge the larger dimensions of debt and gratitude on which the book rests. The International Study Commission on Media, Religion, and Culture (1996–2005), founded by the intellectual partnership of Adán Medrano and Stewart Hoover, did much to advance the intellectual agenda of the humanistic study of religion and media, which this book seeks to register. As a member of the group, I learned more than I can reckon traveling and collaborating with them. Several of its members are among the authors here.

Second, it is important to mention a list of significant scholars who are not among the authors, though they might easily have been, and whose works are repeatedly referenced: Lynn Schofield Clark, Diane Winston, Michele Rosenthal, Faye Ginsburg, Mary Hess, Gordon Lynch, Heather Hendershot, Heidi Campbell, Charles Hirschkind, Brian Larkin, Mia Lövheim, Alf Linderman, Knut Lundby, Christopher Parr, Asonseh Ukah, Robert White, Rosalind Hackett, Sean McCloud, Brent Plate, and Brad Verter. I have learned from each of them and enjoyed their company at many conferences around the world. Several of these colleagues have been actively involved in the "Religion, Culture, and Communication" group at the American Academy of Religion, which is yet another index of the turn documented in this book. Others among them, including several of the authors in this volume, have participated in the Media Religion Culture Project's annual "Global Seminars." A large and very international group of scholars brought together over several years by the entrepreneurial research and leadership of Birgit Meyer represents yet another aspect of the intellectual community that has formed around the study of religion and media. And last it is important to mention the biennial Conference on Media, Religion, and Culture, spearheaded by Stewart Hoover, as it marks perhaps the largest circle of this concentric pattern of associations. I am indebted to all of them for many years of lively and collegial conversations on the field of religion and media.

Introduction

Religion, media, culture: the shape of the field

David Morgan

In recent years, mediation has come to be studied as a range of religious practices in different cultural settings and historical periods around the world. The assumption at work in social and cultural criticism, theology, and mass communication studies before the 1990s was often either that the study of mass media need not include any attention to religion or that mass media compromised, diluted, or eviscerated religious belief. In the United States, the realization that religion is indeed a mass-mediated phenomenon whose social agency and historical significance need to be scrutinized emerged during the 1970s and 1980s under two broad rubrics: the history of the book and print culture and the study of popular culture and religion.[1] There were several noteworthy exceptions to this, especially in the study of visual mass media and religion (Lange 1974; Milspaw 1986; Goethals 1990). But more generally, interest in popular religious media in the United States was bolstered by the rise of the religious Right as a political force that made aggressive use of media in the political sphere.[2] Though work before that time had certainly considered the meaning and effect of media among religious audiences, much of it was theological reflection or investigation conducted by religious researchers for use by clergy and religious organizations (Parker et al. 1955; Marty 1961; Kuhns 1969; Horsfield 1984; Fore 1987).

In Europe, scholars such as Raymond Williams, Stuart Hall, Roland Barthes, Guy Debord, and Jean Baudrillard advanced the study of popular media by developing sophisticated cultural theories that were widely influential.[3] But in large part because of the prevailing secularist sensibility of cultural studies, the study of religion and media in Europe was intermittent during the 1980s, not gathering great attention until the next decade. There were, however, studies of great relevance, such as Benedict Anderson's epochal discussion of nationalism (1983; rev. ed., 1991), which framed print and popular culture as the means of imagining national community; and Colin Campbell's grounding of consumerism in Romantic yearning (1987), which has encouraged scholars to look for religious legacies in consumption and the marketplace (Anderson 1991; Campbell 1987).

Media scholarship over the second half of the twentieth century relied heavily on the theoretical as well as substantive fieldwork by leading scholars in many other countries, including Latin America, Israel, Canada, and Australia. Canadians Harold Innis and Marshall McLuhan dominated the field during the 1950s and 1960s (Innis 1950, 1951; McLuhan 1964). Whereas prominent accounts of mass media such as those advanced by the Frankfurt School at one end of the political spectrum or the critical pronouncements of conservatives such as Ernst van den Haag, at the other, regarded mass media as a menace to democracy, McLuhan celebrated new media as progressive steps in the liberation of consciousness. New media disrupted existing forms of spatial and bureaucratic organization, serving to revolutionize the storage and use of information as well as the social arrangements that invested media with power. Though he was widely criticized for promoting a technologically determinist understanding of media, McLuhan infused new energy in the historical imagination of the social impact of media. If he has not been followed by a school or movement, his influence is nevertheless widely discernible, especially as regards the bedazzlement of media scholars by new media and the tendency to celebrate them for their expansion of personal agency, a process regarded by McLuhan and many since as inherently secularizing. One of the exceptions to this generalization is the work of the Latin American scholar, Jesús Martin-Barbero, which will be discussed below (Martín-Barbero 1987, 1993).

From the 1990s to the present, the study of religion and media in Europe, North and South America, Asia, and Africa has steadily increased.[4] Since the mid-1990s, an academic book series, an international journal, and a series of biennial international conferences have fueled interest and served as important forums for continued research and discussion.[5] A number of useful collections of essays of diverse subjects have appeared since the mid-1990s under the general rubric of "media and religion," serving especially to advance theoretical and methodological considerations of the field.[6] In addition to these, other recent collections of historical studies and influential monographs and essays have contributed to the preliminary formation of media and religion as an academic field of research.

The culturalist approach

If a single moment in scholarship can be said to have birthed a new way of thinking about the relationship between communication and religion, it may be an essay published in 1975 by James W. Carey, "A Cultural Approach to Communication" (Carey 1975, 1989). Here Carey differentiated two alternative conceptions of communication, the "transmission" and the "ritual" views, and pointed out that each was rooted in religious origins. He urged scholars to attend to the latter model as the "cultural approach to communication" because it regarded the purpose of communication "not in the transmission of intelligent information but in the construction and maintenance of an ordered, meaningful cultural world that can serve as a control and container for human action" (Carey 1989: 18–19). This cultural view of communication deeply informs the present book and the scholarly efforts in which its essays broadly participate.[7]

The role of media as practices and forms of meaning making in the construction of a meaningful world characterizes much of the interest of scholars engaged in the study of religious uses of media over the last three decades. By contrast, the transmission model tends to regard human beings as passive receivers of media influences, which direct them to vote, consume, or behave as the transmitter of the media wishes. Scholarship that has stressed this model when studying religion has often been the work of those with ties to religious organizations, which have wanted to know better how to use media to convey religious messages or affect the behavior of believers. But the cultural and humanistic side of the study of media does not wish to lose sight of the human being as a moral agent, as a being capable of choice and concerted effort directed by ideals, reason, feelings, and imagination. To be sure, all of these unfold within environments of strongly assertive, sometimes quite coercive social forces that often appear to leave little room for choice or chance. However, many scholars have noted the place for resistance and its power to carve out alternative or countercultural forms of identity in the popular reception of media.[8] The cultural approach to the study of the religious significance of media and mediated practices therefore proceeds without prescriptive assumptions about what religion properly is or how people ought to use or interpret media.

In an essay published in 1980, Stuart Hall offered a reflection on the historiography of cultural studies, focusing on the work of Raymond Williams, in which he found formulated two different emphases in the definition of culture (Hall 1980). The first was "the sum of the available descriptions through which societies make sense of and reflect [on] their common experiences" (1980: 59). The second, Hall summarized as "those patterns of organization, those characteristic forms of human energy which can be discovered as revealing themselves…within or underlying all social practices" (60). For Hall, cultural studies does right to engage both emphases in "the dialectic between social being and social consciousness" (63). Culture, in other words, is both: the meanings that are embodied in the practices. Or, to push their dialectical relation to the logical end: culture is the meanings and the practices that produce one another in the three-fold dialectical process described by sociologist Peter Berger as externalization, objectivation, and internalization (Berger 1969: 4). This means that culturalism regards culture not simply as the effect of human activity but as the constructive activity that makes social reality. Culture is what people do to negotiate their relationship to natural, social, and economic realities. Cultural studies is the academic inquiry into this interaction of everyday life, especially in the form of class, race, gender, and sexuality as it has been practiced since Hall's founding work.

Shaped as it was by British Marxist thought, cultural studies has almost entirely ignored religion. More recently, however, culturalism in the study of media and religion may be defined as the humanistic form of study that stresses the constructive role of culture in the investigation of religion and media, or anything else for that matter. Always seeking to temper any form of biological, historical, economic, or technological determinism as the basis for cultural interpretation, the culturalist approach seeks to integrate human agency with material factors that condition choice, preference, and disposition. Culturalism regards meaning making as shaped by social conditions such as class and prevailing institutions but not determined by them. Aspects of human identity as gender, sexuality, race, and ethnicity condition but do not prescribe experience, and they do so themselves as cultural constructions, not as biological determinants. The aim is not the study of mechanistic social forces that construct the world for individual agents but rather the interaction of social forces and individuals in the construction and maintenance of life-worlds, where phenomena at both the macro- and microscales combine to shape an ecology in which people live and interpret the world around them.

Carey's delineation of the "cultural approach" was carefully studied and presented for consideration by a key figure in the study of religion and media, Robert White, who contributed instructive literature reviews during the 1980s and 1990s to the journal *Communication Research Trends*.[9] In his assessment of Carey's work, White rightly pointed to the anthropological debt of Carey, primarily to Clifford Geertz and Victor Turner. Carey read Geertz's *Interpretation of Cultures* just after it appeared (1973) and wrote a long review essay on it, arguing for its relevance to the study of communication (Carey 1975a). Of special importance to Carey was the anthropologist's claim that understanding something as vast and detailed as culture could be done profitably by studying a ritual. The whole lies encoded within the part. It was a matter "of making large claims from small matters: studying particular rituals, poems, plays, conversations, songs, dances, theories, and myths and gingerly reaching out to the full relations within a culture or a total way of life" (Carey 1975a: 190). This approach was able to recognize the communicative significance of individual cultural artifacts and practices, and thereby endorsed the cultural studies model of investigating communication.

Geertz also offered a definition of religion that was friendly to humanistic study because it stressed the importance of interpretation. In his widely read account of "thick description," in which he contended that culture consisted of the webs of significance spun by humanity, Geertz asserted that the analysis of culture was not "an experimental science in search of law but an interpretive one in search of meaning" (Geertz 1973: 5). Applied to the study of religion, this meant that meaning was what religion did for its adherents, who needed it as an antidote to the threat of chaos, anomie, or lack of meaning posed by a universe that did not behave as a cosmos, or universal order. Religion, therefore, is a system of symbols that provides its believers with a coherent understanding or valuation of life, a meaningful, ordered world in which interaction and interdependence are enabled. For Geertz and Carey, religion was a shared, communal, intelligible way of life. It was about meaning making, a project of culture rather than society: that is, a cultural system of symbols that consisted of a people's ethos and world view, each of which Geertz explained as "the tone, character, and quality of their life" and "the picture they have of the way things in sheer actuality are, their most comprehensive ideas of order" (Geertz 1973: 89). To this, Carey added the insights of Victor Turner's anthropological study of ritual in order to stress the importance of practice in the definition of religion. Human beings make their worlds through the things they do, such as pilgrimage and a variety of other forms of ritual behavior. Turner and Geertz provided the example and intellectual warrant to apply the study of mass communication to religion, shifting from the heavily quantitative study of transmission to the qualitative investigation of cultural forms of meaning making.

However, the culturalist study of religion and media did not happen in a robust way for another decade or so, when White's articles began to appear and younger scholars began to think culturally about the religious significance of media. Significant works by Stewart Hoover (1988) and Jesús Martín-Barbero (1987) represent two of the earliest book-length studies to turn the corner on the transmission model. Hoover framed his study of televangelism with the concept of "religious consciousness," since he wished to understand how television as medium had changed American religion. Consciousness became the register for his investigation. Though it may seem inherently inchoate and elusive as a matrix for measuring a medium's impact, consciousness allowed Hoover to draw on recent anthropological theorizations of culture that stressed meaning making as the fundamental activity of religion. Furthermore, the term allowed him to avoid the sectarian influences of Protestant Christianity in framing his study, as "consciousness" readily captured the current spirituality of New Age and Eastern thought and practice that permeated American society. The implications for the study of religion and media have been enormous. By situating the parachurch, noninstitutional phenomenon known as "the electronic church" within the marketplace of religion and the self-styling traffic of practices and symbols, Hoover's work has encouraged other scholars to study contemporary non-Christian religious groups in the United States and far beyond for their use of media to gain market share, appeal to their followers, advertise themselves, engage in polemic, and forge new practices of communication as religious community.

Following a quotation of Clifford Geertz's widely cited description of religion as a "system of symbols," Hoover defined the "new religious consciousness" as he studied it in his examination of televangelism as "the individual's relationship to such systems, symbolic and real, and the moods and motivations that evolve with that involvement" (Hoover 1988: 22). He made use of Walter Ong's seminal work in elaborating the definition of religious consciousness as Ong, like McLuhan, stressed the constitutive role of media in the transformation of culture as people experience it (McLuhan 1964; Ong 1982). However, whereas McLuhan and Ong dwelt on broad social trends and cultural epochs to measure the cultural and social influence of new media, Hoover could integrate the study of broadcasters, preachers, and organizations with the much closer focus of qualitative research on individual audience members of the electronic church. The "individual's relationship" to the symbolic system of religion signals the culturalist approach, which relies on the careful study of qualitative analysis to assemble compelling accounts of meaning construction. Accordingly, Hoover invoked Carey's distinction of "transmission" and "ritual" definitions of media, relying on the latter to frame his approach to religious communication (Hoover 1988: 26).

Jesús Martín-Barbero moved the cultural analysis of the religious significance and experience of media ahead by formulating the idea of "mediation." Rather than training attention on the media as fixed genres, rhetorical tropes or message bearers of religious content, Martín-Barbero argued that media are much better understood as the site of religious experience and meaning making. In contrast to a meaning of the term as recorded by Raymond Williams ("where certain social agencies are seen as deliberately interposed between reality and social consciousness, to prevent an understanding of reality" [Williams 1985: 206]), one might combine Hoover's analysis with Martín-Barbero's to define mediation as a consciousness of community or cohort. Rather than positing a discrete media product whose impact might be measured as this or that effect or gratification, Martín-Barbero urges us to reckon mediation as a process of engagement that includes struggle, resistance, and an ensuing transformation of consciousness in which media take a part. This allows him to direct attention to media as forms of emancipation no less than as tools of oppression and social control. Media operate as a site in which different agents, communities, and institutions interact. In the utopian terms of Marxist liberation theology, Martín-Barbero speaks of this entire process as the "resacralization" of a world secularized by modernity. "I am suggesting," he writes in a later essay, "that we should look for the processes of re-enchantment in the continuing experience of ritual in communitarian celebration and in the other ways that the media bring people together" (Martín-Barbero 1997: 108).

This is very much the direction in which a great deal of study has gone since the 1990s. The media are not delivery devices but the generation of experiences, forms of shared consciousness, communion, or community that allow people to assemble meanings that articulate and extend their relations to one another (Shepherd and Rothenbuhler 2001). In fact, this is the way in which media have always performed, but now their operation is not controlled or interpreted by religious organizations but studied as cultural phenomena by social analysts.

Though Geertz's definition of religion was the most widely cited and affirmed approach to the humanistic study of religion in the last quarter of the twentieth century, it has attracted a number of critiques, some of which are quite important to consider for their implications for the study of media and religion. One of these is an essay by Talal Asad in his *Genealogies of Religion* (1993), in which he argues that the search for an essence of religion leads to its insulation as a cultural phenomenon from its actual formation within the social, economic, and political domains of power (Asad 1993: 27–54).[10] Geertz's notion of religion as a cultural system, he claims, promotes this isolation of religion as a self-contained, autonomous domain of human activity. The quest for a single, universal definition of religion can only ignore the social and historical aspects of human experience and does so, Asad argues, in response to the liberal Christian anxiety about the crisis of biblical authority. With the edifice of the Christian faith straining under the attack of historical-critical methods of studying the sacred text, formerly understood to be fully inspired by the deity and therefore the only true religion, Victorian thinkers reasoned that Christianity need not be undermined by scholarship nor bothered by its faulty claim to exclusive truth if the focus of study were not its truth but the way in which all religions responded to the core or essence of religion as most Europeans felt it was most perfectly manifest in Christianity. This allowed them to organize all religions in various taxonomies, usually organized chronologically and with the help of a progressive march from the primitive toward the monotheistic. Beliefs became the focus of the anthropological study of religion in the nineteenth century as local variations on a universal essence. Geertz, Asad points out, inherited the idea and plied it in his universal definition of religion: "Geertz's treatment of religious belief, which lies at the core of his conception of religion, is a modern, privatized Christian one because and to the extent that it emphasizes the priority of belief as a state of mind rather than as constituting activity in the world" (Asad 1993: 47). Instead of analyzing religion as a cultural system of symbols that act on the psychic state of one's beliefs, Asad urges analysts of religion to integrate it with the study of the social exercise of power. It is not symbols alone that construct religious dispositions, as he discussed in the case of St. Augustine's willingness to discipline heretics with the heavy hand of state-enforced authority, but power in all of the forms that shaped Augustine's experience, such as imperial and ecclesiastical laws, such religious sanctions as death, damnation, and penance, and such rewards as salvation and good repute (Asad 1993: 35). By drawing out the stark difference between medieval Christianity and latter-day liberal Protestantism, Asad makes the point very clearly that Christianity is not a single essence but historically constructed as part of a matrix of social forces.

Recent work on religion and media has not defined religion as a discrete and universal essence but has regarded religion as fundamentally mediated, as a form of mediation that does not isolate belief but examines its articulation within such social processes as consumption, cohort formation, political resistance, transnationalism, postcolonial nationalism, and globalization (Meyer 2006a; Hoover 2006; Stolow 2006; Armbrust 2006; Morgan 2005: 220–55). This has meant looking at ways in which the self dissolves in and emerges from mediated practice as unstable, discontinuous, and processual, flowing locally and globally into extended communities and articulated in a great variety of practices. Symbols are in flux and do not crystallize into fixed formations of belief. The constructive action of media receives appropriate attention as scholars move from former preoccupation with firmly defined religious profession of beliefs to practice-centered study of religion as media. Martín-Barbero directed his remarks to the power of the electronic church in Latin America to create a site that was able to reinfuse the modern world with the sacred by recognizing television's ability to visualize "the integrating myths of our societies" (Martín-Barbero 1997: 111). He cited sports events and rock concerts as further examples of mythic resources aptly mediated by television and successfully generating communities among viewers. A very influential study by Daniel Dayan and Elihu Katz argued for the power of television to facilitate such unifying or centralizing effects by televising "epic contexts of politics and sports, charismatic missions, and the rites of passage of the great—what we call Contests, Conquests, and Coronations" (Dayan and Katz 1994: 332). Televised media events are not identical to their contents, though that is often the illusion they exert. A media event is experienced within the bounds of a medium, which condenses time, combines distinct perspectives, expands the experience of presence, and fuses a diversity of contents into a singular field of vision, fashioning a coherent narrative that brings the event to the viewer. Such live events as the funerals of world leaders, presidential inaugurations, papal elections, state ceremonies, or the Olympic Games are retold as "a primordial story about current affairs," resulting in mediated events "that hang a halo over the television set and transform the viewing experience" (ibid.). Media events are fashioned from ritual occasions and therefore exhibit several features: they are live and they are "presented with reverence and ceremony" (336). The awe and aura endow the events with a rhetorical stature that invites a reverent response from viewers and presumes to address them in the uniform and heady tropes of nation, polis, people, world, Christendom, humanity, and so forth, seamlessly extending the bounds of community to the mediated space of the televised rite. Though Dayan and Katz have been criticized for endorsing a myth of the center, a center that does not in fact exist, the criticism fails to recognize the power of myth. States, nations, and peoples commonly rely on such a story to cast a spell of unity, to generate a magnetic field that enables a polity to celebrate its coherence, its imagined community.[11]

A group of media researchers examining and comparing media uses in several demographically different American homes has shown that some groups within American society imagine themselves "at the heart" of the culture, whereas others perceive themselves as off-center or at the periphery, which they believe is a better place to be (Hoover et al. 2004: 103–29 and 79–101). In both cases, media help them do so. An evangelical Christian family selected media for home use that affirmed, in effect, its participation in "a new cultural mainstream in U.S. society," the neoevangelical subculture, which often fondly asserts that America is a Christian nation (103). Contrarily, American Muslim parents in another case study attempted to secure their family's religious and cultural difference from the American mainstream by establishing rules against listening to popular music and strictly limiting the amount of time spent each week watching television or playing video and computer games. Naturally, the children found ways to break or stretch the rules (91).

The investigation of media practices as formations of consciousness allows scholars to understand better the many ways in which experiencing media structures thought and feeling. This is important for several reasons. First, we can learn more about the *mentalités* or encompassing cognitive and aesthetic patterns that media help to construct and maintain by drawing and reinforcing definitive boundaries such as inside and outside, us and them, center and periphery, top and bottom, frontline and rearguard, first and last, old and new. These structures confer fundamental aspects of social identity by mapping out such temporal, spatial, and imagined terrains of church, neighborhood, clan, nation, and world. Second, we can understand how something as local and embodied as sensation—seeing, hearing, and touching—mediates individuals and vast social forces and institutions such as media producers, corporate advertisers, religious organizations, governments, or entire nations, regarding the mediation as neither unilateral nor arbitrary but as nuanced negotiations that must be studied up close, though always with an eye to the macroecology that informs every media commodity. Third, how media practices offer access to and draw from collective imaginaries, the shared cultural resources of symbols, images, sounds, songs, ideas, and personae whose knowledge and symbolic use invest individuals in broad patterns of feeling that constitute their participation in communities of different kinds.

Methodology, disciplinarity, research agenda

Though there is no reason to pit quantitative and qualitative research against each other, as has sometimes happened in various "method wars," much of the work done by those who approach media from a cultural-studies standpoint leans on qualitative analysis. This was thematized in the study of communication in the late 1970s in an issue of *Communication Research*, which carried a set of important essays that argued for the significance of humanistic approaches to communication research, especially as regarded the study of popular culture.[12] Qualitative research is designed to focus attention on individuals and to capture what they say and do in terms of narratives, which exert a compelling evidential effect as ways of explaining what people think and feel. Meaning, the result of qualitative study, is not understood as a rational choice or a consumer preference, which may be very effectively measured by the apparatus of quantitative research as forms of information.[13] Meaning is what people feel, intuit, imagine, fear, repress, narrate, or symbolize. In an important essay on the study of reception, Klaus Bruhn Jensen pointed out that quantitative study is well applied where choices, behaviors, and concepts of value are routine, whereas "qualitative inquiry is called for in the attempt to discern the categories audiences use to decode specific media products" (Jensen 1987: 33). People can reply to a questionnaire by stating their preferences, but how are we to learn their criteria, their conceptualization or interpretive apparatus, and the often unarticulated categories on which they rely unless we engage them in interviews and observation? The cultural approach is one that is designed to cater to meaning making as a lived process, especially one that must be witnessed *in situ*. Yet the two methods of study should not be polarized. In fact, some scholars effectively combine qualitative with quantitative research to understand how preferences are nestled in narratives and communities.[14]

For all the interest in qualitative audience research, none of the scholars represented in this book would deny that media are used instrumentally, and to considerable effect. Advertising, political propaganda, and public relations all work to one degree or another. The challenge is to integrate the study of production, circulation, and reception where possible and to regard reception as potentially creative and resistant forms of response to the preferred reading that producers encode in their media products. That said, popular response may be anything but creative. Sometimes consumers behave exactly as producers and advertisers hope they will. And that may be something to welcome, depending on the cause and one's politics. In any case, recent scholarship has avoided a determinist view of media effects without ignoring the fact that media do work to shape response, even if consumers are not captive to intended influences.

If some cultural critics and media scholars were once inclined to dismiss as "kitsch" the mass-produced items of popular religious belief, that is clearly no longer the case. As formations of religious consciousness that are not to be understood in prescriptive terms, popular media attract enormous interest from historians, sociologists, and anthropologists working on media and religion today.[15] Popular culture is no longer defined in terms of non-elite culture but often as common culture, the everyday practices and artifacts that invest the ideas and feelings that are the cognitive medium of identity and social life. Much of the study of media and religion today trains attention on these ideas and feelings as they are worked out in diverse forms of sensation, as what one might call the *social body*, the extension of the senses to the imagined corpus of groups. This is evident in the way that age, gender, and ethnic and sexual cohorts dress, eat, play sports, dance, listen to music, and consume everything that enables them to behave as a member of a somatic collective.

The study of the religious significance of media was slow in coming to the fore for two important reasons. Cultural studies, as has been noted, was formulated within a neo-Marxist tradition in Britain and therefore had no interest in religion. Moreover, the secularization thesis, long in place among social scientists and cultural critics, considered religion vestigial and reactionary, something that modernity and the media as part of the modern project had jettisoned. Since the early 1990s, however, secularization has been called into question by a burgeoning body of work.[16] Second, the definition of religion that prevailed among many scholars in Europe, North and South America, and Australia was deeply shaped by Christianity. The sacred was associated with authoritative institutions and the creeds they disseminated and endorsed. Religion, in other words, was a message directed by various instruments at believers and nonbelievers and was deeply invested in certain traditional notions of culture as the treasure of tradition, as a sectarian version of Mathew Arnold's characterization of culture as the "best that has been thought and said." In fact, modernity has not been consistently nonreligious. It is more accurate to say that scholars have preferred to ignore it because the theory of secularization told them that it was not there. In the meantime, religion has changed beneath the feet of scholars and institutional establishments alike.

The rise of the religious Right in places as diverse as the United States, the Middle East and India during the closing decades of the twentieth century, the new availability of media to emergent churches and charismatic religious leaders in postcolonial states and in post-Soviet nationalisms, and the global movement of immigrants from the developing to Western states made religion visible in new and unpredicted ways. Religious minorities of one sort and another made aggressive use of media to promote their interests, resulting in "electronic churches," that is, noninstitutional parachurch organizations whose public face was radio and television programs, bill boards, and print. The Internet and desktop publishing vastly expanded the possibility of media access and production, leading scholars to realize that media could no longer be understood only as instruments for message delivery but were inseparable from religious identity and practice. The inquiry into media, religion, and culture, as Jeremy Stolow has rightly pointed out, has shifted to understanding "religion as media" (Stolow 2005). The culturalist approach has raised the importance of the study of practice and reception, which has led many scholars to question the instrumentalist understanding of media and, instead, to look for the constructive operation of mediations. Moreover, "religion" no longer means only Christianity and Judaism but, as Sarah Pike's essay in this volume clearly shows, everything from Neopaganism, New Age, and Hinduism to self-help therapies, personal spirituality, and fandom.[17]

Much of the work in this book represents a broader tendency among scholars of media and religion nowadays to recognize in mass-mediated artifacts such as religious pictures and objects another sense of the word *media*. More than radio, newspapers, and televised news broadcasts, media also means Internet fan sites and blogs, circulating videos or cassette tapes, lithographic prints, billboard advertisements, bumper stickers, mass-produced commodities such as plastic statuary or music CDs, or symbols such as crosses, menorahs, and tapestries picturing the Ka'bah. However, neither is there any need to limit media analysis to mass-produced items. Any medium, even the hand-made and utterly unique, should be included in the definition of religious media. This registers a new interest among some media scholars to look beyond the canonical and taste-bound views of art history, musicology, and traditional aesthetics to the formation of lived aesthetics to understand more about sensation and the senses as forms of cognition.[18] Accordingly, several of the key words included in the present volume signal the growing recognition of the body as the matrix of sensuous cognition. In addition to regrounding research in the body and avoiding the traditional humanist privileging of mind and rational thought, many of the writers demonstrate keen interest in the history of media, seeking to correct the presentist bias in many studies of mass communication and new media.[19]

Finally, the mélange of disciplines, geographies, and media supports the view that no single discipline has commanded the field of study. Sociology, anthropology, and history have contributed major methodological guidelines —quantitative and qualitative research, ethnography, and archival and artifactual study. However, media studies, cultural studies, feminism, art history, visual and material culture studies, and religious studies have brought a host of additional questions and methodological priorities to bear on the study of religion and media, resulting in a range of interests and a conversation that is really a set of conversations, including the study of journalism, mass communication, consumption, visual culture, theology, the public sphere, globalization, transnationalism, political theory, and cultural economy. To date, participants have felt no urgency to limit the discourse or dominate it by discipline, field, or methodology. For many of us, this is a sign of robust intellectual health.

Key terms and the conceptual field they configure

This book seeks to discern the emerging conceptual framework in the recent study of media and religion. Rather than looking for fast boundaries or new foundations in an overlooked or a novel subject matter, the approach is to describe an intersection where no discipline dominates but several are engaged in serious conversation with one another. The writers are scholars from around the world who come to the study from different academic specialties. Their work over the last decade and more has been influential in shaping the field of media and religion.[20] One might add many names to the list and compile a substantial bibliography. The signs clearly indicate that the field is expanding and deepening: all of which makes one pause at the audacity of selecting a mere fifteen words for a list of key terms. Given the many different emphases in the far-from-unified field of inquiry, lists of even a few terms would vary considerably. Rather than trying to be comprehensive or universalizing or equitable, it seemed more important to look across a large number of inquiries, conferences, and consultations in search of patterns that might affirm themes, keyed to concepts and their terms, that have played a recurrent and influential role in the discourse.

Judging from the traffic that has traveled the intersection of disciplines, questions, and studies, the list of key words that comprises the book captures much of the energy and focus. The following remarks attempt to sketch out the conceptual field by clustering several of the terms into smaller groups.

Gathered together for critical definition here, I hope they push the discourse on media and religion to recognize more formally the most influential implications of recent work. The terms have been selected to represent the emergent network of ideas that have shaped investigation over the last three decades. Each of the authors has written within a matrix of ideas, artifacts, institutions, and practices that joins them to a larger framework. For example, one of the threads connecting several words (*audiences, circulation, public, community*) is the power that media practices have demonstrated time and again to create social forms of association. So in writing about audiences, Stewart Hoover considers the history of the treatment of mass media, the eclipse of traditional religious authority, the importance of the marketplace, and the emerging prominence of audiences as powerful agents rather than passive consumers. A significant consequence of these changes has been that scholars have come to focus on the meaning-making activities of media practices. Likewise, in discussing circulation, Johanna Sumiala examines ways in which the mass-mediated framing of images creates relationships between them and viewers. These relations inflect the reception of images, suggesting that scholars train their attention on the circulation and reception of media artifacts to learn how mediated events take on meaning.

Reflection on the social, cultural, and political functions of print and broadcast media has been importantly concerned with the formation of different publics, the public sphere, and public opinion. Joyce Smith examines the mediated construction of publics, asking how they are imagined, disseminated, consumed, contradicted. Where and how do media publics happen? Riffing on Jürgen Habermas's enormously influential study of the role of eighteenth-century coffee shops in forming the public sphere, Smith suggests that mediated publics today arise in the savory taste of coffee and the leisurely privacy of wifi connections. All of the analyses described so far unfold in dialogue with J. Kwabena Asamoah-Gyadu's discussion of the community-forming effects of media consumption. He shows how this applies to face-to-face and urban—but also transnational—communities for whom media maintain an extended set of associations as religious groups take shape in the global flows of immigrants.

A second set of terms (*text, narrative, technology, economy*) responds to traditional approaches to the study of media and religion to show how it has changed. Thus, texts are not stable entities, drawing from abiding genres that provide clear meanings but, as Isabel Hofmeyr shows, are social events, emerging from use, endlessly redacted and circulating. Careful historical study is able to demonstrate how each iteration is suited to particular circumstances and negotiates social and cultural differences. As a dominant structure in human communication and memory, narrative is one of the primary occasions on which news media's public constructs its sense of truth, community, and value. Jolyon Mitchell investigates the role of narrative in journalism, folklore, and the formation of national identity, focusing on the dynamics of narration as the story of a Philippine national hero is retold in word and image. Stories are framed and followed by journalists in the form of various narratives and are rejected, championed, and redeployed by consumers in rituals of communication. Through narrative, events and people are assembled into powerful figures that are linked to myths, religious stories, and other artistic forms in the forging of collective identity. Technology has long been the fetish of social histories of media, adorned with narratives of revolution as the primary trope in discourses on modernity, democracy, and Western supremacy. However, Jeremy Stolow proposes that technology needs very much to be reexamined within an approach that stresses practice, community, and reception. This allows him to argue persuasively for understanding religion as media, touching on perhaps the most fundamental idea in the turn to the humanistic study of media and religion. This shift allows for much greater attention to interpretations and uses of technology in the life-worlds of consumers, which may then, in turn, be instructively compared to ideologies and cultural myths about technological power and promise.

The "power of media" thematic carries with it a strong temptation to reduce media technologies to their commodity value, which is understood commonly as their capacity to deliver corporate profit. A great deal of mass communication research in the twentieth century was dedicated to measuring the intended and unintended "effects" of such media as film, advertising, public relations, and political propaganda—research that was often funded and relied on by business and political interests. This highly instrumentalist approach to media easily overlooks the culture of media reception, which involves the religious significance of consuming media. Production, circulation, and consumption of media form what may be described as a cultural economy of media. David Chidester ponders this as a religious phenomenon insofar as media reception performs such important cultural work as crafting or reinforcing representations of world, home, gender, race, self, clan, and enemy. All media come to people today as commodities, making us consumers engaged in acts of exchange that do far more than provide food or clothing. The culture of media practices may be very helpfully described as a system exchange that relies on different forms of belief, unbelief, and make-believe.

Another cluster of key words revolves around embodiment and sensation (*aesthetics*, *image*, *soundscape*). This represents a distinctive direction of recent research in media and religion, the result of interdisciplinary study by anthropologists, film scholars, and art historians. The body has yet to receive its due as one of the most fundamental registers in the cultural analysis of media, and this is due largely to the lack of methodological resources in the study of media to date. To this end, four scholars trained in appropriate disciplines explore the various ways in which the senses function in media practices as ingredients in the ways of knowing and feeling that interact with media to create their immediacy and effect. Birgit Meyer and Jojada Verrips revisit the modern word *aesthetics*, first coined in 1735 to designate the study of how poetry operates as a form of sensuous cognition. They urge scholars of media and religion to go beyond the question of art as visual representation to the body itself. The implications for inquiry are considerable: How do we study the body's experience, sensation and intuitions, feelings and moods as a principal aspect of the process of mediation? And how does the body enter into the construction of private and public experience and the creation of meaning? David Morgan develops a parallel account of seeing, understanding the image not merely in terms of symbolic forms of representation, that is, as iconography, but as cultural and biological operations that are grounded in the human face, where image meets body. The fear of images arises in just this corporeal registration of visual representation. And this fear has an august history that is deeply invested in the history of ideas about representation. Dorothea E. Schulz investigates the other dominant bodily medium of communication—sound—by framing it spatially as soundscape. This enables her to think productively of the power of sound to construct public spaces but also to study how religion is embodied and felt by believers, becoming a powerful form of sensation and thereby materializing the study of mediated communities.

The key words *religion*, *media*, *practice*, and *culture* are located throughout the warp and woof of the book, each serving to articulate and interpret the direction of the field over the last fifteen to twenty years. The study of religion, as Sarah Pike demonstrates, has shifted from an emphasis on institutions, creeds and the biographies of influential leaders to the stories and practices of groups and individuals who commonly appropriate materials from rival groups and from the past to fashion new narratives. They freely engage in commerce and marketing to position themselves to competitive advantage and make avid use of both new technologies and traditional forms of material and visual culture. Peter Horsfield surveys the dynamic nature of media in recent studies, articulating several influential models for the study and experience of media. In doing so, he is able to demonstrate how the term is a key to understanding lived religion as a set of material practices, as a process of marketing belief, and as a social operation of mediation, in which religion is not simply here or there, invested in the traditional hardware of altar or holy site, but diffused in virtually ubiquitous media artifacts and the practices of consuming them. This state of affairs urges analysts to recognize the importance of understanding practice as the center of gravity of religion, and that is what Pamela Klassen does in her chapter on practice. By reviewing the recent history of theoretical reflection on practice among sociologists, anthropologists, and historians, Klassen shows the importance of the idea for the study of religion as mediation.

To date, many scholars of religion and media have operated with only an implicit notion of culture in mind. This tends to produce under-theorized accounts that stress the dominance of institutions and trendsetting individuals that take the place of more subtle perceptions of the cultural processes of mediation. A more robust account of culture in the study of media and religion will highlight the dynamics of constructing narratives, the performance of ritual practices, the mediation of religious belief, and the role of consumption in crafting communities and social identities. Angela Zito, therefore, conducts her discussion of culture as a history of how major thinkers over the last several decades have successively framed the study of media and religion in different approaches to culture. She argues that culture is more than the static reservoir of meanings and artifacts and the enduring hierarchy of authority that certain groups wish it to be. Culture is also the creative, countervailing, evolving, ever-transient, and always historically constructed range of activities that order and value human experience, forever building worlds up and tearing them down. Culture consists of the practices and epistemologies of embodiment and mediation that endow human experience with its meanings. Religions are prevailing forms of such ordering at work in institutions, markets, individual and collective rituals, various mediated publics and audiences, and the shifting shape of communities that each of these produces.

Notes

1 Major work on the history of the book and religious print that appeared in the 1970s and 1980s includes that of Stout 1977; Hatch 1983; Hall 1989; and Nord 1984. Important work on religion and popular culture at this time includes Real 1977; Williams 1980; and Goethals 1981.

2 The winter 1985 issue of the *Journal of Communication* ran as a special feature entitled "The Mediated Ministry," consisting of six articles by scholars who examined the use of mass media for religious purposes, *Journal of Communication* 35 (1): 89–156. The following studies also register the interest of scholars occasioned by the new circumstances of religious communication

and media marketing during the Reagan era: Frankl 1987, Hoover 1988, and Schultze 1990.

3   See the many references to Williams, Hall, Barthes, and Baudrillard in the bibliography. Two helpful and widely cited surveys of leading theorists, debates, and schools of thought regarding mass media since the 1950s in Europe, though including figures in Canada, Australia, and the United States, are McQuail 1994 and Stevenson 1995. Neither volume makes any mention of religion in the study of mass media.

4   See, for example, Babb and Wadley 1995; Hackett 1998; Eickelman and Anderson 1999; Armbrust 2000; Rajagopal 2001; Ginsburg 2002; Ukah 2003; Pinney 2004; Abu-Lughod 2004; Oosterbaan 2005; Hirschkind 2006; Meyer 2006a; Jain 2007; Larkin 2007.

5   The book series, entitled "Religion, Media and Culture" and published by Routledge (London), is edited by Stewart Hoover, Jolyon Mitchell, and David Morgan. The journal, *Media and Religion*, published by Erlbaum, is edited by Judith Buddenbaum and Daniel Stout. The International Conference on Media, Religion, and Culture has been held on six occasions: Uppsala, Sweden, 1993; Boulder, Colorado, 1996; Edinburgh, Scotland, 1999; Louisville, Kentucky, 2004; Sigtuna, Sweden, 2006; Sao Paolo, Brazil, 2008. The seventh and eighth conferences are scheduled at Toronto (2010) and Amsterdam (2012).

6   Sweet 1993; Arthur 1993; Stout and Buddenbaum 1996; Hoover and Lundby 1997; De Vries and Weber 2001; Hoover and Clark 2002; Mitchell and Marriage 2003; Horsfield et al. 2004; Mitchell 2005; Meyer and Moors 2006; Sumiala-Seppänen et al. 2006; Henriquez 2007; Clark 2007b.

7   Stewart Hoover has recently noted the importance of "the culturalist turn" and Carey's work as well as the relevance of Geertz's approach to religion to his own study of media and religion, Hoover 2006: 16–17, 23.

8   De Certeau 1984: 165–76; Fiske 1987; Jenkins 1992; Radway 1984.

9   See White 1981 and 1994 for two authoritative overviews of current literature; for a helpful overview of the shift that White helped note and characterize, see White 1983.

10 For a philosophical critique of Geertz's definition of religion, see Frankenberry and Penner 1999.

11 Important discussion of the idea of the center begins with a seminal essay by Shils 1975. An instructive set of reflections on Shils's work and the topic is Greenfield and Martin 1988. The idea of a "social center" as developed by Dayan and Katz has been critically analyzed by Couldry 2003: 55–74. Couldry is, of course, correct that no such single center exists, but the appeal and cultural capital associated with the idea of or desire for one articulated in its mediated construction is the point I wish to underscore.

12 The issue was introduced by Hirsch 1978.

13 I borrow the distinction of "meaning" and "information" in regard to qualitative and quantitative method from Jensen 1987: 31. On the explicit distinction of the social scientific study of audience preferences and the cultural studies approach, see Kreiling 1978.

14 See, for example, the large body of work by Robert Wuthnow, such as Wuthnow 2003, which combined interviews with social survey instruments.

15 Examples might be enumerated a great length. Lynch 2007 and Clark 2003 serve to signal the range of recent work.

16 One of the early and widely influential studies that helped turn the corner for many scholars of media and religion was Warner 1993.

17 For discussion of this change and its relevance for the study of media, see Hoover 2006: 50–66. For a variety of reflections about religion and its conceptualization, especially in regard to the study of media, see De Vries 2007.

18 A call for and preliminary conceptualization of this research area is Meyer 2006a. Meyer and Verrips develop the approach in their contribution to this volume, "Aesthetics." See also Verrips 2006. Consideration of a popular aesthetic of mass-produced religious imagery occurs in Morgan 1998: 29–58.

19 Important recent historical studies of religion and media include Winston 1999, Peters 1999, Hangen 2002, Hendershot 2004, and Rosenthal 2007.

20 In addition to several items listed in previous notes, see Pike 2001; Hofmeyr 2004; Asamoah-Gyadu 2005; Stolow 2005; Sumlala-Seppänen and Stocchetti 2005; Chidester 2005; Meyer 2006a; Schulz 2006; Hoover 2006; Mitchell 2006; Klassen 2006; Morgan 2007; Mitchell 2006; and Zito 2007.

1

Aesthetics

Birgit Meyer and Jojada Verrips

From *aisthesis* to aesthetica
Kant's legacy
Religion as mediation and the "aesthetic turn"
Religious aesthetics

Time and again, artists have presented work to the world that has been perceived by believers as shocking, insulting, and hurtful. A famous case in point is *Piss Christ* by Andres Serrano (first exhibited in 1989), which upset many Roman Catholics so much that they initiated lawsuits to have this "obscene" piece of art removed from exhibitions.[1] A few even went so far as to try to destroy it, such as the Melbourne teenager who attacked it with a hammer because his mother had wept on hearing that a judge had ruled it not "offensive *per se*." According to Alison Young, who has dealt with this case in detail, the judge's problem was

> that the image can easily be described in aesthetically pleasing terms (the sunset hues), but it is the ordinary person's imputed understanding of the title and knowledge of the manner of the image's making that might evidence the offensiveness and the possible obscenity. The judge might wish to locate legal obscenity or indecency in the artwork, but is ultimately unable to do so, due to the conflict he finds between the *aesthetics* of the image (the "beauty of its appearance") and the prepositional condition of the artwork (the "disgusting" nature of its creation confessed by the title). And it seems to be this surface "beauty" of the image that saves it from obscenity.
>
> (2005: 32; italics added)

It may seem counterintuitive to some readers to find "aesthetics" included as a key word in the study of religion and media. If so, that could be owing to the limited sense that the word has acquired in its modern career. In the passage above, *aesthetics* occurs with the meaning it gained at the end of the eighteenth century and which it still has in both professional and popular circles, i.e., as referring to the "disinterested beauty" of a work of art. However, before it received this specific (Kantian) meaning, aesthetics encompassed much more, as will be shown here. At present, there is a tendency among scholars with different disciplinary backgrounds (cultural and visual studies, anthropology, cultural criminology, media studies, art history, and comparative religion), who share an interest in the nexus of religion and media, to revisit this broader conception of aesthetics. After a succinct presentation of the ancient genealogy of the term and the shifts in meaning it has undergone over time, we consider the question of how aesthetics is conceived and used in a sensitizing manner to develop deeper insights into the ways in which religious media—understood in a broad sense, encompassing icons, images, texts, films, radio, cassettes, and the like—affect religious practitioners and convey a sense of divine presence.

From *aisthesis* to aesthetica

In *De Anima,* Aristotle deals with the question of how the "psyche," conceptualized by him as a nonmaterial entity with specific powers or a kind of life energy with certain potentialities, uses the material body of human beings and other animals to realize these potentialities or powers through and in their bodies. The psyche is the source of (1) our potentiality to feed ourselves, (2) our potentiality to perceive the world through our (five) senses (*aisthetikon*), (3) the powers to make representations *of* (*phantastikon*), (4) the power to think *over* (*nous*), and (5) the power to develop desires *in* (*orektikon*) this world—all on the basis of our sensations. Of all the senses, Aristotle considers touch to be the most fundamental because it forms the condition of our survival through reproduction (sex) and defense (violence). Though he did not see the other senses as variations of touch, as do some scholars today (see Chidester 2005; Verrips 2006), he understood our perception of the world through our five senses as an undivided whole. This is what he meant by *aisthesis* (directly related to *aisthetikon*): our corporeal capability on the basis of a power given in our psyche to perceive objects in the world via our five different sensorial modes, thus in a kind of analytical way, and at the same time as a specific constellation of sensations as a whole (e.g., an apple with a texture, a taste, a smell, a sound, and a visible shape and color). An apple makes an im-pression or has an im-pact (on us) as a whole and in different sensorial ways at exactly the same time.

Aisthesis then refers to our total sensorial experience of the world and to our sensuous knowledge of it.[2]

In the course of history, this type of knowledge has gradually been pushed to the background in the Western world. Emphasis has come to rest more and more on sensations received by the eye, representations based on the eye alone, and finally abstract thinking and reasoning based in their turn on these representations. Particularly after Descartes presented his *cogito ergo sum*, expressing his sharp division between body and mind (cf. Meyer 2003: 22), the *aisthesis* of Aristotle, the *aisthetic* way of knowing the world, the knowing through our body, rapidly lost ground in intellectual circles. Alexander Gottlieb Baumgarten's introduction of the term *aesthetica* in the middle of the eighteenth century to designate the science of sensuous knowing (*scientia cognitionis sensitivae*) in the classical sense was a milestone, but it did not denote a return to or lasting reestablishment of more balanced relations between *aisthetic* and rational knowing of the world (Baumgarten 1936). It may be that his qualification of the aesthetica as a science that concentrates on the *facultates cogniscitivae inferiores* (inferior or lower cognitive faculties, i.e., the sensorial ones) of human beings, instead of on their *facultates cogniscitivae superiores* (higher or superior cognitive faculties: i.e., the rational or logical ones) contributed to this lopsided development. Whatever the case, it is a pity that Baumgarten's touching plea to philosophers to pay serious attention to the importance of *aisthetic* knowing or sensorial impressions of the world did not get the response he expected (see Schweizer 1973: 108–9; cf. Plate 2005: 19–20). This was a pity, for after him a trajectory was set in which the Aristotelian heritage faded into the background in works on aesthetica, and movement was instigated in a very specific direction. Aesthetica gradually became a cerebral science of the beautiful and the philosophy of art.

Kant's legacy

A major role in this one-sided and rather narrow-minded development was played by Immanuel Kant. Kant was familiar with Baumgarten's seminal treatises on the relevance of taking into consideration ways of knowing through the senses or the body alongside those connected with the faculty of reason or the mind, and he deemed the aesthetic judgment of an object to be based on a subjective feeling of pleasure (*Lust*) or reluctance (*Unlust*), which was the result of an unintended confluence of imagination and reason. Nevertheless, he ventured toward a rather rational approach to this experience, as from his perspective the feeling of *Lust* or *Unlust* was based on a (pure) judgment of taste or on reflection by a subject that disposes of both *Sinnlichkeit und Verstand (Vernunft)* (sensuality and reason [common sense]). Characteristic for the feeling of aesthetic pleasure *or* displeasure (and the experience of beauty *or* ugliness) is (1) that it is not related to an interest or does not generate a specific desire, (2) that it pertains to a single object and never to a class of objects, (3) that it can be judged as having a "*Zweckmässigkeit ohne Zweck*" (appropriateness without purpose), and

(4) that it (unreasonably) requests approval by others (see Kant 2001). In connection with beauty, Kant also dealt with the aesthetic category of the sublime (*das Erhabene*): something observable that generates amazement, anxiety, and awe and transcends the beautiful. It is these two categories that form the pillars of his philosophy on aesthetics.

Though a host of other great thinkers, including Schiller, Schelling, Hegel, Schopenhauer, and Marx, to mention but a few, also dealt with aesthetics, it was Kant's approach that became the most influential for decades to come, especially among art historians and philosophers of art. In fact, it still informs, directly or indirectly, the work of many scholars studying beautiful objects and sublime phenomena. However, the acceptance of Kant's cerebral and rational perspective on how experiences of the beautiful and the sublime could be understood implied a number of problematic divides through which aesthetics was framed as a rather limited field of inquiry.

The most immediately obvious is the further delineation of the split between the realm of the senses or the body and that of reason or the mind, which Baumgarten so ardently wished to bridge. This implied that the senses and the body were of little or no relevance for the understanding of the sensorial and emotional impact of all kinds of imagery and objects, in the sphere of religion, for instance, on their beholders. We might call this process the de-sensualization or disembodiment of aesthetics (see Plate 2005). The eye became a mind's eye and the ear a mind's ear, whereas the rest of the senses were numbed or an-aesthetized (see Buck-Morss 1992). Only with the rise of phenomenology, particularly as it was developed by Merleau-Ponty in his work on perception (1945), *aisthetic* experiences and knowing reappeared once again on centre stage. Merleau-Ponty's *Causeries* (2002 [1948]) explicitly dealt with such experiences in connection with the rise of modern art (see also Dufrenne 1973). Artists were aiming for representations of reality that were more in accordance with the fact that we do not perceive the world through our eyes alone but with all our senses: our entire body. It has been his work, among that of others, that has inspired many scholars from different disciplines in the second half of the twentieth century to design approaches that transcend the bodiless and dematerialized aesthetic theory in the philosophy of art.

The second divide relates to the fact that neo-Kantian aesthetic theory was almost exclusively applied to what became known as high or modern art (i.e., art stored and exhibited in special places and spaces) and not to what was degradingly labeled as low art or kitsch: mass-produced imagery and objects meant to be consumed by vast numbers of people. In this connection, it is important to realize that this distinction between high art and low ran more or less parallel with a third divide that came into existence with the Enlightenment: the separation of the artistic from the religious realm.

According to this view, religion was supposed to gradually lose importance in the course of the modernization and rationalization of society, whereas high art would be the site par excellence for the generation of sublime experience. As a consequence, artworks made by religiously inspired people considering themselves to be serious artists were relegated to the realm of low art or kitsch and therefore deemed not worthy of study by art theorists (see Elkins and Morgan 2008).

As a consequence of these divides, neo-Kantian aesthetic discourse became confined to an exclusive field of study that became rather narrow, at least as seen from an *aisthetic* perspective in Aristotle's sense. It was not only the body that was discounted but a wide range of imagery and objects that were rather arbitrarily disqualified as low-brow or religious(ly inspired)—or both—and therefore uninteresting. In addition, there is a tendency to disregard the social and cultural context in which aesthetic experiences are generated and theorized. All this yielded rather static and disembodied approaches to aesthetics. Taking for granted the gaze as the central sense through which beholders engage with images, these approaches fail to take into account the ways in which the tuning of the sensorium has undergone actual transformations under the influence of the invention of new technologies, especially in the sphere of the production and consumption of, for example, modernist imagery and texts (Danius 2002; see also Crary 2001). In other words, in their insensitivity toward the significance of social and cultural contexts and the sensorium as a whole, such approaches neglect the specific tuning of the senses in consonance with the rise of modern subjectivities.[3]

Religion as mediation and the "aesthetic turn"

Though these typically modern distinctions between mind and body, high and low art, and art and religion long informed approaches of aesthetics, there is currently a trend toward a broader understanding of the term. Recognizing the need to account for the affective power that images, sounds, texts, and other cultural forms wield over their beholders, scholars seek to develop more integrated understandings of sensing and knowing. Obviously, this inquiry no longer locates aesthetics in the domain of the high arts alone (as opposed to popular arts and religion) but rather in everyday life. This implies moving beyond the divides entailed by neo-Kantian aesthetic discourses toward a recognition of the more encompassing Aristotelian notion of *aisthesis*. The emerging field of religion and media is one of the sites where a turn is being made toward a broader understanding of aesthetics. This turn has been instigated by the spectacular rise and circulation of religious audio-visual cultural forms, from cassette sermons broadcasting Islamic preachers to radio programs advertising the Catholic Renewal, from religious sitcoms to charismatic televised preaching, from mass-produced lithographs and photographs that induce a sense of spiritual presence to the emergence of sacred sites in cyberspace.

At first sight, such media and religion may appear to belong to two different ontological realms: one of crude materiality and technology, the other a higher order of the divine or transcendental. Facing the adoption of new media into religious traditions, however, scholars have come to realize that this view itself is highly problematic. The very assumption of a divide between religion and media stems from a dematerialized and disembodied understanding of religion. Indeed, in consonance with the divides sketched above, in the aftermath of the Protestant Reformation, modern religion came to be regarded in terms of an opposition between spirit and matter, inner belief and outward behavior (Asad 1993; Keane 2007). For a long time, questions of representation and interpretation, geared toward understanding inner beliefs and underlying meanings, have held a privileged position. Pondering the nexus of religion and media has yielded an understanding of religion as a practice of mediation (De Vries 2001; Meyer 2006; Stolow 2005) to which media are intrinsic. In this understanding, media form the necessary condition for achieving a linkage between people and the realm of the invisible: that is, the province of the divine or transcendental. Taking mediation as a departure point also implies that media are taken seriously as material forms through which the senses and bodies of religious practitioners are tuned and addressed. In this way, in the field of religion and media, alternative approaches that have emerged transcend the disembodiment and dematerialization of modern religion and pay due attention to aesthetics, recapturing the broad Aristotelian sense.

For instance, in his analysis of the relation between images of Jesus and their beholders in the context of American popular Protestantism, David Morgan (1998) advocated a more contextualized, embodied understanding of religious aesthetics. Highlighting the affective power of images, Morgan stresses the corporeal immediacy through which Jesus pictures achieve a compelling presence, rather than featuring as mere depictions. Christopher Pinney's (2004) exploration of the ways in which central Indian villagers relate to mass-produced lithographs of deities takes this alternative approach of aesthetics further still. Situating these "photos of the gods" in a bodily praxis of worship—"a poetry of the body"—through which images get "what they want" (Mitchell 2005a), Pinney shows how in Hindu image practices, the experience of the effect and efficacy of the image on the part of the worshipper accounts for its power. Stressing that a neo-Kantian aesthetic approach (as outlined above) is geared too much toward the disinterested bodiless beholder to grasp images' appeal and perceived efficacy, Pinney coins the alternative term *corpothetics*. With this term, he seeks to recapture the ancient Greek meaning of aesthetics as "perception by feeling" grounded in the corporeal and material and as mobilizing the senses simultaneously (2004: 19). Corpothetics, to him, means "the sensory embrace of images, the bodily engagement that most people (except Kantians and modernists) have with artworks" (22). His book shows beautifully how this broader understanding of aesthetics opens up new possibilities of inquiry into mass-produced religious images that reveal not so much how images look but what they can do (8).

As a great deal of research on religion and media focuses on visual culture, it is not surprising that critiques of conventional aesthetic approaches emerged as a result of researchers' dissatisfaction with the incapacity of these approaches to grasp the affective power of images and their capacity to trigger religious experience. However, a search for a broader understanding of aesthetics can also be found in work on nonvisual media, such as radio and cassettes. Of special importance here is Charles Hirschkind's work on the ways in which mass-produced cassette sermons speak to embodied repertoires within their young Islamic listeners, who adopt these tales into an "ethic of listening" (2006). Stressing that people's capacities for speaking and hearing are shaped in a shared disciplinary context that produces particular affective dispositions, Hirschkind shows how the realization of Islamic moral personhood is linked to the resonant body (102). Adopting a broad corporeal understanding of aesthetics that is inspired by Shusterman's notion of "somaesthetics" (2002), Hirschkind is particularly concerned with highlighting how the interface of aesthetics and ethics is grounded in the body; hence his analysis of the "soma-ethical" grounding of religious experience.

It needs to be stressed that these new approaches, though emphasizing bodily sensations, are somewhat distanced from theories of the genesis of religious experience in private feelings, as developed following William James. The fact that he and those working in line with his ideas take the existence of a primary, authentic and, in this sense, seemingly unmediated religious experience at face value is problematic. This locates concepts such as will, emotion, and aesthetic judgment exclusively in the individual believer rather than taking into account how transmitted and shared social forms, such as language, contribute to shaping individual experience (Wittgenstein 1958; see also Shusterman 2002). In addition, James's perspective fails to realize the extent to which structures of repetition, as they are safeguarded by religious organizations, play a central role in affirming specific religious subjectivities (Taylor 2002: 116). An understanding of religion as mediation regards such practices and structures as a *conditio sine qua non* for the genesis of religious experience (including a highly individualized spirituality). Rather than attributing primacy either to the individual or to social forms, the point is to understand the genesis of religious experiences and subjectivities as a process in which the personal and the social are inextricably bound up with each other.

Religious aesthetics

Religious aesthetics, in the current sense, refers to an embodied and embedded praxis through which subjects relate to other subjects and objects and which is grounded in and offers the ground for religious experience. To grasp the link between aesthetics and experience, we propose to take as a starting point those religious forms that organize encounters between human beings and the divine, as well as with each other, and make individual religious experience intersect with transmitted, shared forms. To get at this process of intersection, through which the personal and the social are aligned, we introduce the notion of *sensational form*. We understand these forms as relatively fixed, authorized modes of invoking and organizing access to the transcendental, thereby creating and sustaining links between believers in the context of particular religious regimes.[4] Sensational forms are transmitted and shared; they involve religious practitioners in particular practices of worship and play a central role in forming religious subjects. We outline here a number of key dimensions of sensational forms so as to highlight our understanding of aesthetics as an embodied and embedded praxis.

First, sensational forms organize encounters with an invisible beyond, the realm of spirits or the transcendental. By authorizing certain practices of mediation as truthful and valid, religious traditions endorse specific modalities through which this realm can be accessed (and, from a more distant perspective, produced), entailing certain restrictions and suggesting appropriate modes of getting in touch that involve the senses in various ways. In the example of Hindu image practices given above, worshippers attribute a certain spiritual power to the photographs of the gods. The gods are not only rendered present via mass-produced representations but are held to engage with worshippers via a mutual process of seeing and being seen, or *darshan*. Though there is a lot of work on images and icons as particular sensational forms that render present a divine force (Meyer 2005, Morgan 2005), it is important to look further than the nexus of pictures and vision, as pinpointed by current work on matters such as spirit possession wherein a person embodies a spirit (e.g., Morris 2000; Sanchez 2001; Van de Port 2005, 2006) or the linkage between voice and charismatic power in Christian (De Abreu 2005; De Witte 2005; Wiegele 2005) and Islamic settings (Schulz 2003). The point is to establish how certain material forms are vested with the capacity to render present divine power. The aesthetic appeal of these forms lies in the specific ways through which they affect their beholders via the senses and the body.

Second, as already intimated, sensational forms address and form people's bodies and senses in distinct ways. Morgan has shown that religious images are embedded in a specific didactics of vision that entails particular "looking acts" (1998: 8), while Hirschkind (2006) has emphasized that listening is a practice that is far removed from mere "hearing" in that it depends on the genesis of specific dispositions and sensibilities. In both instances, piety is achieved via a sustained work on the body and the senses that mobilizes the eye and the ear. Liz James has analyzed the Byzantine church as a "space that appeals to all the senses," "a space that places the body and the body's relation to the spiritual at the centre of its display" (2004: 504). Showing that the material and sensual intersect in achieving the spiritual, she highlights the centrality of "lower senses" such as smell, touch, and taste to Byzantine religiosity. That it would be mistaken to exempt texts from having a sensory appeal is clarified by Jeremy Stolow's (2007a) analysis of how Jewish text books (sold via the Internet) are made to embody a sense of gravity that seeks to anchor readers in a tactile, rather than a merely intellectual, relationship with the text. In all these examples, the sensorium and the body are shown to be key sites for shaping religious subjectivities, in which personal inclinations and shared sensational forms merge into a distinct habitus.

Third, the bodily and sensory modes that are implied in forming religious subjects are also key to invoking and affirming links among them. In this sense, aesthetics is also central to the making of religious communities that thrive on a shared aesthetic style (Maffesoli 1996; Meyer 2004; Morgan 2007). Inducing as well as expressing shared moods, a shared religious style—materializing in, for example, collective prayer, a shared corpus of songs, images, and modes of looking, symbols and rituals, but also a similar clothing style and material culture—makes people feel at home. Sharing a common aesthetic style via a common religious affiliation generates not only feelings of togetherness but speaks to and mirrors particular moods and sentiments. Such experiences of sharing also modulate people into a particular, common appearance and thus underpin a collective religious identity, which becomes a gestalt. Shared religious aesthetics may also play a key role in vesting hitherto secular spaces with religious power, as shown by Allen and Mary Roberts' (2003) analysis of the sacralization of urban Senegal that occurs through the omnipresence of images of the Sufi Saint Sheikh Amadou Bamba in public space. The role of aesthetics in the formation of shared religious identities and their public appearance will certainly require more attention in the future.

Conclusion

To account for the appeal— and disgust—that images invoke for beholders in our media-saturated, postsecular world, aesthetic theory needs to be pushed beyond the divides between body and mind, high art and low art, and art and religion. A broad understanding of aesthetics, as we have argued, allows one to focus on the relationship between people and religious images and other forms and to inquire how this relationship is shaped by authorized modes of invoking divine presence and power and by sensorial practices through which it is incorporated (see also Verrips 2008). From the vantage point of the broad understanding of aesthetics proposed here, believers' distressed reactions vis-à-vis *Piss Christ* appear in a different light from that of a conventional neo-Kantian approach, as mobilized by the judge who regarded this image as a piece of high art with its own "beauty of appearance." Whatever our position with regard to charges of blasphemy, the "aesthetic vertigo" (Young 2005: 20–45) it may generate, and the political debates surrounding it may be, the approach of aesthetics advocated here sensitizes us to the fact that people may be hurt—literally—by exactly those images that violate their embodied religious sensibilities and accepted modes of representation. Controversial imagery thus spotlights the point we have sought to make throughout this chapter: Religion is not confined to the sphere of ephemeral spirituality and mere abstract beliefs but entails solid materials that form religious subjects through a process of embodiment.

In closing, we stress that our plea to turn to an embodied and embedded aesthetics seeks to go further than privileging the body and the senses at the expense of "the mind." Owing to the dematerialization and disembodiment of religion and aesthetics, it is certainly important to reclaim the body and the senses. However, in so doing we need to avoid reinstating the mind–body divide. In our understanding, as also pointed out by Merleau-Ponty, the production of meaning and knowing (which is usually associated with the domain of the mind) always involves bodily experiences and emotions *as well as* reflections on it—a process that may well be characterized, following Baumgarten, as "aestheticological" (see Schweizer 1973: 42–4). In other words, to grasp the immediacy and power that religious sensational forms wield over their beholders, we plead for an understanding of aesthetics that incorporates body and mind as an undivided whole.

Notes

1   That watching taboo-breaking art can trigger visceral reactions in viewers is nicely illustrated by the warning in the folder distributed by the Brooklyn Museum of Modern Art in New York at the occasion of the "Sensation" exhibition in 1999.

For consideration of how the content of the works shown may lead to shock, vomiting, confusion, panic, euphoria, and anxiety, see Verrips 2008.

2   For a more detailed account of *aisthesis*, see Verrips 2006.

3   Critiques of modern perceptual regimes, as launched by Benjamin (1977) and Buck-Morss (1992), are well founded in that they contextualize the transformation of the sensorium, which led to foregrounding a sense such as vision, and attempts to anesthetize other sense perceptions. Nevertheless, ocularcentrism should not be taken at face value, as this implies a numbing of our understanding of the modern sensorium. The point is to explore the tuning of the senses, and their synaesthetic interferences, in specific historical settings, such as the modern one.

4   For a more detailed outline of the notion "sensational form," see Meyer (2006a).

2

Audiences

Stewart M. Hoover

Media change and religious change
Religious authority and media authority
The religious "marketplace"
"Religious" and "secular" media
The culturalist turn in media studies
Audiences in context
Religion, spirituality, and the "common culture"

Audiences are essential to the media. The entire notion of mass communication depends on the existence, or cultivation, of a large number of people interested in attending to a given medium. There is, further, a relationship between generally accepted conceptions of the various media and the audiences that are attracted to them. For example, newspapers such as the *New York Times* or the *Washington Post* enjoy the devoted readership of the intelligentsia and managerial elites, whereas Web logs (or "blogs") command far greater attention among youth. Thus, media influence varies according to audience.

Our received ideas about mass communication, and thus media audiences, are the products of particular times and particular media structures. The term *mass communication* best describes a few particular media and particular conditions of audience practice. It applies to broadcast television over large networks particularly well but also fits large-circulation newspapers, film, and the popular music industry. "Mass communication" does not work so well with other aggregations of media audiences that nonetheless share commonalities with these examples, such as music performance venues, specialized videos or DVDs, limited-circulation newspapers and magazines, and print literature.

A process of rethinking mass communication and media audiences has been underway for at least three decades. This rethinking has coincided with—and to some extent has also been encouraged by—the reconceptualizing of a particular mode of audience practice: the consumption of mediated communication in relation to religion and spirituality. Seeing audiences anew has involved a shift in the way in which media scholars and critics characterize those audiences. Instead of regarding "religious audiences," whose identities and motivations toward religious or spiritual material would be assumed to reside in an essential, definitive religiosity, it has become important to think of the *audience for religion* (or spirituality). This moves the focus away from the presumed nature of the audience to the observed nature of the practice and as a consequence opens up to scrutiny a wider range of phenomena, media, and audiences.

Media change and religious change

More and more, the media are diverse and interconnected structurally, economically, and thematically. There are obvious differences and less obvious similarities between them, particularly when we consider their audiences. The print media of newspapers, magazines, books, and pamphlets and the screen media of television and film are prominent and obvious in these considerations and are what come to mind when "the media" are invoked in public discourse. However, radio broadcasting has had a long history as a platform for religion, particularly in the United States. These more traditional media are now joined by emerging settings and platforms which share affinities of context, taste, and consumption with their predecessors. Popular music has always been important in religious expression but now constitutes a distinct medium through its economic and material force in the media marketplace and its interactions with other media platforms and contexts, including radio and its increasingly important—and profitable— live performances. These other media are also increasingly interrelated with a larger range of products of visual and material culture, many of which constitute the elastic and growing symbolic and iconographic inventory of contemporary religion and spirituality. Finally, and most prodigiously, the emerging media of the digital realm, the Internet, the Web, digital downloads such as podcasts, interactive media, user-generated content, and the range of emergent platforms now appear to be important—even determinative— contexts for the development of contemporary media cultures (Brasher 2004; Campbell 2005).

There is a historical trajectory to these media and an implied view of these audiences that are important to articulate. Audiences for the earlier media were treated as more passive and perhaps reactive than audiences for the more recent media have been, particularly those of digital media. For example, advertisers distinguish between the so-called "push" media of television and radio as being displaced by the "pull" media of the digital age. Some media are thought to be able to carry information and messages that directly motivate behavior (they can "push" audiences) and other media that put audiences more in control (audiences can "pull" out what they want). The digital media are prominent examples of the second sort, in that they are claimed to constitute contexts of more or less infinite "supply" of resources from which audiences are more or less free to select.

The central emerging arguments about the nature of audiences for religion and spirituality in fact see such a shift in focus as paramount. This is rooted in changes that are fundamental conditions for both "religion" and "the media."

For nearly two decades now, religion scholars have been charting a decline in the importance and authority of religious institutions and a simultaneous rise in the authority and autonomy of individuals in charting their own religious and spiritual lives (Warner 1993). The resulting mode of religious and spiritual practice has been called "seeker" or "quester" religiosity (Roof 1999). This mode of practice is rooted in a contemporary cultural logic that encourages a quest for the ideal "self." Prominent social theorists, including Anthony Giddens (1991), have argued persuasively that the conditions of social life today encourage the individual to turn inward for the resources that were once found in the external social environment to support the development and maintenance of selves and identities.

This view puts the individual in a particular kind of position with reference to religion and spirituality. Though traditional sources of authority are losing their power to define and determine, individuals nonetheless must find meaningful and coherent sources to their quest (Clark 2003). Religious traditions of various kinds are ready sources but, in the present era, it is the individual who authorizes them in terms of their meaningfulness and legitimacy. There is a kind of dialectical relationship between the autonomous actor and the historically rooted symbolic and other resources. The individual's autonomy is not absolute in that there are limits to the range of things that might qualify as "religious" or "spiritual," those limits set to an extent by received categories of what defines "the religious." What is questioned in religious authority is not the nature or content of the symbols but the power and authority of religious institutions and leaders to define and determine the meanings of those symbols.

Religious authority and media authority

The decline in religious authority has two kinds of implications. First, there is the implication of the legitimacy of the symbols themselves (i.e., the stability or institutional fixity of their meanings and associations). Second, there is the question of the legitimate contexts for their presentation and consumption. Emerging audiences for religion and spirituality are then composed of people for whom the media context is a potentially legitimate source of religious and spiritual resources in ways that are unprecedented and, at the same time, this context provides new and novel symbolic and other resources. There is a homogenizing or "horizontalizing" effect of this situation, and audience preferences and practices bring the historically legitimate symbols into a context where their particular claims are understood to stand alongside other interpretations and other symbols. The aggregation of these seeking individuals into audiences also then supports the formation of the symbolic marketplace itself (Hoover 2006).

These media changes occur against the backdrop of an earlier, more stable, and centralized media context. The structure of television in the United States, Europe, and those national television systems influenced by the American and European models (which is by definition most of the rest of the world) had assumed a certain relationship between religion and broadcasting. Religious and cultural authorities believed that religion must necessarily have a place in the television landscape, and television authorities, eager to secure a role in social and cultural life, provided for it. At the same time, the potential for religious conflict and controversy encouraged arrangements that favored the established religious institutions as partners to broadcasting in these endeavors.

This situation favored certain approaches to programming and certain conceptions of the audience. Media and scholarship about the media for most of the twentieth century commonly regarded audiences as more or less passive recipients of television content whose religious mediascapes were defined by the policies and practices of programming authorities at the centers of culture and of media power. Furthermore, conceptions of the audience were rooted in the notion that religion should be primarily a "private" matter. The provision of religious materials by public authorities was done on the assumption that these would be consumed privately by audiences.

At the same time, both sets of authorities operated within a framework of choice that limited the range of offerings in two ways. First, as was common at mid-century, there was a widely shared sense that media producers would be programming for a mass, heterogeneous audience and thus that their productions were to be necessarily general in nature. Second, a kind of paternalism that prevailed saw the broadcasting context as suited to programming intended for the religious enlightenment or edification of audiences more than to programming that might serve religious experience or piety. Even though the broadcasting of religious services predominated, these were more formal and less experiential, more general and less particularist, and done with a broad, national audience in mind.

The prevailing framework suited religious authorities in that it symbolized their centrality to the culture. It worked for broadcast authorities by insulating them from the necessity of making choices between competing (and potentially conflictual) religions and religious claims. In this way, broadcast policies on religion reified formally what had been the case with prior media cultures informally (particularly the prodigious religious publishing industries): a preeminent place for formally constituted and established religious authorities at the center of the culture and of media culture (Rosenthal 2007). The role of audiences in this conception was as more or less peripheral participants in the public arena.

The religious "marketplace"

There was, of course, religious publishing and later religious broadcasting and religious film production that took place alongside and outside this system. Beginning with independent and nondenominational pamphlets, tracts, and other educational and inspirational materials in the nineteenth century and later as the evangelical impulse in (particularly American) Protestantism motivated increasingly independent and paradenominational publishing and radio and film production in the twentieth century, a parallel system of religious supply began developing audiences for this more informal, alternative material. These audiences then aggregated around media materials (and material culture) whose functions spread beyond the kind of paternalism that defined the material produced by the established institutions.

This system and these assumptions began to change in the 1970s with the advent of new video production and transmission technologies. Technology interacted with broadcast policies in the United States, Europe, and elsewhere intended to increase audience "choice" in screen media and intended to encourage the economic development of new screen media industries. There was growing dissatisfaction with the relatively limited range of television options (limited to a few commercial broadcast channels in North America and a few public service channels elsewhere), and advocates of broadcast deregulation were able to point to evidence of potential audiences and markets that would flourish under a new structure and regime.

The proliferation of channels and services that resulted significantly undermined the centrality of the former system wherein commercial and public service broadcasters largely determined practice both in overall philosophy or approach and in its execution. The alternative or parallel religious mediascapes also came into play in this era, as evangelical Protestant broadcasting, for example, found new platforms and markets in North America (and increasingly in Europe as well) and emergent audiences for these materials became accustomed to a range of religiously inflected materials available in the screen media marketplace.

The "decentered" character of religious production is significant because from the earliest days of the so-called media age, their commercial basis has given the media industries an autonomy that established their threat to other cultural and institutional authorities, including religion. This spreading economy cultivated and aggregated audiences across its new range of offerings, altering the basis on which earlier arrangements had rested. And these emerging audience centers have continued to develop and flourish, constituting a profound challenge to interests—such as religious authority—committed to the power and prerogatives that accrue to a single "center."

These changes coincided with rising "seeker" religiosity. Though it is not the case that the alternative religious content (evangelical broadcasting, the growing and vigorously commercialized Christian publishing industry, etc.) has competed in a real sense with the secular mainstream in ways that its proponents claim, it has expanded the range of offerings and demonstrated that a "market" for religion exists.

"Religious" and "secular" media

One of the consequences of these developments has been a subtle emergence of religious and spiritual content within "secular" media. Even though deregulation has undermined the former relationship between dominant religious and media institutions, they have not faded away. They remain the dominant players in the global "screen" marketplace in production and distribution. What has changed is their self-understanding. Mainline religious bodies, government agencies, and the media industries have gradually retreated from their presumptive position of centrality in cultural discourse, gradually integrating themselves into the broader economic marketplace and letting the logics of that marketplace determine practice and policy. Increasingly freed from the cumbersome and expensive burden of providing time to religion, broadcasters have also been relieved of the expectation that their policies represent determinations of the relative symbolic values of competing religious claims. As a freer marketplace of media choice has emerged, audiences and broadcasters alike have become comfortable with the notion that the marketplace might well determine the nature and extent of the religious mediascape.

Audiences have been empowered in the American religious landscape longer than in the media landscape. The commodification of religion was not new at the time of the video revolution in the 1970s and neither was the notion of a symbolic marketplace of choice in religion and spirituality. Developments in what has come to be called the "multi-channel era" have deepened and extended these trends. The convergence and concentration of media, leading to greater interaction between channels and developing synergies in the various markets, along with the increasing numbers of sources, services, and channels, has led to an impression of diversity. In fact, the diversity has become actual with the emergence of the digital media marketplace, further deepening and extending the integration of media into religious/spiritual seeking, and vice versa.

The culturalist turn in media studies

These changes militate in the direction of a new conception of medium, the audience, and audience relationship to these media. The fields of media and cultural studies have undergone a shift in focus as the media themselves have changed. Culturalist media studies are rooted in conceptions of the audience that shift the focus of scholarly inquiry from the "passive" to the "active" conception of consumption. The earliest work focused on received ideas about hierarchies of culture within media, critiquing them from the perspective of their relation to class, class tastes, and the cultural capacities of the classes presumed to make up "the mass audience." Opening the door to conceptions of the audience as active and to inquiry into audience tastes, motivations, and meanings at the same time opens the way to consider a range of tensions and contradictions within media culture. One of these tensions is that which we have identified in relation to what we might call "the establishment era" in religion and media. Just as culturalist scholars have pointed out the extent to which the network and public interest models of broadcasting defined and constrained audience subjectivities through their genre and programming strategies, we have seen how this process worked in relation to religion and spirituality. At the same time, though, there are important and intriguing contrasts.

I noted earlier that the overall sensibility has seen a shift from medium to audience as the focus of inquiry. This shift has been described as a change from an "instrumentalist" or "effects" paradigm to one that stresses practices of consumption by audiences. This has led to a broad range of inquiries into various classes, means, and modes of audience practice. Provocative studies of gender, families, youth cultures, politics and civic engagement, commodification, and the political economies of various kinds of media culture have resulted.

Work in the area of religion and spirituality was signaled for some in James Carey's (1975) call for the transformation of media research from a "transportation" to a "ritual" paradigm. There has been a good deal of discussion of the question of whether Carey meant his notion of ritual in anything other than metaphoric terms (Rothenbuhler 1998). However, for the present purpose, looking at the construction, practices, and meanings among audiences, such a distinction is not of great concern. The question of whether the media constitute a substantive sphere of religious practice (whether they become a kind of religion or function as a civil religion or replace religion, for example) is an empirical one that would direct inquiry toward such fields of activity.

Carey and his interpreters have joined the discourse on the side of the "active" audience. His model, focusing as it does on the way that media are consumed, experienced, and exist within the cultures to which they relate implies that the focus should be on audience practice. It is important to note that, though such paradigmatic conceptions of the role of media in late modern cultural life point to practices and consumption that might have a kind of normative status (they might constitute the imagined "object" such as religious practice), there is a wider field of conceptualization involved. It is important to make a distinction between intention and function in this regard. Regardless of what is intended by certain mediated texts and genres, what matters is what results from these expressions and their consumption. Thus, the question of who the audiences are and what they do becomes the central one.

Defining things in this more expansive way takes account of both the empirical-methodological issue of what to study and how to do it and the more theoretical question of how emerging modes of religious and spiritual practice are finding particular and enhanced expression in a media sphere that is evolving to accommodate, even encourage, them.

Audiences in context

There is a question about whether what we have been calling the audience for religion or spirituality can be thought of as distinct within the overall media landscape. This is important because of the long-standing patterns and practices whereby media audiences are made. There is both a historical and contemporaneous dimension to this. Historically, the emergence of the electronic media was far from tacit or unproblematic. Significant efforts were necessary to integrate media into the warp and woof of daily life. Contemporaneously, media audiences find in their practices significant points of identity and meaning, serving to provide stable "sources of the self." Along these dimensions, audiences are "made," they do not just evolve through some natural means.

As the new media objects and devices of the twentieth century were introduced into the domestic sphere, they were not necessarily easily or tacitly accepted there. Though it is true that each new medium has in a way been built on what went before, in a process of imbrication (Morgan 2007), some technologies have been more problematic than others and have required a degree of negotiation. Early phonographs intended for the home, for example, were marketed as fine furniture (Siefert 1994) as were early radios (Smulyan 1994) and television sets (Spigel 1992), and the content of each of these was directed at emerging class and taste sensibilities. Early phonograph recordings tended toward the classical, and much of early radio was also addressed to bourgeois aspirations in the moral and cultural spheres. Audiences were further cultivated by formats and genres intended to locate these media at the center of the culture. During the great depression and the two world wars, film theaters presented the newsreels through which American and European audiences experienced the wars and radio flourished as more expensive entertainments were less available.

By the 1950s, national media audiences had been well established, with a range of conventions and routines that firmly lodged them in the context of daily life. Thus, it came to be the case that the media were domesticated, and the domestic sphere mediated (Spigel 1992). Thus, audiences in the twentieth century revealed both acceptance and resistance, a seeming contradiction that continues to underlie public attitudes about the media today (Hoover 2006; Hoover et al. 2004).

Religion, spirituality, and the "common culture"

Audiences are self-conscious about their practices, and this self-consciousness plays an important role in modern identity formation. Simply put, we are today well prepared to describe ourselves in terms of the media we consume and in terms of the kinds of media we reject or consume as a "guilty pleasure." These reflexive self-descriptions are in a way a function or a result of the processes whereby the media have been "domesticated" and the domestic "mediated." There is a sense in which this project is incomplete. Narratives of media in private life are far from tacit but carry specific and focused critiques of the media, critiques that are often religiously inflected. These critiques are complexly and incompletely related to behavior, and it is this contrast that is evidence of the extent to which the media are not fully domesticated," and the domestic sphere is not comfortably mediated.

It is a widely shared stereotype that religious people tend to be the most prudish or moralistic about media culture. Experience has led public discourse to expect that the more religious the audience, the more likely they are to find fault with entertainment television, popular film, popular music, and other popular arts. These critiques serve the issue of identity in that such viewers are also likely to think of their view of media as important to describing who they are, that is, "...I am the sort of person who finds such-and-such program objectionable...." Popular discourse around the film *The Passion of the Christ* in 2004 clearly revealed these connections between media preference and identity, as many, many conservative Christians coalesced around this film as an important theological statement and as an opportunity for the expression of identity through aggregation around this important alternative media expression. These audience identity claims thus form important framing devices both for audience practice (conservative religious parents claim certain kinds of rules and behaviors surrounding media in their homes) and for identity (the sort of affinities discussed above). Those on the other end of the religion-spirituality spectrum have proven just as likely to narrate their media consumption, though with different objects. In 2004, for instance, they were more likely to identify with *What the Bleep Do We Know* or *Farenheit 9/11* than with *The Passion of the Christ*. And, they were also likely to actually derogate the media on the other side, wishing to make themselves distinct from the latter film and similar materials.

Both religious liberals and conservatives resemble others in their social class in their attitudes about media. Spiritual seekers, likely to be better educated and higher-income than those who are more conservatively "religious," are attracted more to elite media than to popular forms. Thus, their identity statements regarding media frame public television and radio, art films, and other such materials as preferred. They also tend to take a particular view of the major popular-media framing categories: questions of "sex" and "violence" in television and film. It is commonplace to expect religious conservatives to be more concerned about sex and religious liberals to be more concerned about violence. This does tend to be the case, but more important to our discussion here, those on the Left reflexively understand the stereotype and have been known to make openness to sexuality in media an important point of identity.

Across audience categories, there is a rather consistent tendency for these identity statements *vis-à-vis* media to be contradicted by behavior. People tend to say one thing and do another when it comes to media consumption. A widely circulated example of this is the success of the salacious prime-time drama *Desperate Housewives* in the U.S. Bible Belt during its early seasons. Though it had lower ratings there than elsewhere, its viewership in this conservative region of the country was higher than one would have expected if the widespread religiously conservative critiques of popular culture were also determining viewing behavior. Many studies find this to be the case at the individual household level as well, that even in households where the media critique is the most explicit and focused, derogated media are nonetheless consumed. Thus, we can say of audiences that their attitudes about specific genres and forms are important, historically lodged statements of identity and meaning, while at the same time, the attractions and pleasures of actual media consumption is a different, though related, matter. And, as religiosities and spiritualities often necessarily carry with them commitments to certain normative ideas and values, those who would identify with religion or spirituality as important dimensions of their lives are particular audiences within these landscapes. In general, though, spirituality and religiosity seem to relate more to the reflexive identity questions than they do to actual audience behaviors (Hoover 2006).

This distinction between belief and behavior among audiences obviously complicates the study of media audiences and the study of media audiences in relation to religion and spirituality in particular. Much empirical work depends on various kinds of self-report of media behavior, and these reports tend to be unreliable as precise measures of actual behavior. The point is not that people are inconsistent, which is widely known. The more profound issue is the question of how and why such audience identities are formed and maintained and what purposes they serve. Though much remains to be done on this, the outlines of it are becoming clear, as we have seen, and some more insights will do so with further investigation.

As I said before, there is a way that the media serve as a kind of "cultural center" of society, a gathering place for the representation of a common conversation that spreads across contexts and localities. This is a function that is lodged in historical circumstances in the mid-twentieth century, and this common culture and "the media" can be said to have evolved together in such a way that there exists within both the media and media audiences a rather firm and stable expectation that among the genres, structures, and functions of the various media will be those media and those moments where this sense of centrality is important. It is expressed, of course, at moments of crisis such as the 9/11 and 7/7 events. It is also expressed in significant moments of cultural ritual, such as major sporting events and political campaigns. However, it also aggregates around purely "media" events of celebrity and charisma. For audiences, it is important on some level to be able to be part of a common conversation about these things, and there are important cultural currencies that attach to the ability to be conversant in the common culture. This is particularly important for young people, but it is a cultural affinity that other generations share. And, there are "common cultural" resources for these subcultures as well. Youth want to be part of the common discourse about popular music, for example. Women are aware of, and attracted to, a common discourse about "women's issues." And, equally important, there are media devoted to these tastes and interests (motivated in part by their economic logics and economies of scale).

The history of the audience for religion provides a certain structural dimension to this picture that is significant. As we saw earlier, there have been continuing efforts for most of the last century for religious particularism to develop its own media. The "radio preachers" of rural America are an example of this, as are the Billy Graham organization's film projects (Hendershot 2004). More recently, specifically religious productions and production goals have been expressed in other ways, for example through the expanding offerings of the Christian Booksellers' Association and high-profile books for the Christian market such as the "Left Behind" series. *Left Behind* was also made into motion pictures for theatrical release. In many of these efforts, there is an objective of "crossing over" between the religious and the secular markets, to infuse the latter with the values of the former.

In fact, such crossing over is rarely successful. What tends to happen instead is the continuing aggregation of audiences around distinct "general" and "religious" media. Where the crossing over takes place is with audiences for religion. That is to say that those among the audience who are most morally committed to the values of the "religious" media marketplace nonetheless are also in the audience for the "general" media marketplace. It seems to be the case that the major reason for this is the appeal of the "common culture." Religious audiences want to be able to maintain their particularist identities, but at the same time they are drawn to the larger, more general, conversation and discourse.

The pressures in this direction are profound. Their children and adolescents are drawn to the media of youth culture. Their friends and neighbors are aware of—and talk about—the latest films and television programs. Their class identities and loyalties come into play as well, as American evangelicalism has long been deeply culturally articulated with its geographies and classes of origin, and the media are adept at marketing to such identities that for most adherents are mostly indistinguishable from their religious identities. Media turn even derogated symbols and values into "guilty" pleasures, and religiously motivated audiences are amenable to such influences. This situation is compounded by the fact that many religious viewers seem not to be particularly attracted to specifically "religious" media, thinking it is good that it is there, but good that it is there for "…someone else, who really needs it" (Hoover et al. 2004; Hoover 1988).

There is further evidence of this "common cultural" phenomenon when we investigate directly what kinds of media (outside the specifically "religious" media) religiously motivated audiences would find to be positive. Whether we look at the specific examples of media suggested by individuals in the audience or at more general statements of what constitutes "good" television, film, or popular culture, the thing that seems to link these ideas is that such media need to be "inoffensive." That is, they need to fit into a general or heterogeneous marketplace and carry general, least-common-denominator values. They tend not to say that specifically or self-consciously religious content needs to be part of the mix. They might feel that it is important that such programming be produced by religious people or that such people be part of the entertainment industry. At the same time, though, they accept and recognize that media culture is a common culture, intended for a heterogeneous audience.

As we saw earlier, this "common media culture" serves as a place wherein contemporary religious and spiritual sensibilities can find resources fitted to their quests. This tends not to work in a categorical way, where strict boundaries can be seen between cultural interests such as religion, spirituality, gender, or politics. The contrasting prospects of the *Left Behind* films and *The Passion of the Christ* provide examples of this complexity. As we noted, the *Left Behind* franchise was immediately coded as "religious" and, in spite of its production values, did not achieve the "crossover" effects predicted. *The Passion of the Christ*, by contrast, did achieve greater crossover success, attracting Catholic and other non-evangelical audiences in large numbers.

Among *Passion's* effects was an apparent renewed interest in religion on the part of Hollywood. More religious products were predicted for the film mainstream. However, media culture operates according to its own logics with a certain elasticity. In the years after its release, *The Passion* has faded in effect, subsumed into a media marketplace where a number of trajectories streaming out of it illustrate the complexity that audiences encounter there: The "Mel Gibson" trajectory led toward *Apocalypto*, and the "religious spectacle" trajectory toward *What the Bleep Do We Know?* and then to James Cameron's pop archaeology. The politics trajectory flowed to Michael Moore's *Farenheit 9/11*. An effect of the mediated public sphere, then, is the destabilization of the category of "the religious" in media audience terms. People are attracted to common culture media of various kinds, and at the same time the media marketplace provides media products in trajectories that direct interest and combine interests and values according to "Are audiences for religion or spirituality unique?" As we have seen, there is reason to believe that they are not that different from the audience in general. The difference is a matter of interest and practice. Though we find within the audience those who we can typify according to religiosity, spirituality, or religious interest, these do not turn out to be definitive of action. This is owing in part to the imperfection of our understandings of how identity and action should be related in these regards. It is also owing to the changing nature of the religion and spirituality and of the media marketplace. At this point in time, it seems, there is good reason to continue to focus on audiences in terms of their identities and motivations. Otherwise, we will find ourselves once again missing an important dimension—the media dimension—of emerging patterns of religion, spirituality, and the range of sensibilities and practices that bear a family resemblance to religion and spirituality, but are at the same time bursting out of our formalized and essentialized categories.

3

Circulation

Johanna Sumiala

Tracing circulation
Circulating gaze
Circulating imagination
Circulating religious associations
Circulating ethics

If we have been able to show that glorified sites like global and local were made out of circulating entities, why not postulate that subjectivities, justifications, unconscious, and personalities would *circulate* as well?
(Latour 2005: 207; original emphasis)

We live in a network society; a society in which everything is always in circulation; items, ideas, and even social relations—without rest—liquid, as Zygmunt Bauman (2004) calls it. The *Oxford English Dictionary* defines circulation as

the transmission or passage of anything (e.g. money, news) from hand to hand, or from person to person (with the notion of its "going the round" of a country, etc.); dissemination or publication, whether by transmission from one to another, or by distribution or diffusion of separate copies.

The simplest way of defining circulation is, thus, to say that it is about "going the round" or "passing on" something (or both)—whether it is material or immaterial items, goods, artefacts, ideas, or beliefs that are being distributed and disseminated.[1] In today's world, circulation could not be understood without the strong role of the media. The anatomy of mediated circulation consists of a number of *encounters* with different actors: new and old media, images, texts, viewers, subjects, venues, consumers, vendors, markets, experts, journalists, producers. In short, circulation in today's world is acted out in cultural and social *networks* shaped by the communicative logic of the new media technology. Networks enable people to communicate individually from one to one, but even more important, they make it possible for individuals to participate in communication exchanges in which their mode of address is semi-public rather than private (Lister et al. 2003: 172). To paraphrase Manuel Castells, to live in a network society means to be invited into a new, informational mode emphasizing knowledge generation, information processing, and symbol communication (Castells 2000). The network society is made out of numerous new technologies that diverse people use in diverse real-world locations (Miller and Slater 2000: 1). It is within these networks that people form, transmit, and modify their self-understanding (or mis-understanding!) about the world they live in and in which their lives are formed, transmitted, and modified by others (see also Morgan 2005: 149). This is to say that circulation is a form of the cultural work of the network society (Castells 2000).

How these encounters—crucial in understanding the dynamics of circulation in network society—are constructed in the media is the topic of this essay. The central element of the encounter is its ability to construct relationships between different actors (Latour 2005). My analysis focuses here, namely, on the circulation of images and relationships established around them. As David Freedberg reminds us,

> We must consider not only beholders' symptoms and behaviour, but also effectiveness, efficacy and vitality of images themselves; not only what beholders do, but also what images appear to do; not only what people do as a result of their relationship with imaged form, but also what they expect imaged form to achieve, and why they have such expectations at all.
>
> (Freedberg 1989: xxii)

In this essay, I present a typology of three types of relationships between (1) the image and technology, (2) the image and the artefact, and (3) the image and the spectator. By emphasizing "the visual aspect" in circulation, I take seriously the challenge proposed by scholars of visual culture who argue that the study of contemporary way of life should take a broader look at how images or visuals (or both) are part of our ways of relating to this world and establishing relationships in it (see e.g., Mirzoeff 1999; Jay 1988; Mitchell 2005a; Sumiala-Seppänen and Stocchetti 2007).

In this essay, I am especially interested in images of large circulation. Even in the culture characterized by constant flow of media images, as ours, there are types of images that have a potential of striking more public attention and get wider public circulation than others. Images of the Abu Ghraib (AG) torture scandal belong to this category.

Immediately after becoming public in 2004, the images started to circulate among different mediated spaces. In the era of digital revolution, these images were easy to reproduce, distribute, and disseminate through different channels of communication (see e.g. van Dijk 1999: 6). They were shown on several Internet sites and international and national television channels; printed in numerous newspapers; and eventually published in books dealing with the scandal (see e.g., Danner 2004). An event that first took place inside a U.S. army prison ended up affecting the network society on a global scale.

One of the most prominent images of AG featured in the media was an image of a hooded man (Jabar) positioned on a box, having wires attached to both hands and supposedly to his penis.[2] In another AG image, a naked man stands in front of the camera with his arms spread wide, feet crossed, and his naked body covered with dirt and excrement. At the level of the obvious, what are being circulated here are the two torture images as objects, but there is more than that. As Latour points out, it is *subjectivities, justifications, the unconscious* and *personalities* that circulate as well (2005: 207). Drawing on Latour's (2005: 217) terminology, I consider the AG images to be actors operating in a large web of circulating mediators communicating with one another, constituting new kinds of associations and relationships. For Latour, circulation involves a process of making connections between disparate actors and of making sense of these connections. In other words, an actor can gain strength only by associating and establishing relationships with others (see e.g. Latour 1988: 160).

In the first part of the chapter, I explore the role of the new media technology and images establishing encounters with each other. In the second part of the chapter, my focus is on one specific type of an encounter: a relationship between the spectator looking at the image and the tortured represented in the image. I argue that to understand the circulation of the relationship between the spectator and the other in the image one needs to analyze a visual practice structuring the act of seeing: the gaze (see e.g. Morgan 2005: 2–6, 2007a; Seppänen 2005). In this connection, I apply Arjun Appadurai's (1997) idea of *social and cultural imagination* describing the dynamics of fashioning imagined association stimulated by different visual interactions with the image (see also Burke 2001).[3] I ask what kind of religious associations potentially circulate through the practice of imagination between the spectator and the image. Finally, I draw some preliminary conclusions about circulation and its ethical implications in contemporary network society.

Tracing circulation

My analysis starts with a basic Latourian notion that circulation of the two images is established around a series of encounters between technologies, artefacts, and humans (see e.g., van Loon 2005: 9). According to Latour,

[i]nformation technologies allow us to trace the associations in a way that was impossible before. Not because they subvert the old concrete "humane" society, turning us into formal cyborgs or "post human" ghosts, but for exactly the opposite reason: they make *visible* what was before only present virtually.

(2005: 207)

In Latour's thinking, circulation is strongly affected by technological agency. The two AG images are themselves enabled by their translation into particular technological operations. In other words, they are mediated by various interfaces and switches, establishing digital connectivity. The process of distribution is complemented by countless cross-references and cross-fertilizations between new and old media; newspapers and television referring to Web sites and vice versa (see also van Dijk 1999: 165). However, also as van Loon points out, every medium is by its very nature "interfacial"; it performs translations between different types of forms (2005: 11). The process of image circulation can thus be described as a continuous multiplicity of flows that are only partially and temporally stabilized in emergent assemblages. In the case of the two AG images, this results in numerous opportunities for various actors to get invited into associative contacts with them.

Second, circulation is acted out on condition, wherein relationships are between different images as artefacts. The two AG images are *photographs* taken by soldiers using their camera phones. Latour argues:

...[o]bjects occupy the beginning and the end of a similar accumulation cycle; no matter whether they are far or near, infinitely big or small, infinitely old or young, ...[t]hey all take the shape of a flat surface of paper that can be archived, pinned on a wall and combined with others.

(1987: 227)

In the case of the two AG images, this is especially true with photographic reproductions that were printed in news media or were published in books and articles on the issue (see e.g., Sontag 2004; Danner 2004). On the Internet Google image archive, one can find several images of the same event and cartoons commenting on "the original" images. It is in these encounters between the images that different kinds of associations potential for circulation are made possible. What kinds of associations are eventually activated depends on variation, order, and context of portrayal. For example, when the two AG images are put side by side and "read" from left to write, one can assume that what is represented is a torture narrative of one and the same man. There is no face shown in the first image to prove that he is not the same man as in the other image. This means that the change in the order of representation may change the narrative, which again affects the associations established around the story.

The third dimension of circulation has to do with relationships established among individuals. There are two paths to follow here: relationships between spectators and the tortured men pictured in the images and relationships among individuals, who are looking at the tortured in the images. Common to both categories of relationships is that they are established in conditions that are not very much tied to the parameters of time, place, or territory. Instead, spectators living in diverse locations and cultures are invited to connect with these images and with one another in "a complex mosaic of differently sized overlapping and interconnected public spheres" (Keane 1995: 8 in van Dijk 1999: 165).

Circulating gaze

The spectator's ability to establish a relationship with the tortured is always tied to the fact of what is put on view; in other words, what is circulated and disseminated to the public (see also Boltanski 1999: 128). It is also tied to the ways and practices of looking at the images (Sturken and Cartwright 2005); in this case, especially the ways of looking at the images of torture (see e.g., Seaton 2005; Chouliaraki 2006). Drawing on David Morgan and many other scholars of visual culture, I approach the practice of looking by applying the idea of the gaze (see e.g., Morgan 2005; 2007a; Brennan and Jay 1996; Bryson 1983). The gaze is understood here as a visual field—a network in itself —that constitutes a social act of looking (Morgan 2005: 3). According to Morgan, several elements are included in this field: a viewer, a fellow viewer, the subject of viewing, the context of the subject viewed, and the rules that govern the particular relationship between viewers and viewed. This means that gaze *activates* certain possibilities of meaning, certain forms of experiences, and—most important—certain *relations* among participants of the visual event. It is the gaze that relates the one seeing and the one to be seen, conventions and structures of seeing to physical, historical, and ritual contexts of seeing (Morgan 2005: 3–4; see also Seppänen 2005).

In the case of the AG images, this means that different gazes are constructed depending on a spectator's historical, cultural, political, ethnic, religious, and social background; emotional involvement; condition of looking, whether he or she is looking at the images in private or in public space, alone, or with other people, what kind of media he or she is using; the structure and convention of looking, how he or she approaches the images as a genre of news, information, entertainment, propaganda, spectacle, harassment. The type of gaze can vary greatly; there can be an emphatic gaze, a sympathetic gaze, destructive gaze, male gaze, sadistic gaze, tourist gaze, Western gaze, an Oriental gaze...

When giving a closer look to the practice of gazing, one realizes that the relationship between the spectator and the tortured is rarely symmetrical. The asymmetries are shaped by different ways and hierarchies of looking and being looked at. In his analysis on historical portraits, Allan Sekula argues about "shadow archives" containing images of the heroes, leaders and moral exemplars of society and images of its poor, diseased, insane, criminal, and somehow radically "inferior" members (Sekula 1986; see also Lury 1998: 44). According to Sekula, every portrait has to take its place either implicitly or explicitly in this social and moral hierarchy of types of genres:

> The *private* moment of sentimental individuation, the look at the frozen gaze-of-the-loved-one, was shadowed by two other more *public* looks: a look up at one's "betters" and a look down at one's "inferiors."
>
> (Sekula 1986: 10; emphasis in original)

The two AG images can be considered portraits subjected to looks (whether private or public) that *categorize* the other stimulated by Sekula's *shadow archives*. However, it is worth noting that because of the complexity of circulation, the "shadow archives" themselves are also pushed into a move. Another source of asymmetry has to do with *scopic regime*—a concept coined by film scholar Christian Metz and further developed by Martin Jay (1988)—the idea that every era is characterized by certain kinds of visual structures that suggest some interpretations more likely than others. I argue that in the two AG images, there is an explicit structural asymmetry between the representations of the tortured as a passive victim subjected to the gaze of an onlooker. In the first image, the tortured is hooded, blinded, and objectified for a penetrating gaze; in the second one, the tortured is escaping the eye of the spectator by looking away from the camera. Composition in both images favors a superior gaze that looks down at the tortured as inferior, as also described by Sekula.

Another source of asymmetry has to do with recognition. There are at least two ways of approaching the question of recognizablity. The first one has to do with the physiological and mental perception of the image, such as we can recognize that there are humans in the AG images (see e.g. Pylyshyn 2006). The ability to recognize such an element is a first precondition for making sense of the images but not enough to understand them. The second approach to recognition has to do with the cultural and social perception of the image. It can be called "a politics of recognition," referring to a demand to be seen as an actor with a status acknowledged by others. In a classical model, the process of mutual recognition is about constructing identities. It is a crucial part of the reciprocal relation between subjects (see e.g., Fraser 2005: 243–51).

In the case of the two AG images, we can make the following observations. First, the spectator may recognize that the two humans are men and that they are portrayed as objects of torture. In this process, the men are given an identity of victim. Second, the spectator may recognize that the ones committing those acts were American soldiers. They are given an identity of persecutor. However, this information is not in the pictures. The persecutor is visually absent in the images, and the only person portrayed is the one tortured, and we can not even be sure whether there are two different men tortured or just one and the same in both images. So to recognize the persecutor, a spectator requires contextual knowledge of the event. Without it, one is unable to realize that the acts of torture were carried out by American soldiers abusing Iraqi prisoners, that there were many of those tortured, and that pictures were created to be further circulated among colleagues, friends, and relatives of the soldiers.

Another, more complicated, argument draws on the assumption that the tortured person and the persecutor are recognized, given identities of a victim and a victimizer, but are nevertheless *identified* differently, depending on the gaze of the spectator. Identification means here a psychological process whereby the subject assimilates an attribute of the other and is transformed, wholly or partially, after the model the other provides (Laplanche and Pontailis 1973, 2006: 205). The spectator is offered the possibility to give the tortured the identity of a sufferer—but not to identify oneself with his position. As a result, the identity of the victim is recognized, but his social status is *misrecognized* (see e.g., Frazer 2005: 247). It is my argument that the blindness and passivity of the victim in both images emphasizes the asymmetry in the relationship between the viewer and the viewed. Neither of the victims is gazing back. This fact underlines the tortured's inability to establish a reciprocal relationship with the spectator: to be able to give the viewer an identity and a social status from a perspective of a victim or actively refuse to identify himself with the identity given to him by the spectator.

Luc Boltanski (1999) reminds us that the process of identification is affected by the length of the mediated chain that is established between the spectator, the one tortured, and the agent who causes the suffering. According to Boltanski, the situation becomes more and more delicate as the distance between the spectator, the persecutor, and his or her victim becomes greater (1999: 62). This is especially true with the AG images. Owing to a complex circulation process fragmented into different mediated spaces and spheres, different kinds of physical, cultural, social, and historical distances are established between the spectator, the tortured, and the persecutor, making the processes of recognition, misrecognition, and identification even more heterogeneous.

Circulating imagination

The emphasis in the Latourian approach is on the analysis of different *conditions* of circulation, acted out in various relationships established in connection with numerous actors (spectators, media technology, and photographic images). Furthermore, these relationships are to be traced through careful description of associations characterized by visibility and the ability to leave traces: verbal and written debates around the images, visual comments such as cartoons on the topic, iconoclastic or political acts (or both) around them.

But what about the circulation of associations that do not leave visible or material traces? In other words, how do we grasp the circulation of associations when they are first and foremost *imagined*? And even more important, how should the media analyst make sense of those associations?

Arjun Appadurai offers an interesting insight into a problem of nonvisible associations by claiming that images are to be considered sites of imagination:

> The image, the imagined, the imaginary – these are all terms that direct us to something critical and new in global cultural processes: **the imagination as a social practice.** No longer mere fantasy (opium for masses whose real work is elsewhere), no longer simple escape (from a world defined principally by more concrete purposes and structures), no longer elite pastime (thus not relevant to the lives of ordinary people) and no longer mere contemplation (irrelevant for new forms of desire and subjectivity), the imagination has become an organized field of social practices, a form of work (both in the sense of labor and of culturally organized practice) and a form of negotiation between sites of agency (individuals) and globally defined fields of possibility. It is this unleashing of imagination which links the play of pastiche (in some settings) to the terror and coercion of states and their competitors. *The imagination is now central to all forms of agency*, is itself a social fact, and is the key component of the new global order.
>
> (Appadurai 1997: 31; bold face in the original; italics added)

In Appadurai's interpretation, images can be treated as actors establishing connections with other actors (e.g., spectators establishing relationships with the image representations). However, unlike as in Latour, the emphasis in

Appadurai's insight is on *imagination as a social practice*. For Appadurai, imagination serves thus as a catalyst for unfulfilled participatory needs and desires, but it also has an ability to establish controversial imaginaries powerful enough to shape and reshape social relationships. This calls for the analysis of *imaginal linkages* and *connections* with *the spectator and the image activated potentially in the social and cultural practice of looking.*

Circulating religious associations

The imaginary or imaginal associations that spectators make are heavily drawn—either consciously or unconsciously—from memories, which are culturally, socially and historically conditioned (see e.g. Burke 2001). Especially interesting are associations of religious connections. In the story line of AG, it was an acknowledged fact that both tortured men were Muslim and that the images were taken by U.S. soldiers, representing a nation of strong Christian inheritance and influence.

The analysis of religious traces in the AG images shows that they both are filled with many religious references that are culturally and historically grounded. In the image of a hooded Muslim man called Jabar, one can see references to public executions. There are explicit visual signs of the death penalty and the use of electric shock (still in use as one means of execution in the United States). As a historical, cultural, and/or political institution, public execution is found in all three religious traditions: Islam, Judaism, and Christianity. In all of them, the victim can figure as an innocent martyr, sacrificed for the sins of the others; or as an evil enemy deserving destruction, as the shape of the hood in the first image recalls the robes used by the Ku Klux Klan during ritual lynching or execution of African Americans as what might be called, according to the KKK's racist ideology, race-criminals.[4] In the other image a naked man standing before the camera and covered with dirt and filth resembles representations of Christ on the cross or being scourged by Roman soldiers. The humiliated Muslim prisoners may appear to some viewers to echo the Christian visual tradition by occupying a subject position similar to the innocent and unjustly mistreated Jesus, who was abused and then executed in a state of abjection and bodily violation (cf. Sontag 2003: 40-46).

Media historian Jean Seaton discerns an explicit linkage between media and Christian conventions of regarding suffering. I call this type of gaze emphatic. Seaton states:

> [C]hristianity did provide a vehicle for relating to, and expressing, what could be called the interests of suffering. This has had an enduring impact.

Themes involving pain and redemption are an abiding feature of modern media.

(Seaton 2005: 87)

And she continues later on:

There are some continuities that are hardly ever even recognized. These may be at the level of values, but there are also powerful visual conventions that merit examination. At the very simplest, the composition of images plunders motifs invented by Christian art. But the attitude which we bring to the assessment of real events is more complicated than is allowed by our necessarily shallow everyday acceptance of them as part of life.

(Seaton 2005: 89)

However, cultural imagination drawing on Christian tradition has many other layers than just that of imagining the sufferer as a victim. An observation that holds true also with many other religious traditions. As David Morgan argues, in Christianity and, for example, in Hinduism, there is also a long tradition of treating the images as a part of contemplation and meditation (Morgan 2005). The emotional attachment established in a contemplative relationship with the image can be constructed also through a sympathetic gaze, helping the spectator to create a more reflective relationship with the suffering individual (see e.g. Morgan 1998). This can invite the viewer to make ethical and moral judgments based on his or her worldview and to establish a relationship with the tortured structured around perhaps more abstract and general principals concerning how one should treat others.

Furthermore, religiously inspired cultural imagination can stimulate iconoclasm, that is, the practice of destroying images when they fail to tell the "truth" and are for that reason found dangerous and/or offensive (see e.g., Freedberg 1989: 421–8; Morgan 2005: 141–6). Iconoclastic imagination can come in many forms and can be found in many religions and in secular movements. Controversial images such as the AG images can stimulate a deconstructive gaze and call for action, suggesting the need to defend the values of one's own religion and worldview. With the AG images, this holds true especially when discussing the imagination potentially stimulated and associations supposedly circulated by and around Muslim tradition, as the tortured men were Muslim. An example of an iconoclastic association could be imagined in the look of a devoted Muslim who sees the rules of his religion being violated through the public exposure of nakedness and impurity.

Circulating ethics

My analysis suggests that circulation as a cultural logic (as described above) is especially powerful because we live in a network society. The communicative logic of the new media technology makes it possible for us to get invited to such a media spectacle as the AG image scandal on a scale unlikely or even unimaginable for earlier generations. In this process of circulation, we are asked to establish relationships with the images disseminated and with the ideas and beliefs attached to those images circulating around us.

I have argued here that to understand the logic of circulation, we need to analyze the conditions of relationships established between different actors, including relationships between images and new media technology, images and other visual artefacts, and images and spectators. In my closer analysis of the relationship between the AG images and the spectator, I have explored the idea of visual practice: the act of gazing and its relation to cultural imagination.

Religion as a source of cultural imagination is of great relevance when the subjects of circulation are images of Muslim men tortured by soldiers representing a culture of strong Christian heritage. In the eyes of the viewer, religious aspirations can suggest the emphatic gaze: that is, identifying emotionally with the suffering of the victim. Or it can stimulate the sympathetic gaze, which reflects deep values of human life. However, it can also call for the deconstructive gaze, urging iconoclastic action—a need to defend one's religious beliefs through destroying or trying to stop circulation of the images.

In a Latourian perspective, all these relationships constructed in the circulation of images are far from being totalizing, stabilizing, or symmetrical. Instead, they change constantly and, at their best, they can be grasped only for a very few scattered moments in time and space. In this sense, a Latourian approach is a useful tool for thinking about new *conditions* for circulation and asymmetries between different actors, shapers and consumers in contemporary world (see e.g., Couldry 2008: 3–4).

Drawing on Zygmunt Bauman, this type of imaginal association can be called "liquid." Bauman describes the essence of liquidness in the following manner:

> Liquid... (the term I prefer, since it emphasizes the processuality of relationships; it calls to mind patterning rather than patterns, structuring rather than structures, something constantly in-the-state-of-becoming, unfinished and revocable) manifests itself as much in the assembling of relations as in keeping them eminently "dismantable."
>
> (Bauman 2004: 22)

In this perspective, it is circulation of liquid imagination as a multi-currented, scattered, and flowing the social practice that flourishes in conditions of the continuous multiplicity of translations, as in the case of the two AG images.

To sum up, analyzing the dynamics of circulation in contemporary society is of great importance because circulation heavily emphasizes the complexity and multiplicity of the problem of distribution and dissemination in the network society we are living in, whether it is dissemination of material objects such as photographic images of AG or religious ideas attached to them. The process of circulation can be described as an endless chain of associations and relationships developed in those encounters. As a consequence, the problem of framing becomes unavoidable—what kind of potential associations are relevant and from which perspective? Where to draw the line in the analysis of different relationships? In my view, circulation of associations stimulates and nurtures the interpretation of relationships with spectators and with the tortured others. These interpretations are characterized by heterogeneous and fragmented cultural imaginaries potentially activated in the act of looking but remain difficult to trace empirically. Yet it appears that it is through engaging a never-ending chain of circulating imaginal associations that we establish a common world. As a cultural work of network society, circulation seems to play an unexpectedly significant role in that enterprise.

Notes

1 *Distribution* and *dissemination* are used here often synonymously. The difference between the concepts is that distribution refers more often to circulation of goods and items such as news images, whereas dissemination refers to circulation of ideas, and beliefs (see e.g. Peters 1999).

2 The case of Abu Ghraib where Iraqi prisoners were abused and tortured by American soldiers first came to public attention in spring 2004 after the publication in U.S. media of some disturbing images. These images had been shot by American soldiers using new media technology, digital cameras, and videos. Because they are widely available on the Internet, they have not been reproduced here.

3 Latour on imagination and digital traces; see e.g. Latour 2007.

4 Ku Klux Klan is the name of several American organizations advocating white supremacy, anti-Semitism, anti-Catholicism, racism, homophobia, anti-communism, and nativism. These groups have a history of murdering, terrorizing, intimidating, and oppressing other social and ethnic groups (see e.g. Kellner: 46).

4

Community

J. Kwabena Asamoah-Gyadu

Community, media, and religious experience
Religious quest: Individual and communal
Religious pluralism, media, and community
New media and community
African religion, migration, and community
Media ministry, actual institution (ministry), and community
Community media

Contrary to earlier predictions of the "death of God" by the turn of the twenty-first century, religion is flourishing. Increased religious fundamentalism and proliferation of new religions and religious media means our world remains enchanted. Through the media, religion has gained increased visibility and space in public discourse in spite of attempts in the West to keep it as a private endeavor. Its core ingredients, concerns, and defining characteristics include belief, worship, faith, sacrifice, transcendence, doctrine, offering, mediation, pilgrimage, prayer, community, creeds, icons and images, symbols and other relational elements, and devotions to sacred objects and practices. "Transcendent reality" and "community" remain the two axes around which the others revolve. Along one axis religion presupposes the existence of a transcendent unseen realm, the source of life, power, comfort, sustenance, and strength. Along the other axis is the earthly realm of human beings commonly associated with weakness, limitation, powerlessness, helplessness, the search for meaning and, ultimately, with death. The two axes intersect in revelations and human responses as people search for salvation in a precarious world. Religious groups constitute community in its quintessential form because shared aspirations for deliverance from the human predicament throw people together. Indeed, in traditional cultures such as those of Africa and Australasia, the sacred and secular realms of existence remain inseparable, and the key word is "participation." Religious community here potentially includes the living and the transcendent ancestor who may be physically dead but remains an active participant in the religious life of the community.

Community, media, and religious experience

Thus, religion, as I understand it in this chapter, should not be defined apart from the relationship that exists between "transcendent realities" and the human "communities" that embody them. The very expression *community* recalls such relational concepts as "common," "share," "engage," "interest," "identity," "interaction," and "encounter," all having something to do with a sense of "belonging" and "participation." The sense of belonging engendered by the community of living beings enables the definition and construction of identities. A human community is a fellowship or association of persons sharing common grounds on matters of mutual interest. Religion means that this identity is inspired by shared religious experiences. In her work on *Religious Sensations,* Birgit Meyer draws attention to the fact that dichotomizing subjective and primary religious experiences on the one hand and the religious life of the community on the other is problematic. The disposition of the individual in search of God, she points out, is "part and parcel of a discursive, and hence shared cultural construction" (Meyer 2006: 8). This is the thinking that will direct the thrust of this chapter on "community." Without the community that depends on what Meyer refers to as "sensory regimes"—that is, the bodily techniques, doctrines, and practices that make up a religion—the searching individual craving for experiences of a transcendental nature would be nonexistent (Meyer 2006: 9). The media play a central role in providing the "symbolic resources" through which we make meaning out of our social worlds and "religion and spirituality are important parts of that meaning-making" process (Hoover 2006: 56).

In traditional African philosophical thought with its religious orientation, the individual exists because others do, too: "I am because we are and because we are I am." Sensational forms, Meyer rightly argues, are "transmitted and shared," and this is particularly evident in one of the key themes of religion: worship. In Pentecostal worship, for example, where the experiential presence of the Holy Spirit is coveted, a lot is made of "feelings," "sensations," and "transformations" in the divine-human encounter. However, these elements are not restricted by time and space. In our hi-tech world, television and radio programs "address anonymous viewers" and listeners, asking them to participate in televised and radio-broadcast events. It is not uncommon to hear testimonies of "feeling God's presence" and being healed through those media. In one case from Ghana, a viewer even spoke in tongues merely by listening to a television sermon on that theme and, in another, a stomach ache was healed by touching a radio at the request of the preacher. The two experiences formed the subjects of testimonies in church on the following Sunday, validating the community's orientation toward those media as extensions of their ministry. Access to the media means the boundaries of religious community are being constantly redefined. In Africa, Pentecostal-charismatic communions now influence the dominant modes of representation, that is, the formats, styles, and ways of framing in the public sphere leading to a gradual "Pentecostalization" of that sphere. One way in which this has been achieved is through the film industry, wherein worldviews of mystical causality are sustained. This ever-popular African film industry is dominated by story lines that privilege Pentecostal Christianity over traditional religions by demonizing the latter as the domain of the devil.

Birgit Meyer writes that "collective rituals are prime examples of sensational forms, in that they address and involve participants in a specific manner and induce particular feelings" (Meyer 2006: 9). Her observation recalls the Muslim practice of praying at set times facing a particular direction, wherever one may be around the globe. It also brings to mind the Pentecostal religious practice of the "prayer chain." Here, individual members of the community are charged to pray on particular topics, during particular hours, and for the same length of time. During that period, people may be praying individually but, in fact, they do so as participants in "community" separated only by distance and space. They remain one in spirit and in the Spirit. Similarly, the world of media has seismically altered the way in which sacred realities are encountered. Members and nonmembers of religious communities have become consumers of mediated religion, making the mass media leading players in the field of religious belief and practice. Defining religion within the context of visual practice, for example, David Morgan refers to "configurations in social relatedness and cultural ordering that appeal to powers that assist humans in organizing their collective and individual lives." Further, religion is a way of controlling events or experience for the purpose of living better, longer, more meaningfully, or with less hazard (Morgan 2005: 52). For many, then, particularly in non-Western primal cultures, religion is a survival strategy and usually something that involves the entire community.

However, religion as expressed in the modern West can also be a highly intellectualized activity. The very conscious and sometimes aggressive attempt to keep religion private and to restrain it from encroaching on public space has led partly to the innovative "mediatizations" of the sacred we find in the modern world. Community-based religions such as Christianity and Islam feel under siege. One Internet web site is named "Indians against Christian Aggression": www.christreview.org. The two religions have reacted in different ways, including the creation of virtual religious communities that access religious resources through the media. A sense of shared belief and purpose and of mutual support, for instance, helps televangelism's viewers to face threats to their faith (Alexander 19994: 85). In the aftermath of 9/11, the world was treated to a systematic demonization of Islam through the media. Through the same media, Muslim communities have bonded together to ensure their own survival and for the preservation of the holy things they hold dear. The public expression of religion such as church attendance may be declining in the West but on television, on radio, and on the Internet, it is now possible for Christian communities to access religious resources for daily consumption. The media play important roles in the formation of religious identity, and its resources are used "to proclaim the truth, mobilize the masses, protect the faithful and lay down the gauntlet to non-believers" (Thomas 2005: 4). The deep and innate human desire to link up with, or even feel touched by, a meta-empirical reality has led to the reinvention of religion in many ways, including the formation of new communities, and the media are being used to great effect for religious purposes. Several African pastors of independent churches now text daily words of inspiration to the mobile phones of their members. And "religious broadcasting constitutes a religious activity that is produced and viewed by people who share common symbols, values, and a 'moral culture' they celebrate" (Hoover 1988: 21). That is the essence of community: to produce a sense of identity, belonging, and comfort—virtues that are not discontinuous with the aims of religion.

Religious quest: Individual and communal

Modern media democratize access to the sacred, the quest for religious fulfillment and salvation or whatever "rewards" expected from encounters with transcendent realities. Particularly in the West, this contributes to what Stewart Hoover refers to as "personal autonomy" wherein increasingly religion is seen as "a project of the autonomous, reflexive self" (Hoover 2003: 11). In the West, religion has thereby moved "away from situations in which religious institutions and histories are definitive to situations in which individual questing and practice have become more definitive" (Hoover 2003: 12). This trend is heightened by three main developments: the religions-under-siege mentality, religious pluralism, and the intrusive and overbearing nature of modern media. The media in all its forms has developed as a "midwife" between the world of transcendence and the world of humans. Thus, an insightful foreword to Hoover's *Mass Media Religion* notes how television religious broadcasts, for example, "can 'strengthen' and deepen the faith of viewers by providing them with instruction, exhortation, inspiration, hope, encouragement, entertainment, example and opportunity for service" (Martin, in Hoover 1988: 11).

In *The Sacred Gaze*, Morgan also serves us well by recognizing "images and visual pieties" as vital parts of religious practices that put beliefs to work in the experiences of both the individual and community. More often than not, the experiences of the individual are meaningful in terms of shared religious experiences of the community. Thus, the community is an "important site for visual culture" (Morgan 2005: 54). Morgan's basic argument is that religious images are better appreciated as integral parts of visual practice, explained in terms of "a visual mediation of relations among a particular group of humans and the forces that help to organize their world." His explanation that images and objects can operate very powerfully in religious practice "by organizing the spaces of worship and devotion, delineating certain places as sacred, such as pilgrimage sites, temples, domestic spaces, and public religious festivals" may be illustrated by the following practice (Morgan 2005: 55). In the reinvention of the Wesleyan camp meeting tradition in my native Ghana, I have often been struck by the innovative transformation of secular spaces into sacred ones by the installation of a cross. Camp meetings among Ghanaian Methodists take place in public parks. To set that space apart from its previous profane uses, a giant wooden cross is erected in the center of the park to signify that space as temporary sacred space.

The cross usually remains there for the entire duration of the camp meeting as the focus of community and ritual. The worshipping community believes in the newly acquired status of these usually grassless parks and would often collect the sand used to mount the cross for whatever therapeutic purposes they can serve after the camp meeting. The image, Morgan states,

> declares by virtue of its signage or its iconic presence or its incursion into otherwise profane space or its complete isolation from everyday traffic that something significant is happening, or once did, that the devout should pay special heed.
>
> (Morgan 2005: 56)

The enthronement of the holy book in Sikhism, as cited by Morgan, and the presence of images in worship such as the cross in African Methodist camp meeting traditions and on local and international pilgrimage sites such as Mecca and Lourdes thoroughly vindicate his exposition. And among the import of images to religious communities, Morgan refers to how they have been employed as media of communication with the "unseen, mysterious, and potentially uncontrollable forces that are understood to govern life" (Morgan 2005: 59).

Religious pluralism, media, and community

All the empirical data point to the fact that modern media, particularly in its electronic forms, have been at the center of the resurgence of religious consciousness since the middle of the twentieth century. Evangelically minded Christians are renowned for their innovative uses of the media motivated by the belief that technologies remain gifts of God for Christian mission. For example, non-Western Pentecostal-charismatic religious communities emerged as a direct result of contacts with North American televangelism. The powerful theology of "sowing and reaping" and the "health and wealth" gospels in these contexts are traceable directly to people like Oral Roberts and the Copelands. The availability of religious television has not only engendered a sense of belonging to international organizations, but the distribution of audio and video tape recordings of the international ministries synchronized messages and led to the development of important networks.

The new religious communities that have emerged in the non-Western world as a direct result of religious media are by no means restricted to Christianity. New religious communities of Hindu, Buddhist, and syncretistic persuasions have formed in these contexts too. They include Eckankar, a middle-class neo-Hindu movement with a North American guru or "living master" called Harold Klemp, the Nichiren Shoshu Soka Gakkai of Buddhist lineage, and the Hindu movement, International Society for Krishna Consciousness. These are movements with roots in Asian traditions, but most of them have come to the Third World through American devotees. New religious communities in non-Western contexts thus very often owe their origins to the influence of the Western media. In many cases, a "seeker" after alternative ways of being religious has listened to a tape, seen a documentary, read a book or magazine written by a North American devotee, and has proceeded to request more material. These media-instigated contacts have eventually culminated in the establishment of branches of such movements in Third World contexts.

New media and community

Because the element of "communing" is implied in communication, the goal of communication is partly a call to community (Lehikoinen 2003: 254). In an article on *Living Word* hosted by Pastor Mensa Otabil of Ghana's International Central Gospel Church, Marleen de Witte enables readers to see how new kinds of media theology from the stables of Pentecostal-charismatic religions allow virtual communities to participate in religious discourses and practices (De Witte 2003). In instances known to me, healings and breakthroughs have occurred through prayers offered on television and radio programs. The new media available include posters, overhead street banners, and car bumper stickers that not only advertise the programs of churches but, most important for our purposes, tell the world about the benefits of joining a particular church community (Asamoah-Gyadu 2005a).

The use of car bumper stickers issued by churches immediately identify owners with specific religious communities. There is no doubt that new forms of mediated religiosity have contributed to creating and extending forms of community, strengthened personal self-esteem, and given people hope in the context of the disruptions in modern urban life.

Rather than challenge the new traditions, mainline churches have joined the trend and are offering similar mediated religiosity. In African mainline churches, this has been taken to another level with car bumper inscriptions such as: "I am a Methodist and I love my Church" and "I am proud to be a Presbyterian." Those familiar with the hemorrhage suffered by these historic mission denominations at the emergence of the new Pentecostal churches would appreciate the church stickers as defensive mechanisms against the popularity of the newcomers. Pentecostal-charismatic pictorial images on religious billboards, for example, are also chosen to reflect particular theological moods and identities. They usually would have large portraits of the pastor and his wife in their best clothes and sometimes shots of members at worship selected to portray the large numbers of people in that church community and how happy they are together. In Pentecostal-charismatic Christianity in particular, numbers are important indications of God's favor and indices of the viability of the messages of prosperity they preach. Congregations, in keeping with prosperity mindsets, must be mega-sized to reflect the potency of the anointing of leaders, and members speak proudly of these numbers as signs of God's blessing. God is advertised as such. This perception and interpretation of community goes against the grain of conventional thinking that communities must be kept to manageable sizes for people to have a sense of belonging. In these newer Christian religious contexts, belonging to a large "family" is what is important; being personally known is usually secondary.

The transition from radio to television in the middle of the twentieth century was nothing short of an electronic revolution as far as information and communication are concerned. The invention of the transistor radio virtually moved listening to that medium from being a communal to a "privatized" affair. However as Mitchell explains, radio's potential to involve people in depth, increased flexibility resulting from portability and ease of access have contributed to the continuing commitment to radio listening (Mitchell 1999: 62). Today, radio goes with people wherever they are, as they are found in every automobile and on mobile phones and computers. Religious communities can be reached by their leaders through radio religion, ensuring that the religious menu intended to keep the faithful on course is not restricted to regular places of worship. The use of the media and the availability of religious resources outside the boundaries of the church, mosque, or ashram enable the continuing "feeding" of the flock not just through radio but via sermons on video and audio cassette tapes, CDs, and DVDs that members can even circulate as a way of selling the viability of their own religious persuasions and communities.

Religious communities may have evangelical or political agendas or both, and the media are used to pursue those aims. In this vein, Pradip Thomas shows how the meticulous, systematic uses of the media by Hindu nationalist forces in India, the Vishwa Hindu Parishad and the Bharatiya Janata Party, by the Taliban, backed by the technologies of marketing, have played key roles in their visibility in the public domain. Further, Hindu fundamentalists in India, he reports, have used video to great effect and more recently satellite television. Their mass leaders such as Sadhvi Rithambara are what they are today, Thomas notes, because of their cassette ministries (Thomas 2005: 7). Christians belonging to the revivalist and evangelical streams still dominate the new forms of media in terms of religious usage, but the examples here demonstrate how competitive the field has become in the attempt not simply to win souls but to enable people to belong to national and transnational religious communities. Through television, radio, and the circulation of audio and video cassette tapes and CD and DVD recordings, the media have been employed to literally transform and revolutionize religious communities. In some cases, the revolution has been literal as communities adopt militaristic tactics to reinforce their beliefs and claim lost territories.

African religion, migration, and community

Compared to the kinds of private religious practices that North Americans are familiar with, Rosalind Hackett has noted that religion in Africa is less individualistic and more group-related (Hackett 2000: 103). Further to this, whereas primal societies generally conceive of religion as a system of power and of living religiously as being in touch with the sources and channels of power in the universe, Christian theology in the West seems on the whole to understand the Christian Gospel as a system of ideas (Bediako 1985: 106). These distinctions are important because they have implications for the way in which religion and community engage with each other in the two contexts. Non-Western traditional cultures connect better with religious systems that focus on rituals of intervention, so movements that focus too much on personal reflection and meditation never enjoy mass followings among people. One way to appreciate the interface between religion and community in African life and the focus on power is to look at it from the perspective of migrant communities from the continent in the Western Diaspora. Their lives are full of uncertainties, but hope is kept alive through the availability of sermons on Internet web sites and receipt of recorded church services from pastors back in their home countries through whose prayers the journey to the European and North American "paradises" are made possible.

In her groundbreaking work in this field, Gerrie ter Haar is emphatic that religion is central to the existence of African communities. This position challenges previous definitions of African immigrant communities in terms of their ethnic identities. The result of defining African migrant communities in terms of their ethnic identities is that "groups of migrants who consider themselves bound by a shared religious faith may be defined by others in their new homeland as connected primarily by a common ethnic origin" (Ter Haar 1998: iii). This position, which is challenged by Ter Haar, amounts to a misunderstanding of the critical and almost non-negotiable role that non-Westerners in general and Africans in particular assign religion in community formation. In the precarious immigration environment in the Western world today, religion is for many African immigrants "an outstanding way of coping with difficult surroundings" (Ter Haar 1998: iv). There are many ways in which immigrant churches express the sense of community gained from practicing their faith in the Diaspora. One of these is the giving of testimonies. This involves sharing personal stories of God's deliverance amid the uncertainties of life in Europe. Gerrie ter Haar's explanation of the relationship between religion and community among African immigrants in the Netherlands is representative of such communities elsewhere:

> While giving testimony [in church], individual witnesses are surrounded by friends and fellow-believers who were close to them in their time of trial. They are a visual representation of the moral support needed in these circumstances. For example, a person may have applied for a residence permit and visited the immigration police for months, without making any progress. If one day the request is unexpectedly granted by the authorities and the applicant provided with the precious documents, this turn of fate is ascribed to divine intervention. ...There are abundant stories of divine intervention in seemingly hopeless cases form a source of inspiration to those who are still waiting for a solution to some intractable problem or negotiation with the government.
>
> (Ter Haar 1998: 45)

Thus, the immigrant church is now the context within which Africans and Latin Americans demonize and fight immigration authorities. At one such prayer service in Chicago during the 2006 Easter service, the immigration authorities in the United States were all "soaked" in the blood of Christ that they would be restrained from "touching" any soul connected to the African Christian community whose status was irregular. These ways of expressing faith within community keep religion alive in African life and existence.

Giving testimonies clearly fulfills an important role in mutual support and encouragement among migrants. Through testimonies, individual believers are able to share their concerns with others in the congregation and thereby receive mutual support both material and spiritual through the combined efforts in prayer.

Media ministry, actual institution (ministry), and community

Taisto Lehikoinen also refers to attempts in the study of religious media communication to distinguish between "media ministries" and actual or church-type institutions or ministries as I designate the latter (Lehikoinen 2003: 250–3). There is a tension, he notes, between mediated ministries and actual church ministries, a tension that he crystallizes into the following questions: "Do media ministries serve as constructive religious suppliers for already churched people? Or do media ministries and church ministries compete against each other in ways that erode the authority of church bodies?" Lehikoimen concludes by referring to the established view, arguing from a Western viewpoint that "active consumers of religious media are also active members in their local congregations" (Lehikoinen 2003: 251). He refers to Peter Horsfield, who echoes the mainline position that the electronic church cannot be a genuine Christian community (Horsfield 1984: 52–63). In the developing world, there are very few ministries that are predominantly media based. Most media-based ministries are representatives of actual ministries or churches, so members are actually encouraged to "participate" together with their families in the ritual of viewing as a continuous aspect of church life. The influence of religious media on non-Western communities is thus very strong and far reaching.

The questions raised by Lehikonen arise because of the ability of religious media not only to influence religious orientation but to generate religious communities. It is not uncommon for members of media-generated communities to divert financial resources—tithes and offerings—away from their regular church communities to the ministries of television, radio, and book evangelists who may be reaching them at their points of need through those media. In the words of Lehikoinen, "Media ministries have been a successful new form of mediated religion, which guarantees their influence and continuity, because they can fulfill genuine religious needs through the use of media" (Lehikoinen 2003: 252). Generally giving, including tithing, offerings, and donations, is a big theological practice in Pentecostal-charismatic religion. The sacramental value of seed sowing so passionately regarded by Oral Roberts has greatly influenced the theology of giving in this type of religion across the world. In the Western world where ministry could be completely media based, the strength of the religious community dedicated to that particular ministry could be assessed through the sacred practice of giving. Though the followers of media ministries may not be able in every case to participate immediately in the activities of a given ministry, they may do so remotely or vicariously through their giving. Such donations serve three main purposes in the religious practices of the sorts of ministries that use the media most. First, donations serve as "points of contact" or channels of blessing for the donors. A person's salvation and success in life have virtually become dependent on the material investments he or she makes in the kingdom business of modern radio and televangelists. In return, donors are integrated into a virtual community of religious consumers of the pastoral products of particular evangelists. They receive books, audio and video cassette tapes, and recordings of sermons. Second, the community of donors helps to perpetuate and extend the influence of the ministries concerned. Third, donating money legitimates a ministry, helping the "minister" to see how his or her ministry is appreciated and helping the donor to participate in feedback mechanisms that facilitate the success and longevity of media ministries.

Community media

Community media have been with the Western world for many years. Here community radio stations and newspapers were the main means of relaying information to people and articulating concerns with which communities could immediately connect. As with other forms of media, community radio and newspapers made people feel important and gain a sense of recognition that then enhanced their sense of belonging and care. The chief objective of community media, as Robert White explains, is to create *dialogue* in the community. They have a strong commitment, he notes, to become a "voice for the voiceless" and make a special effort to develop the communication competencies of less-educated minorities (White 2003: 287).

Community media developed in Africa from the early years of the colonial period where they gradually replaced the periodic visits of Ministry of Information vans that toured villages bringing news from the seat of government. The distance between the government and the grassroots was quite wide, but information and documentary cinema vans brought things closer by bridging the gap. It used to be a great pastime in many African villages as they congregated in the village park on weekend evenings to watch documentaries on the nice things and developments going on in their capital cities. Community media also have a strong educative agenda. That was its essence, so in African countries they tend either to be owned by churches or else have a very strong religious orientation. Community media, which in Africa tends to be radio and the local newspapers in vernacular languages, therefore served as extensions of church-based informal education programs and other religious services. They are greatly improved now and, with the increase in the rate of literacy, a number now combine the vernacular and foreign languages as the mediums of expression. The use of the vernacular in these media ensures a sense of affinity and ownership between the media and grassroots communities. The Roman Catholic Church is a leader in the provision of religious services through community media, and it explains in part why that church continues to have a strong presence in Africa in the face of the challenges from Pentecostal/charismatic communions and Islam.

Conclusion

We have noted that there are two core ingredients of religion: the world of transcendence and that of the community of worshippers. The survival and identity of any religion depends on its community of believers and how they express faith in the worshipped. The media play an important role in identity formation. Moreover, religions and new religious movements use media not only to proclaim the faith but to redefine and extend community, often understanding community as a form of mediation. The "evangelical imperative" is strongest in new religious movements because of the need to offer innovative menus that have the ability to draw from existing communities, and the media is used to great effect in the pursuit of that agenda. The essence of religious communication is to motivate audiences to join the actual community. This guarantees the need for effective media evangelism and the effective instrumental use of media to recruit members of the listening audience into becoming active in the services of the church. The main challenge of any media-enabled religious community, then, is to develop technique and content which in effect motivates the audience to participate in the activities of the actual community.

The global Christian media ministry is dominated by the evangelical stream encapsulating the Pentecostal-charismatic varieties with their strong orientation toward experiential religion. The attractions of this type of religion under the heat of Western secularization and non-Western sacralizations of life are obvious. In the Western world, people are searching for alternative ways of meaning beyond materialism and, in non-Western contexts, people look for religion that connects with traditional spirituality with its emphases on experience and existential salvation. In both worlds, the media have become the frontier and location within which identity and meaning are sought. Thus, whether we are talking about Western societies or non-Western, media have become important for community formation and identity, both virtual and real. The alluring effects of media religion have proven too much to resist; the religious menu offered through the media constitutes extensions of actual ministries. In today's media world, no religious organization can lay absolute claim to the allegiance of its registered members. The media have not only universalized religious belief and practice but have democratized access to the sacred, making it possible for the use of media to deepen, advertise, and even hype the formation of communities.

5

Culture

Angela Zito

Religion and media
Culture (and religion) as meaning
Culture (and religion, and media) as practice
Culture as mediation
Some examples

"...The project of the Enlightenment philosophes was radical revision of the nature of culture that would displace religion from its dominant position...The institutions and media of civil society: philosophy, literature, the arts, sciences, journalism and popular culture also gained at religion's expense and became the prime venues in which ethical and aesthetic issues are seriously engaged...the chief battlegrounds in the cultural conflicts of modernity."

Bruce Lincoln, "Culture"

"Culture is one of the two or three most complicated words in the English language... partly because of its intricate historical development, in several European languages, but mainly because it has now come to be used for important concepts in several distinct intellectual disciplines, and in several distinct and incompatible systems of thought."

Raymond Williams, *Keywords*

"The concept of culture is such a weak and evanescent notion in American social thought....This intellectual aversion to the idea of culture derives in part from our obsessive individualism, which makes psychological life the paramount reality; from our Puritanism, which leads to disdain for the significance of human activity that is not practical and work oriented; and from our isolation of science from culture: science provides culture-free truth whereas culture provides ethnocentric error."

James W. Carey, "Communication as Culture"

What can a concept as weak and baggy, as ambiguous and conflicted, as "culture" possibly offer a new field beset by enough of its own problems? As scholars began taking up the study of religion and media in tandem in the 1970s, they were burdened by the attitude illustrated above by Lincoln: that, in modernity, religion and "the media" (as a secular institution of civil society) were in conflict. And behold, the very object of their epic struggle was over the role of arbiter of culture as a quintessential value in modernity. Yet the last decade has seen early scholarship on "religion and media," which had assumed that the domains of "religion" and "media" were in collision and competition, give way, somewhat ironically, to an understanding of the two in terms of a larger frame, usually glossed as "culture." The difficulty becomes apparent: are we speaking of culture as the discursively and historically specific object of fraught struggle in human communities or culture as designating an object of critical method and analysis?[1]

The world today is bound in a matrix of very complex media whose infrastructure allows ever more complex global interconnections. At the same time, religious life has a larger admitted public presence than ever before in modernity. The discourses of individualism, utility, and scientific rationality that Carey points out in the excerpt above as dominating communications studies, crowding out a version of "culture" associated with meaning and religion, are, if anything, stronger than they were in 1975, the year of his seminal essay. In this quick discussion of "culture," I deal with "several distinct and incompatible systems of thought," as Williams notes in what must be the primordial example of a "Key Words" volume. To glean something useful from this reframing of religion and media in cultural terms, I propose that we must understand cultural analysis itself through several phases: culture as meaning, culture beyond meaning as practice, and finally, culture in terms of "mediation." We might also see something interesting, something new, in the very invisible and unrepresentable at the edge of "meaning," the secret that religious practitioners seem constantly to imagine themselves verging on as they seek to mediate their worlds (Meyer 2006)—something that presents a sense of limit even as it opens, organizes, and politicizes the senses in specific ways for specific, collective life-worlds.

Religion and media

As religion and media were brought into simultaneous view (from the fifties through the seventies), they were, according to Stewart Hoover, construed in conflictual opposition as a "dualism," each half of which was considered to be "coherent, transhistorical, unchanging...independent and potentially acting independently upon one another" (Hoover 2006: 8). Lincoln notes that this perception had its grounding in precisely the version of post-

Enlightenment history in what Jeremy Stolow calls a "powerful myth about social modernization," one that credits print media especially with the "disembedding of religion from public life and its relocation within the private walls of bourgeois domesticity, or the interior, silent universe of individual readers" (Stolow 2005: 122). Hoover has written that this historical moment has given way, empirically, to a world wherein media and religion are drawing ever nearer in terms of functions: "[T]hey occupy the same spaces, serve many of the same purposes, and invigorate the same practices in modernity" (Hoover 2006: 9; see also Hoover and Clark 2002: 3).

Regardless of whether one invests in this version of the historical Enlightenment rearrangement of culture, there remains the problem of the implicit theory grounding such dualistic approaches as *analysis*. Stolow links this powerful "myth" of Enlightenment culture to Jürgen Habermas's work on the public sphere and rightly reminds us that, though the secularization thesis that religion will gradually disappear before various aspects of modern rationality has lost its explanatory cachet, its corollary—that modern media are inevitably agents of secularization—still carries on. In the zero-sum game notion that mass media compromised and diluted religion, we see religion privileged as an ideal matter of belief, paralleling the notion of "culture" as mental, meaningful, circulation of ideas. The implicit theoretical underpinning at work is a Parsonian isolation of culture (as meaning) from society (as function; Parsons 1966). Thus, it is not obvious that a recognition of the empirical shift in the relations of religion and media as domains of social life that increasingly interpenetrate in the world (Hoover's point, and well taken) will automatically push forward new theorization past this notion of culture-as-meaning.

In fact, James Carey's famous critique of 1975 staged an early intervention that, though pioneering for its time, called for exactly such inclusion of the dimension of meaning. He rightly accused communications theory of reproducing an account that was strictly functionalist, what he called a "transmission" view of communication: individualist, utilitarian, instrumental. In his prescient article "Communication as Culture," Carey proposed instead that communication should be seen anew in a "ritual" mode, one that privileges "symbolic" production. In considering modes of theorizing culture relevant to our studies in religion and media, I begin from that point, a moment indebted—as Carey himself notes—to Clifford Geertz and an earlier version of cultural anthropology that emphasized culture as meaning (1975: 35).

Culture (and religion) as meaning

One can hardly overestimate the influence of Geertz's version of culture as symbolic on disciplines outside of anthropology proper, including history, media theory, cultural and literary studies, and various area studies far beyond his own fieldwork sites of Indonesia and Morocco. He was himself much influenced by philosopher Suzanne Langer and burst forth with his anti-functionalist meaning-centric anthropology on an era saturated with the (re)discovery of "meaning" as the key philosophic problem.[2] The late sixties and the seventies were an era of the "discovery" of the culture concept in this new guise—as a symbolic dimension, liberated from any taint of functional usefulness and instrumentality—and much reduced from its more holistic use by earlier social anthropologists.[3]

A relatively obscure essay from 1977 by theologian John Morgan strikes the celebratory tone of the era. He puts Geertz in dialogue with the "cultural theologian" Paul Tillich (as Tillich called himself) over "Religion and Culture as Meaning Systems." Morgan notes that, having "set(s) out to articulate the distinction between culture and social system…[Geertz] seeks to come to grips with dimensions of human culture, particularly of meaning which except for Weber, have too frequently gone unattended by traditional functionalism" (Morgan 1977: 367). As religion and culture are both taken to be "meaning systems," it was possible for anthropologists and theologians to embark on a conversation about analytics. Thus, we see produced a festive tangle among meaning, religion, and culture. Tillich's own contribution to this ferment was the concept of "meaning-reality," which, according to Morgan, "cannot be expressed in the raw, but rather, must be experientially expressed through *religiocultural media*, that is, *symbol systems*" (Morgan 1977: 369; italics added).

It was Geertz's beginning from the symbolic itself that seemed to offer so much promise, and indeed provides still, today, a fine pedagogical starting point for understanding the salience of the materiality of the symbolic for cultural analysis. In his famous article, "Religion as a Cultural System," first published in 1966, he applied his symbolic analysis model to religion, providing an oft-quoted definition. A religion is

(1) a system of symbols which acts to (2) establish powerful, pervasive, and long-lasting moods and motivations in men by (3) formulating conceptions of a general order of existence and (4) clothing these conceptions with such an aura of factuality that (5) the moods and motivations seem uniquely realistic.

(1973: 90)

Geertz's most lasting contribution for our purposes in thinking of the nexus of religion and media comes through his emphasis on the symbol as the materially and publicly available means of discerning thinking and the workings of mind. As he says, "Cultural acts, the construction, apprehension, and utilization of symbolic forms, are social events like any other; they are as public as marriage and as observable as agriculture" (1973: 91). Symbols were (and are) media that are susceptible to semiotic analysis and decoding. They form structures that in turn structure consciousness (Swidler 2001: 75–6). This approach clearly opens up a world of possibility for studying religious media: those material artifacts including things and performances of all sorts. It presents them as crying out for interpretation, for a hermeneutics (Masuzawa 1998: 79–82). Geertz's attention to the aesthetic dimension of human activity—which he seems to have wanted to rescue from consideration merely by literary and art historical scholars—led him, however, to slight dimensions of social life imbricated in politics and power, and for this he came under increasing attack.

Indeed, the 1970s also saw the beginnings of the critique of the hermeneutics of culture as meaning read as though it were a text. This critique proceeded in at least two interrelated directions: from within literary studies, attack was mounted on structuralism and semiotics as too fetishizing of the interior of textual meaning—as though it were given once and for all and thus was ahistorical. Pierre Macherey's *A Theory of Literary Production* appeared in English in 1978 (having been published in French in 1966). Because of Macherey's close ties with the Marxist cultural theorist Althusser, his critique opened up "culture" to even closer susceptibility to study as "ideology" and thus to questions of power and politics. From another angle, this overemphasis on "interiority" and the decoding of meaning was felt to lead to neglect of analyzing the *processes of the production* themselves of the text or artifact or ritual—for understanding the material, institutional, or indeed "social" production of these symbols that had come to loom so large in the landscape of the human sciences as to have hijacked the entirety of "culture" as an analytic. Both angles of critique were affected by Marxist scholarship on ideological production.[4]

Talal Asad has twice critiqued Geetz's work on the religious as symbolic (1983, 1993). In the first essay, Asad faults Geertz for neglecting religion and power

> in the sense in which power constructs religious ideology, establishes the preconditions for distinctive kinds of religious personalities, authorizes specifiable religious practices and utterances, produces religiously defined knowledge.
>
> (1983: 237)

It is not only Geertz's attempt to construct a "universal, a-historical definition of religion" that annoys Asad; his very definition of culture seems to Asad to suggest a "distanced spectator-role" for those living within it as they "use symbols" to "develop their knowledge *about* and attitudes *toward* life." This leads to imagining a cultural form like religion as isolated from "material conditions and social activities" and reduced to consciousness (1983: 238–9). Asad instead proposes that we break down the (false) distinction between technical and expressive action (1983: 251) so key to the version of "culture-as-meaning" to which James Carey invited communications study. Asad regrets that:

> Religion itself is rarely approached in terms of "technical action"—the disciplining of the body, of speech, which is used to produce religion in its variety. Such disciplines are preconditions for specific forms of thought and action, but they must be taught and learnt, and are therefore themselves dependent on a range of social institutions and material conditions.
>
> (1983: 251)

Wrapped up in that statement is a new approach to culture, growing out of the post-structuralist critique, that is, that culture must be approached as process and not as thing; that it is produced through the social organization of material life, in time, and through human efforts; that this is all accomplished through the agency of persons whose very subjectivities are one of the products of this process. In short, that cultural life is conducted through "practice," another idea with a Marxist pedigree.

Culture (and religion, and media) as practice

If the first round of the critique of meaning, which cast it as ideological production, emphasized the "ideological," this round raced toward "production." By the time Asad's second critique of Geertz appears in 1993, in his *Genealogies of Religion: Discipline and the Reasons of Power in Christianity and Islam*, the "practice turn" in theory had overtaken the old paradigm. As Asad puts it:

> ...the formation of what we have here called "symbols" (complexes, concepts) is conditioned by the social relations in which the growing child is involved in which other symbols (speech and significant movements) are crucial. The conditions (discursive and nondiscursive) that explain how symbols come to be constructed, and how some of them are established as natural or authoritative as opposed to others, then become an important object of anthropological inquiry.
>
> (1993: 31)

Asad cites Marxist theorist of language L.S. Vygotsky on how "symbols organize practice," and are intrinsic to "signifying and organizing practices" of all kinds (1993: 31–2).

The translation of Pierre Bourdieu's *Outline of a Theory of Practice* into English in 1977 became a touchstone for practice theory generally. Sociologist Bourdieu inveighed against the reification of society as a series of structures that overwhelmed actors, turning them into prisoners of a previously ordained, always already written "script." Accordingly, his sense of practice emphasized the strategic, constantly changing ways in which people seized a symbolic repertoire and constantly remade it. Emphasizing embodiment itself as the site of discipline and practice, Bourdieu held out the promise that his models could deliver us from that split between mind and body. In terms of the study of religion, it could free us from the trap of thinking that a theory of practice was reducible to its understanding as "ritual" in the older sense of how "belief" leads to "practice," which would be tantamount to treating religious life as merely the expression of a timeless set of cultural assumptions.[5] This would still enshrine a split between belief-doctrine-text and action-ritual-performance, between thinking and doing.

Meanwhile, the last twenty years have seen a slow shift in religious studies itself, which parallels the shift from meaning to practice in cultural theory. Scholars have criticized the Enlightenment emphasis on cognitive and intellectual aspects of religious life (belief in ideas and doctrine) and moved toward an interest in wider applications. One of the primary figures in this critique has been Donald Lopez, a scholar of Buddhism, whose essay on "Belief" in the volume *Critical Terms for Religious Studies* (1998) makes the point that the expectation that religion is based primarily in "belief" is Christian. To be even more specific, it is Protestant, as Eric Reinders notes in his article on Protestant missionary attitudes toward ritual and bowing in China. Their criticisms of the Chinese reiterated their criticisms of Catholic popery and ritual-obsessiveness (Reinders 1997).

Lopez's series of "Religions in Practice" published by Princeton University Press, whose first volume on Buddhism appeared in 1995, stands as a serious corrective to the "belief" paradigm. These books act as emblems of the trend in the study of religions of turning away from philosophy, with its attention to scriptural sources of a literate elite and toward examining the things that many different sorts of people did. Overwhelmingly historical in scope, the collections present many sorts of text-media: hagiographies, gazetteer stories, stele inscriptions, merit books, folk legends, fictions, economic contracts, writings of spirit mediums, and ritual handbooks and texts.[6] Though Lopez led the editorial charge in promoting practice through Asian materials, David Morgan's work on popular visual media as objects and organizers of Christian devotion in the United States grows from similar theoretical insights (Morgan 1998; Morgan and Promey 2001).

The orientation to practice theory in religious studies also lined up with a growing interest in embodiment, a trend whose first era culminated with the publication in 1989 of the three volume collection in the Zone series, *Fragments for a History of the Human Body* (Feher et al. 1989).[7]

In media studies, Nick Couldry has recently called openly for "Theorising Media as Practice," finding it necessary to demand a project to "decentre media research from the study of media texts or production structures (important though these are) and to redirect it on the study of the open-ended range of practices focused directly or indirectly on media" (2004: 117). By now, this wish to move a field away from such dualisms as text-structure should seem quite familiar. That Coudry published this piece in the journal of *Social Semiotics* is telling. He feels that a turn to practice will encourage focus on "what people are doing in relation to media across a whole range of situations and contexts" (2004: 119). He rehearses, as we have here, the promise of rescue from an "older notion of culture as internal ideas or meanings" but draws our attention to the routine and unconscious dimension of practice, its embeddedness in discursive systems that regulate the do-able, and the fact that certain practices anchor others, creating a hierarchy.[8]

Coming as it did at the end of a thirty-year period in the social sciences of devotion to structure and symbol as the centerpiece of cultural analysis, the new emphasis on practice allowed a less reified, more dynamic understanding of social life as produced in time. Humans engage as social actors, become persons, in the materiality of communication itself, a ceaseless process of linguistic and physical labor that produces themselves and the world in simultaneity. They become subjects in those socially material worlds through the forms of language and gesture—a process intimately connected to how bodies have been imagined and lived (Zito and Barlow 1994: 9). This approach even more importantly moves cultural theory to a frontal engagement with subjectivity and personhood, one moment in the process of "mediation" in the theoretically most expansive sense of that term. It allows more sustained and theoretically informed attention to other moments such as reification and objectification itself.

Culture as mediation

As analysts of culture have restlessly propounded theories ranging from functioning holism, to culture as specifically about meaning and from there to culture as practice, the fields of religious and media studies have likewise been shaped by insights that have benefited from cultural theory's peregrinations. The study of religion has critiqued belief as a starting point, widening the field of inquiry beyond texts and beyond the elites who have historically controlled them. Media studies has benefited from a turning away from reified ideas of "the" media toward understanding it as a particularly volatile and reflexively powerful product of cultural practices. I press this trend farther: The particular nexus of religion and media can especially benefit from a deepening and widening of the notion of practice as occurring as part of the *mediation* of social life.

Here I use *mediation* not in the sense of reconciling two conflicting things because that would return us willy-nilly to the dualisms that the turn to practice, rooted in the production of self and social world in simultaneity, supposedly delivered us from. It would take us right back to media and religion as conflicting forces that needed somehow to be bridged. That is not the sense in which I propose to use *mediation*. Theodore Schatzki emphasizes the push to overcome such dualisms in his introduction to *The Practice Turn in Contemporary Theory*. He offers this useful formulation of "practices as embodied materially *mediated* arrays of human activity centrally organized around shared practical understanding" (Schatzki et al. 2001: 2; italics added). Practice theory delivers us to the doorstep, and we arrive, arms full of a grab-bag of concepts: agency, subjectivity, personhood, material things and, most important for me, process. If we take seriously the notion that culture is not a *thing* but a *process*—even though it may seem like a congeries of things, and even though we can analyze only through the materiality of things—we must get it in analytic motion. Much in human life—including "the social"—remains empirically directly unavailable. Yet we know it is "there"—in fact, a good deal of human life is about making the invisible visible, that is, *mediating it.*

I have discussed mediation elsewhere as

the construction of social reality where people are constantly engaged in producing the material world around them, even as they are, in turn, produced by it. Every social practice moves through and is carried upon a material framework or vehicle.

(Zito 2007: 726)

Marx's own dialectical vocabulary consistently "views things as moments in their own development in, with and through other things" (Ollman 1976: 52), leading to the Frankfort School's view of culture as that which "mediates the interaction between the material and the mental, the economic and the socio-political" (Mendieta 2006: 5). By emphasizing the marvelous slippage between "media" and "mediation," I want to focus our attention upon the paradox of *materializing process* (Zito 2008). For analysis, this comes down to grasping the importance of the choices we make of which moments we focus on in the general dialectical construction of social reality.

Shall it be the moment of subjectification, when embodied persons are disciplined, formed, and interpellated in their social locations? The moment of agency, when people self-reflexively take initiative? The moment of production, often contested, over what shall be the proper mode of creation of material things, social relations, and the connections among them? The moment of reification, of things themselves perceived as commodities or as bearers of meaning in precious fullness in the eyes of their users? The moments of language and gesture, which are the microbuilders—*as practices*—of these other moments? How, especially at the level of everyday life, such practices are unnoticed and naturalized and thus hide the production of social life from its makers? That all of these moments are saturated with contestation, conflict, hierarchy making, and the microfilaments of power? Finally, we must ask how do these mediated moments of social life relate and intertwine? The possibility for connections will vary depending on what one's analytic objective might be and how the social domains of the life-worlds at issue are themselves arranged.

Each of these moments in cultural production that provide foci for cultural analysis illustrate how viewing culture as the process of mediation is vastly different from seeing culture as thing-like. Providing "culture" itself with some intrinsic content—like meaning or practice—perpetuates a similar reification of one of its mediating moments, a stoppage of the circulation of its powerful force. Though this is precisely what we do unconsciously every day, to live, it should not be the (unconscious) stuff of our analytics.

Social science categories such as "culture" are products of European practices themselves, and so we must ask how it is that they are produced, how mediated in material processes that mobilize things and people. [9] The concept of culture is most useful when we pay precise attention to its intricate mediations as processes of achieving "truth effects"—the myriad practices that generate a ground of commonsense and normal everydayness—and how they are controlled and subverted. I would venture that this is a process of gradual forgetting and reification. This "forgetting" is very important in creating the "reifications" that we then live with as *the real*—because they seem natural and, most important, beyond the reach of human agency.

To take any concept such as "body" or "religion" or "media" or "culture" backward in time or abroad to another society not only risks naming reality wrongly, it covers over the most important and interesting aspect of studying society—this very process whereby the power of truth effects, good descriptions, reifications and normativity are produced and felt. Religious life plays a profoundly important role in social life in fixing these horizons of agency, as does the production and circulation of mass media. However, one never finds the productive, working reifications of others if one enters armed with one's own.

Some examples

Two projects show what can be accomplished by situating the nexus of religion and media within the field of culture as mediation: the work of Faye Ginsburg and other anthropologists of media, and Birgit Meyer's project in Ghana on Pentecostal uses of media technologies.

Cultural anthropologists have done the most to theorize media studies as culture closest to the terms I am after here. Deborah Spitulnick (1993), Sarah Dickey (1997), and especially Faye Ginsburg (1999) have founded the field of "ethnography of culture and media." Ginsburg's goal has been:

> To resituate ethnographic film as part of a continuum of representational practices [which] aligns our project with a more general revision in a number of fields...that are concerned with the contested and complex nature of cultural production.
>
> (1999: 295)

Key to their contribution to media studies is the insight that media, in their modern, mass forms such as newspapers, film, television, radio, are themselves important cultural artifacts—not transparent utilitarian representations of other aspects of social life but important moments of mediation that actually impact the very life they are commenting on.

> If we recognize the cinematic or video text as a mediating object—as we might look at a ritual or a commodity—then its formal qualities cannot be considered apart from the complex contexts of production and interpretation that shape its construction.
>
> (Ginsburg 1999: 296)[10]

Ginsburg places actors at the center of the politics of media engagement—including the producers and consumers, as well as the analysts who wish to understand their forms of self-fashioning. Thus, choosing the emphasis of the analysis, deciding where one's analytic intervention should be staged, is now more than ever part and parcel of cultural analysis.

> One can see a trajectory in the theorizing of the relationship between culture and media over the last half century as the objectification of the category of culture becomes ever more widespread and the observer becomes increasingly implicated as a participant.
>
> (1999: 313)

Ginsburg's own project on indigenous media as it has enabled the formation of new forms of community and subjectivity provides a fine example of such intervention. Her essay, "Re-thinking the 'Voice of God' in Indigenous Australia: Secrecy, Exposure and the Efficacy of Media," analyzes the shift in documenting (on film and then video) that has occurred in aborigine communities in post-war Australia. This work moved from the hands of outsiders who captured native religious life "on film primarily as texts for Anglo-Euro consumption and study" to aboriginal activists' own media-making activities (2005: 193). She analyzes the filming of the important Walpiri fire ceremony on several occasions: the first film by anthropologist Roger Sandall in 1977 was viewed by Walpiri male elders and "unexpectedly re-signified and actively appropriated as authoritative" (2005: 194). The elders decided to perform the ceremony again, filming it themselves. It was then shot a third time, in 1991. Each of these films circulated in fits and starts, moving in and out of visibility. In contradistinction to Euro-American expectations of informational transparency and flow, the Walpiri are compelled to balance need for religious ritual secrecy with authoritative transmission of cultural knowledge.

Because Ginsburg so carefully and flexibly follows several moments of mediation, charting the agencies at work *through* the moments of *practices* of objectification in film of other cultural practices like ritual, she can show "that moving image media technologies carry within them contradictory potentialities..." and raise "key questions for us regarding religion, media, and the public sphere, and offer a cautionary tale regarding the profound ethnocentrism that too often blinds the ways in which we understand media and its relationship to collective religious expression" (2005: 200–1).

Birgit Meyer's ongoing work in Ghana likewise approaches culture (and religion) as practices of mediation in the broad sense I am encouraging.[11] In her early fieldwork among Ewe Pentecostalists, she noted how their appropriation of Christianity depended heavily on the mediating figure of the Devil. His centrality paradoxically allows for the ongoing tangible presence of Ewe traditional gods and spirits, now considered demonic but existent and formidable nonetheless (Meyer 1999, 2005, 2006a). In her later work on Pentecostalist videos that intersect with the rising market for entertainment and broadcast media, wide open since state monopoly was relaxed, she writes of

> taking as a point of departure an understanding of religion as a practice of mediation, creating and maintaining links between religious practitioners as well as between them and the invisible, inaudible, untouchable, or simply, spiritual world which forms the center of religious attention. This realm is constructed by mediation, yet—and here lies the power of

religion—tends to assume a reality of its own which renders problematic its very representability.

(2003: 1)[12]

In her inaugural lecture at The Free University in 2006, Meyer pursued further the rich contradiction in cultural production that the mediation of religious life makes particularly apparent—that much of what is most human about being human (i.e., thinking and the imagination, the "social" itself as relations *between* people) must be concretized through material mediation: what I have called above "materializing process." Indeed, Meyer calls it a "materiality that is not opposed to, but rather a condition for, spirituality" (2006a: 32). Possibly the study of the religion-media nexus can, in fact, offer something back to cultural theory itself, speaking to this central problematic of its processual dynamics that involve us inevitably in mediation of all kinds.

Notes

1 Tomoko Masuzawa, in yet another "Critical Terms" book, notes that "the categories religion and culture...are both historically specific, fairly recent formations, and our daily employment of these terms...is in fact mobilizing and energizing a powerful ideology of modernity..." (1998: 71).

2 In texts such as *Philosophy in a New Key: A Study in the Symbolism of Reason, Rite, and Art*, published in 1942 and *Feeling and Form: A Theory of Art* (1953), Langer linked new work in symbolic logic based in mathematical and linguistic forms to aesthetics and drama.

3 E.B. Tylor in *Primitive Cultures* (1874: 1) is credited with that first definition: "...that complex whole which includes knowledge, belief, art, morals, law, custom, and any other capabilities and habits acquired by man as a member of society." This anthropologically inclusive notion of culture emerged into wider social circulation after World War II, with Ruth Benedict's work (1934/1959; Masuzawa 1998: 79). When I first came to graduate school in the mid-seventies, I recall being given Geertz's essays by a fellow student who was, of all things, a geographer! This was part of my own motivation for pursuing an education in anthropological theory.

4 In England, the Birmingham School of cultural studies, in many respects, picked up where Frankfort School critical theory left off (Agger 1992: 1–23) and was deeply influenced by the writings of Raymond Williams (e.g., 1981) and Stuart Hall (e.g., 1985).

5 See Catherine Bell's book, *Ritual Theory, Ritual Practice*, indebted to Bourdieu and influential in religious studies (Bell 1992).

6 These titles include *Religions of India in Practice* (1995), *Buddhism in Practice* (1995), *Religions of China in Practice* (1996), *Religions of Tibet in Practice*

(1997), *Religions of Japan in Practice* (1999), and finally *Religions of Korea in Practice* (2002).

7   Of the forty-eight essays spanning several disciplines, at least twenty-four explicitly reference obvious religion material in their titles (terms such as God, soul, sacrifice, Upanishad, religious, Christ, Hungry Ghost, Heaven, Bible, divine, consecrated etc.). In their substance, however, virtually all of them discuss matters from the archive designated as "religious." The field of embodiment studies is vast: for overviews pertaining to religious studies, see Coakley 1997 and LaFleur 1998.

8   He relies heavily on Swidler 2001.

9   A very powerful and concise essay that tries to accomplish this for the concept "culture" is Masuzawa 1998.

10 She notes the debt to Bourdieu's notion of "the field of cultural production" (2002: 3; 1999: 296) and calls this "the social life of media" (1999: 295). "One might think of these linked processes of the cultural production of media, its circulation as social technology and the relationship of mediated worlds to self-fabrication as existing on a continuum" (1999: 299). This continuum ranges from self-conscious activism, to reflexive but less strategic engagements of self-fashioning to institutionalized mass media. Ginsburg and I cofounded the Center for Religion and Media at New York University in 2003, and her influence is obvious in our shared work http://www.nyu.edu/fas/center/religionandmedia/

11 In 2000, Meyer opened a collaborative project on "Modern Mass Media, Religion and the Imagination of Communities." Visit http://www2.fmg.uva.nl/media-religion/

12 For an excellent discussion of this problem through its philosophical genealogy, see De Vries 2001: 4–32.

6

Economy

David Chidester

Expanding economy
Secret, sacred
The political economy of the sacred

Modern economists, who claim specialized expertise in the scientific study of the capitalist economy, have no privileged role in defining or deploying the key word *economy* in the study of religion, media, and culture. So, if we cannot rely on economists for our understanding the economy, what can we do?

Within cultural studies, economy has been integrated into a wider field of practices that are simultaneously material and symbolic. In his *Outline of a Theory of Practice*, the influential French sociologist Pierre Bourdieu insisted that we must "abandon the dichotomy of the economic and the non-economic," because the conventional assumption that the economy can be distinguished from its wider field of symbolic, material, and social relations "stands in the way of seeing the science of economic practices as a particular case of a general science of the economy of practices." Dissolving this dichotomy promised radical results. Modern economic science, with its laws of supply and demand, financial interest, exchange value, market competition, and so on, could be recast as a particular set of symbolic practices in a social field. Social practices, including religion, the arts, and media, could be recast as "economic practices directed towards the maximization of material or symbolic profit" (Bourdieu 1977: 183). This notion of symbolic profit, which could be produced by symbolic labor and realized as symbolic capital, effectively integrated economic practices into the entire field of meaningful cultural productions (Urban 2003).

At the same time, cultural practices, including the practices of cultural media for the storage, transmission, and reception of information, could be incorporated within this expanded understanding of economy. Meaning-making enterprises, such as religion and media, emerged as economic practices of production, circulation, and consumption. Though modern economic theories, such as rational-choice theory, might seek to explain the proliferation of cultural meanings within a conventional economic framework, the cultural meanings of "economy" have dramatically expanded within recent cultural theory to such an extent that they cannot be so easily contained.

Religion, mediating the transcendent and the sacred, ostensibly situated beyond or apart from these economic considerations, is intimately embedded in the symbolic and material economy of media, culture, and social relations. Though institutionalized as a separate domain in modern social arrangements, religion is a key word, or focusing lens, for directing our attention to productions, circulations, and contestations of transcendent claims and sacralizing practices that operate within any network of social relations. For the study of media and culture, this broader understanding of religion is crucial. It allows us to explore not only the ways in which religion, organized within distinct religious institutions, relates to media but the ways in which religion, as mythic traces of transcendence, ritualized practices of sacralization, and orientations in sacred time and space, might permeate or animate a cultural field. This broader but also rigorously theorized understanding of religion, which recognizes religion as mediation and media as incorporating discursive and ritualized practices of religion, fits the broader understanding of "economy" that has emerged in cultural analysis.

Pierre Bourdieu wanted to develop a "political economy of religion" that would advance "the full potential of the materialist analysis of religion without destroying the properly symbolic character of the phenomenon" (Bourdieu 1990: 36). The study of religion and media, however, necessarily requires us to attend to the dynamics of symbolic and material mediations within any economy that I call the "political economy of the sacred."

Expanding economy

In academic analysis and ordinary language, the key word *economy* continues on its long history of expansion to incorporate and encompass more and more of human life. In Greco-Roman antiquity, the term had a relatively small focus, referring to the management of a household. During the eighteenth century, however, with the rise of modern states, the term was redeployed to refer to the management of resources and the accumulation of wealth within a larger collectivity that Adam Smith called "the great body of the people." Economy, in this sense, was political economy, the power relations within which a society "arranges to allocate scare resources with a view toward satisfying certain needs and not others" (A. Smith 1776: 161). Within this expanding scope, the political economy of capitalism could be described as a system for the production, distribution, exchange, and consumption of wealth through the management of scarce resources and potentially unlimited needs. However, this political economy could also be subjected to critique, most notably by Marx and Engels, as a system of alienation that appropriated labor value as a surplus for satisfying the needs of a privileged social class.

Both of these approaches to political economy—the descriptive and the critical—differ from the modern science of economics, which bases its calculations on the notion of abstract individuals who are motivated by a desire for goods that are regulated by the pricing mechanisms of the market (Gregory 1982). However, all of these modern understandings of the economy, whether they focused on political order, contending social classes, or atomized individuals in a free market, all participated in what Max Weber identified as the modern differentiation of specialized social institutions. As a result, the economy could be regarded as a separate domain, which certainly affected any network of social relations but was in principle independent of other spheres of human activity such as religion or aesthetics.

During the twentieth century, critical theorists of political economy challenged any privileging of the economic as a separate sphere. In a variety of critical interventions, accounts of economy that were developed embraced basically aesthetic categories of display and reciprocity in a gift economy (Mauss 1969), of excess, extravagance, and sacrificial loss in a general economy (Bataille 1991), of desire in a libidinal economy (Lyotard 1993), and of representation, circulation, and interpretation in a symbolic economy (Goux 1990). In a dramatic and influential reevaluation of economy, Jean Baudrillard's political economy of the sign proposed that late capitalism was essentially a signifying practice, circulating signs, rather than primarily a mode for producing material goods (Baudrillard 1981; 1994). As sociologists Scott Lash and John Urry argued, "What is increasingly being produced are not material objects, but signs" (Lash and Urry 1994: 5). Economy, therefore, was increasingly being recast as an economy of meaning.

In this expanding economy, which embraced aesthetics, desire, and imagination as an economy of signification, the aesthetics of cultural media, in all of its various forms, could also be rendered as an economy of production, circulation, and consumption. On the production side, during the 1930s the critical theorist Theodor Adorno called attention to the "culture industry," the machinery of mass cultural production in a capitalist economy (Adorno 2001). As cultural production becomes an industry, the artwork is transformed into a commodity that is created and exchanged for profit. In the process, all cultural productions bear what Adorno called "the stigmata of capitalism" (Bloch et al. 1977: 123). In this production-oriented model, popular culture serves the interests of capital—profitability, uniformity, and utility—by entangling people in a culture industry in which a character such as "Donald Duck in the cartoons...gets his beating so that the viewers can get used to the same treatment" (Horkheimer and Adorno 1973: 137–8).

On the consumption side, the popular reception of cultural forms, styles, and content calls attention to the many different ways people actually find to make mass-produced culture their own. Following the critical theorist Walter Benjamin, many cultural analysts argue that the reception of popular culture involves not passive submission but creative activity. Recognizing the capitalist control of mass-produced culture, Benjamin nevertheless found that people develop new perceptual and interpretive capacities that enable them to transform private hopes and fears into "figures of the collective dream such as the globe-orbiting Mickey Mouse" (Benjamin 1972–89, 7: 377; Hansen 1993: 31). Where Adorno insisted that the productions of the culture industry were oppressive, Benjamin looked for the therapeutic effects, such as the healing potential of collective laughter, and even the redemptive possibilities in the reception of popular culture. In the case of Mickey Mouse, for example, Benjamin suggested that audiences were able to think through basic cultural categories—machines, animals, and humans—by participating in a popular form of entertainment that scrambles them up. As Benjamin observed, Mickey Mouse cartoons are "full of miracles that not only surpass those of technology but make fun of them." For an audience "grown tired of the endless complications of the everyday," Benjamin concluded, these "miracles" promise a kind of "redemption" in an extraordinary world (Benjamin 1972–89, 2: 218; Hansen 1993: 41–2).

Between cultural production and consumption, the space of media and popular culture is a contested terrain. Popular culture is a landscape in which people occupy vastly different and often multiple subject positions, subjectivities grounded in race, ethnicity, social class, occupation, region, gender, sexual orientation, and so on. As the cultural theorist Stuart Hall has established, popular culture is a site of struggle in which various alternative cultural projects contend against the hegemony of the dominant culture. Though subcultures develop oppositional positions, perhaps even methods of "cultural resistance," social elites work to appropriate and assimilate the creativity of alternative cultural formations within the larger society. Not a stable system of production and consumption, popular culture is a battlefield of contending strategies, tactics, and maneuvers in struggles over the legitimate ownership of highly-charged cultural symbols of meaning and power (Hall 1980a; 1981).

These struggles over interpreting and appropriating highly charged, perhaps even sacred symbols look a lot like religion. In trying to understand the expanding economy, many analysts have found that religion has reentered the picture, not merely in relation to economic activity, such as the "elective affinity" Max Weber traced between Calvinism and the rise of capitalism

(Weber 1958), but in the inherently religious character of capitalism. From Walter Benjamin's reflections in the late 1920s on "Capitalism as Religion" (Benjamin 1996) to recent debates about the "religion of the market" (Loy 1997; Foltz 2007), the expanding economy of capitalism has been engaged as if it were a religion, emerging in Europe, developing in North America, and now global.

If the capitalist economy is a religion, its sacred texts, its canonical scriptures might very well be discovered in animated cartoons. Both Adorno and Benjamin, for different reasons, found Disney cartoons revelatory in reinforcing capitalism's ethos of conformity and promise of redemption. Though all modern media are entangled in these cycles of production, consumption, and contestation, animation is a particularly plastic medium for testing and transcending limits, for taking a beating, like Donald Duck, but also for playing with transformations, like Mickey Mouse, in an alternative world that is "full of miracles." To illustrate these animations of the constraints of the culture industry and its miraculous promises of redemption, I focus here on one animated film, *Destination Earth*.

Secret, sacred

Destination Earth (1956) is a thirteen-minute animated cartoon, brilliantly illustrated by a team of creative animators, produced by John Sutherland, and financed by the American Petroleum Institute, in which Martians learn the secret of American power. Opening with an expansive display of planets in outer space, with traces of a whizzing spacecraft, the film settles into a stadium, where the supreme Martian leader, Ogg, the Exalted, announces that all Martians are "commanded—er, invited—to attend." Accordingly, the stadium, Ogg Memorial Stadium, in the city of Oggville, with its Oggmart, Ogg Café, and many other Ogg enterprises, is filled to capacity with subservient, obedient Martians, cheering their "Glorious Leader, Ogg the Great," in response to prompters instructing them to cheer and applaud on cue. Surrounded by banners that herald the glorious Ogg as "friend, leader, crusader," the Great Ogg begins by thanking the people for their "unsolicited testimonial" to his greatness.

This gathering was convened to hear the report from a Martian who had recently returned from outer space. As Ogg announced, "by special permission of the commander-in-chief—me—here is Mars' first space explorer, Colonel Cosmic." As the colonel explained to the crowd, he was sent into outer space by Ogg, the Magnificent, because the supreme Martian leader has become dissatisfied with the speed and efficiency of Ogg power, coerced slave labor, "which runs most of our industry." Particularly, the great Ogg was frustrated that his official limousine was too slow drawn by slaves and too dangerous if propelled by explosives. Therefore, as Colonel Cosmic explained, he "ordered our first expedition into space to bring back the secret of how other planets got their state limousines to run smoothly."

Undertaking this interplanetary mission, Colonel Cosmic had headed for the Earth, finding himself in "a country of Earth called the United States of America," where he was immediately astounded by all of the "Earthmobiles" driving around as if they were state limousines. These vehicles, he soon discovered, were fast, efficient, and owned by everyone. Searching out the secret of all of this power, he went into a library, read a few books, and found that the Earth's "code was remarkably easy to break."

Here was the secret: oil. Power was drawn from drilling oil, transporting oil, refining oil and, through the "magic of research," transforming oil into a "whole galaxy of things" that made life in America better "than in any country on the whole planet."

However, this secret would have remained locked deep under the Earth's crust if it had not been liberated by the key of free-market competition. As Colonel Cosmic discovered, the competition of entrepreneurs, taking risks, exploiting opportunities, and seeking competitive advantages against each other necessarily turned scarce resources into surpluses. Market competition, he found, was the key not only for success in the oil industry but for "almost every successful business enterprise in America."

In concluding his speech to the Martian rally in Ogg Stadium, Colonel Cosmic announced that his exploration of the Earth had revealed that the "big secret is of course oil, which has brought a better life to all the people in the USA. But the key to making oil work for everybody is competition." Over the Great Ogg's objection that competition was "downright un-Martian," the rally breaks up as Martians start rushing around drilling for oil under new signs as "Martian Oil Explorers" and "Martian Oil Pioneers." Even the old Ogg Café is suddenly reopened, "under new management," as Joe's Café.

Against the background of this explosion of oil drilling and free enterprise all over Mars, the Martian dictator also explodes, somehow easily blown up, by a push of a button, as Colonel Cosmic says to the Great Ogg, "You are through." In the coda for the film, the colonel addresses a wider audience, extending from Mars to Earth, by drawing out the obvious moral of the story: "Yes, the real secret is not only a great source of energy, but also the freedom to make it work for everybody. And if you have both of these things, any goal is possible. It's destination unlimited!" As the music expands and swells, and the film displays this new banner—"Destination Unlimited!"—we learn again, in the rolling credits, that this beautifully animated and richly entertaining film was presented by the Oil Industry Information Committee of the American Petroleum Institute.

Nothing in this film, we might think, has anything to do with religion. We see no churches, mosques, temples, or synagogues. We hear no priests, imams, gurus, or rabbis. Therefore, this film is not religious, as religion is conventionally defined, as it is commonly understood as something located in specialized religious institutions, arbitrated by recognized religious leaders, and adhered to by religious followers. Based on such a conventional definition, the analysis of religion and media is straightforward. We look for media representations of religion and religious uses of media. However, as historian of religions Jonathan Z. Smith has observed, such a conventional, common-sense definition of religion is circular: religious organizations, with their religious leaders and followers, are religious because they are engaged in religious activities (J.Z. Smith 2004: 375–89). So, we are left with the problem of thinking more carefully about what we want to mean by "religion," for purposes of analysis, for our struggles in trying to understand the material and symbolic economy of religion, media, and popular culture.

If we define religion, following Emile Durkheim, as beliefs, practices, and social relations revolving around the sacred, that which is "set apart," we find that religion is set apart at the center of personal subjectivities and social formations (Durkheim 1995: 44). In the context of the expanding economy, we can explore this definition of religion as a political economy of the sacred to understand the ways in which the sacred is produced, circulated, engaged, and consumed in media. Not merely given, "the sacred" is produced through the religious labor of interpretation and ritualization as both a poetics of meaning and a politics of power relations.

In exploring the political economy of the sacred, we need to identify the means, modes, and forces involved in the production of sacred values. In *Destination Earth*, these features of production were explicitly represented— industry run by Ogg-power was contrasted with industry running on oil; communist collectivism was opposed to capitalist competition; and a Martian (or Marxist) totalitarian dictatorship was overthrown by the liberating spirit of American freedom. Since the late 1940s, producer John Sutherland had been animating these themes for early Cold-War America. *Make Mine Freedom* (1948), for example, depicted a group of Americans rejecting the utopian promises of a snake-oil salesman, Dr. Ism, because their capitalist system gave them the freedom for "working together to produce an ever-greater abundance of material and spiritual values for all." In the conclusion to this film, Sutherland directly referred to the production of spiritual values, but the spirit of capitalism was also present as a transcendent force of production in other films by Sutherland productions, such as *Going Places* (1948), *Meet King Joe* (1949), and *What Makes Us Tick* (1952). Clearly, capitalist competition was invoked in *Destination Earth* as a spiritual mode of production.

Of course, we must notice the role of material forces of production in these films. *Make Mine Freedom* was sponsored by a former chairman of General Motors, *Destination Earth* by the American Petroleum Institute, so the oil and auto industries were clearly driving these productions. However, their instrumental and interested roles were mystified in these films by rendering capitalism not only as spirit but as secret, a sacred secret at the heart of America. The capitalist production of material and spiritual values, *Make Mine Freedom* concludes, "is the secret of American prosperity" (Sutherland 1956). In *Destination Earth*, as we have seen, the entire storyline was premised on discovering, decoding, and deploying a secret. Colonel Cosmic was sent to "bring back the secret"; he found that the "code was remarkably easy to break"; and he concluded that "the real secret" was oil and competition, a source of energy and an economic system.

Secrecy plays an important role in the production of sacred values within any political economy of the sacred (Mathewes 2006). Even open, public secrets, such as those displayed in the films of John Sutherland, are important in generating the mystery that invests values with a sacred aura. Scarce resources, like oil, are heavily invested with secret, sacred meaning. However, a secret, sacred aura attaches to all the commodities of the capitalist market. As Karl Marx observed, the political economy "converts every product into a social hieroglyphic," a secret code that might not always be so easy to break as "we try to decipher the hieroglyphic, to get behind the secret of our own social products." According to Marx, capitalism made deciphering the secret meaning of products difficult by transposing relations among human beings into mysterious relations among things, as if commodities, "abounding in metaphysical subtleties and theological niceties" (Marx 1867: 76), were animated objects, with a life of their own, which enveloped human beings in an economy that resonated with the "misty world of religion."

The political economy of the sacred

As a counterpoint to modern economics, anthropological accounts of economic relations in small-scale, indigenous societies, formerly known as "primitive," have found systems of exchange based on the reciprocity of the gift, a ritualized regime of gift giving that entails sacred obligations rather than economic debts. Durkheim's colleague, Marcel Mauss, outlined this contrast between primitive and modern economies in his classic book, *The Gift*. As the anthropologist E.E. Evans-Pritchards observed, this investigation of alternative economic relations showed

> how much we have lost, whatever we may have otherwise gained, by the substitution of a rational economic system for a system in which

the exchange of goods was not a mechanical but a moral transaction, bringing about and maintaining human, personal, relationships between individuals and groups.

(Mauss 1969: ix)

Though gift giving persists under capitalism, it is subsumed with an overarching economic rationality.

Entertainment media are poised between sacred gifts and economic calculations. In the animated world of *Destination Earth*, with its corporate sponsors and capitalist propaganda, the secret, sacred gift—oil—is celebrated as the ultimate standard of value. Oil is represented as a gift, as something that is just given, as a natural resource that is available everywhere for anyone and everyone. Though the film draws a stark opposition between the economic systems of totalitarian communism and free-market capitalism, *Destination Earth* actually represents a gift economy, an economy based on "moral transactions" of competition that promise to transform "relationships between individuals and groups" from oppressive conformity into liberating and unlimited freedom.

While invoking the moral, transformative, and even redemptive power of the gift, the entire range of media operating in a capitalist economy also celebrate the power of extravagant expenditure, which the perverse Durkheimian theorist Georges Bataille identified as the heart of a general economy that was based not on production but on loss, on a sacrificial expenditure of material and human resources. For Bataille, the general economy of capitalism was ultimately about meaning, but meaning had to be underwritten by sacrificial acts of expenditure, with the loss as great as possible, in order to certify authenticity (Bataille 1985).

Obviously, entertainment media thrive within this general economy of expenditure. Big-budget extravaganzas, exorbitant publicity, and trans-gressive superstars all participate. However, this sacrificial economy, based on loss, also demands sacrificial victims. Underscoring this point, Georges Bataille proposed to revitalize the society and economy of France in the 1930s by officiating over a human sacrifice in Paris. Though he found a volunteer, Bataille was frustrated by the Parisian municipal authorities who refused a permit for this sacrificial ritual. In nationalist rhetoric and popular media, however, this impetus of redemptive sacrifice is a common, recurring motif, with many heroic individuals, from Jesus to Bruce Willis, willingly sacrificing their own lives so that others might live. However, the sacrificial victim does not have to be a willing victim. In *Destination Earth*, as we have seen, the dictator Ogg is killed, effortlessly but necessarily to bring freedom to his people by liberating their oil.

In these mediations of the gift and the sacrifice, we find traces of religious economies that cannot be contained within rational economic calculations of self-interest and market-exchange. The gift and the sacrifice evoke powerful and pervasive religious practices of receiving and giving. However, these religious resources, with their deep histories, are not immune from commodification. Like art, poetry, music and other creative human enterprises, religion operates within a productive economy. Official spokespersons for religion and other cultural productions might insist on their autonomy from market relations but, in a mediated world, religion has no such pure place in which to stand.

Under the conditions of a capitalist economy, religion intersects with electronic media in producing the multiple mediations of a political economy of the sacred. Intending to be suggestive rather than exhaustive, I point to some of the basic features of three mediations in this political economy—the mediations between economic and sacred values; the mediations between economic scarcity and sacred surplus; and the mediations among competing claims on the legitimate ownership of the sacred.

First, electronic media are engaged in symbolic labor by mediating between economic values and sacred values. As we have seen in *Destination Earth*, an animated film can celebrate an economic system as if it were a religious system of sacred or spiritual values for human flourishing and ultimately for human liberation. Clearly, many American films and television shows, even when they are not so blatantly designed as propaganda, can be read as reinforcing free-market capitalism as a sacred orientation.

Money, at the heart of this mediation between economic and sacred values, is itself a medium, a medium of exchange. Though it is also a store of value and a unit of accounting, money is a meaning-generating medium invested with a sacred aura, a symbolic system, following anthropologist Clifford Geertz's definition of religion, which generates powerful moods and motivations and clothes those dispositions in an aura of factuality that makes them seem ultimately real (Geertz 1973). As a medium for religion and electronic media, money has been a nexus for transactions between economic and sacred values. Enthusiastically, the popular television evangelist Reverend Ike proclaimed a gospel of money based on the principle that "the lack of money is the root of all evil." Cynically, the Internet Church of the Profit$ has claimed to be the only honest religious group in America because it openly admits that it is only in it for the money (Chidester 2005: 112).

In between these extreme cases, electronic media are inevitably involved in a cycle of symbolic labor mediating between contingent and changing economic relations and enduring values that must appear to be stable, unchanging, and perhaps even eternal. Assessing the production and consumption of values, the fetishism of commodities, which must also include commodified media productions, has often been cited as the engine that drives this apparent stability of values by transposing human relations into exchange relations amongst objects. Howeveer, the very notion of the fetish, which arose in the intercultural and interreligious trading relations of seventeenth-century West Africa, was originally invoked by Europeans to signal the absence of any stable system of value for mediating exchange relations among people of different religions (Pietz 1985). As the term developed in Europe during the nineteenth century, it was turned back on the instability of values in the capitalist economy by Marx and the sexual economy by Freud, signaling for both a gap within the reality of modernity.

Though Marx and Freud worked against religion, they identified an economy of desire, alienated and perverse desire perhaps, but with profound religious resonance. Every religious form of life has a logic of desire. For example, the Christian economy outlined in Dante's *Divina Commedia* was based on directing desire toward God and away from the world. The *Bardo Thodol* of Tibetan Buddhism was based on eliminating desire. In both cases, however, sin was defined as perverted desire (Chidester 2002: 141–2; 214). Electronic media, as multisensory, self-involving mediations of desire, are engaged in a kind of religious work by mediating the gaps between contemporary economic relations that are based on the manipulation of desire and the desire for sacred values.

Second, electronic media are engaged in building symbolic capital by mediating transformations of economic scarcity into sacred surplus. In *Destination Earth*, the finite and nonrenewable geological resource of petroleum is revealed as an infinitely available surplus. However, scarcity can be transformed into surplus only through the spirit of free-market capitalism. In that spirit of capitalism, a scarce resource becomes miraculously transformed into a sacred abundance of unlimited wealth and power.

As anthropologists Jean and John Comaroff have observed, religious life all over the world, struggling to adapt to globalizing capitalism, has been drawn into "occult economies," economic beliefs and practices based on the expectation of abundant wealth from mysterious sources (Comaroff and Comaroff 1999; 2000). During the twentieth century, cargo movements in Melanesia, which developed myths, rituals, and spiritual preparations for the miraculous arrival of wealth, anticipated this development under conditions of colonial oppression. Now, in a global economy, where the locations of production are dispersed and the rituals of consumption seem to add value (McCracken 1988: 84–8), many people find themselves in a cargo situation.

If cargo movements provide a precedent, we must recall that they went through three basic stages in trying to access the sacred surplus. First, when colonial administrators told indigenous people of the islands to work for wealth, they worked but did not get it. Second, when Christian missionaries told the people to pray for wealth, they prayed and did not get it. Though people sometimes found new ways to combine work and prayer by building piers, docks, and flagpoles and integrating indigenous and Christian ritual, the failure of work and prayer to produce the cargo left a third option: steal it (Chidester 2000: 515–16).

This truth of theft is a recurring theme in the history of religion and economy, from Prometheus stealing fire from the gods to the butter thief Krishna, even if it has not necessarily been underwritten by the Marxist generalization that all private ownership of property is theft. Electronic media, however, with their immediacy, availability, and propensity for personal engagements, place the ownership of sacred surplus in question and at stake. A popular guidebook for screenwriters and filmmakers, *Stealing Fire from the Gods*, explicitly invokes the truth of sacred theft in its title (Bonnet 1999). However, the problem of theft is more widespread and more profound in the economy of religion, media, and culture: who owns the sacred surplus?

Third, electronic media are engaged in mediating conflicts over the legitimate ownership of the sacred. As we saw in *Destination Earth*, this question of legitimacy was easily, quickly resolved in favor of private ownership in a competitive environment. However, this principle of legitimate ownership could be certified only by eliminating the central symbol of opposition, Ogg the Magnificent. An undercurrent of violence, therefore, runs through these mediated negotiations of legitimacy. However, the question of violence can also be easily, quickly resolved by distinguishing between us and them, by highlighting their illegitimate acts of violence, such as Ogg's tyrannical rule, coercive manipulation of public opinion, and exploitation of his people as slave labor, to draw a stark contrast between their violence and our judicious exercise of legitimate force in killing the tyrant, liberating the oil, and freeing the people to participate in a competitive economy based on private ownership.

Modern media, from news media to entertainment media, are actively engaged in these contestations over the legitimate ownership of sacred symbols. Drawing on the insight of literary theorist Kenneth Burke into the cultural process of stealing back and forth of symbols (Burke 1961: 328), we can enter into the economy of religion, media, and culture as an ongoing contest over the stealing back and forth of sacred symbols. Not only made meaningful through interpretation, sacred symbols are made powerful by ongoing acts of appropriation. However, no appropriation goes uncontested. Therefore, the field of religion, media, and culture is contested terrain, a conflictual arena in which competing claims on the ownership of sacred symbols are asserted, adjudicated, and reasserted. As no claim can be final, the struggle over the legitimate ownership of sacred symbols continues to be negotiated through religion, popular culture, and their intersections with media.

7

Image

David Morgan

Moral policing and the power of images
Pictures and children
Visual epistemologies
Public opinion and visual persuasion
Hyperreality: the continuing menace of images

The status of images in the history of many religions and in modern media is an embattled one and generally for a single reason: images are thought to be untrustworthy—they lie, cheat, and steal. Whether in Socrates or in the many critiques of images mounted by Jewish, Muslim, or Christian writers, by Hindu reformers or by Marxist revolutionaries, suspicions circle around a tenacious distrust of images (Latour and Weibel 2002). Images lie inasmuch as they selectively tell the truth, exaggerating aspects of it, commonly distorting what they portray into whatever priests, tyrants, or vendors want pliant viewers to believe. Images dupe the unsuspecting, lulling them into views or opinions that are untrue, cheating viewers of access to truth or power. And images steal belief from words, the revealed medium of divine self-revelation in the so-called religions of the book. As Socrates might have put it, images rob belief in the logical procedure of discourse—the progressive movement of intellectual inquiry from opinion to truth, cheating reason of its rightful place in ascertaining the truth of a matter.

Yet the distrust of images presumes something deeper about them. Images work their magic by a subtle and often irresistible effect on the body: provoking fear, envy, pride, desire, obsession, rage—all the strong feelings and passions that grip the chest or rise in the blood, creep over the flesh, well up as tears in the eyes. Images appeal to and rely on the body. It is precisely this that philosophers, teachers, moralists, clergy, and parents have resented about the power of images. Images are understood to traffic in the body's energies and to threaten to overturn the strictures of thought and conscience that moral authorities work hard to nurture and inculcate.

However, images do not wage a psychomachia in and of themselves. In fact, they are the visible part of an entire apparatus, which consists of biological operations interlaced with epistemological templates and the practices of social institutions. Images do not merely symbolize these unseen dimensions of personal and collective identity. They are the material interface with them—surfaces that turn seeing into feeling and vice versa. Images do this on the model of the most important surface in human experience: the face. Rather than a symbol linked arbitrarily to a referent, the human face is better characterized as the thick surface of the invisible interior, the countenance that bares the hidden heart of things. As such, images are over-determined, regarded as the face of a social or cultural body. "Heads of state" are more than arbitrary signifiers. They are the living faces of the states or nations they lead. We want to believe faces because we assume that they are organically connected to heart and will. Human beings—like many mammals—look at eyes, mouths, and other facial features and at the gesture of the head for vital information. In doing so, they are often able to discern intent and disposition in potential allies or foes. Faces are not texts to read but sites of revelation, the place to witness truth as it happens, or even before it does. Faces are the place where abstraction and feeling become visible. As such, they are the physiological origin of images. Faces are the thick surface that makes images sentient disclosures. It is probably a biological inclination for human beings to look at images as if they were faces and bodies with tactile interest for our own faces and bodies, as if they were beings looking back at us (Elkins 1996; Guthrie 1993).

Vision is a carnal way of knowing, and that is just what bothers the detractors of imagery. Feeling, memory, and abstraction are thoroughly intertwined. Emotions enhance memory formation and learning. Human imaging studies have shown that vision is routed through two discrete neurological systems—one that relies on the visual neocortex, which enables awareness; the other through a more ancient midbrain system that is not connected to awareness, though it is linked to the amygdala, which governs emotional response, especially fear, which obviously finds its way quickly to consciousness, though often as an indeterminate sensation in search of an object. This visual system does not include reason or conscious reflection but informs involuntary reaction to perceived threats (Thompson and Madigan 2005: 175). The two systems may interact when I watch a horror film—one system instinctively directs my fear while the other resists the urge to flee. I tell myself "It's only a movie," but the more primal response urges me to think otherwise: the image I see is the real thing. I compromise by perspiring, biting my nails, and hunkering down in my seat.

Western thought about representation has generally traced its origins to Socrates since Plato's *Republic* develops a distinctive account or, better, interrogation of representation. There we find what has remained an enduring suspicion: images indulge the passions and therefore threaten reason. To control the beguiling appeal of the arts of representation, Socrates proposed the stringent regulation of musical and poetic enjoyment. The ideal was to match a noble soul to a beautiful body (Plato 1992: 79). Most music, poetry, and virtually all visual art, he regretted, failed to strike that all-important balance between psyche and soma, tipping the favor instead to the body's unruly passions.

The Socratic critique has enjoyed intermittent revival over two millennia and, as we shall see, informed several influential twentieth-century critics of mass culture. However, in recent years scholars and critics have recognized the embodied nature of seeing, inquiring into the body's role in making sense of film and other visual media (Sobchack 2004). W.J.T. Mitchell has even argued that the term *visual media* is deceptive because it occludes the important way in which film, painting, or television rely on the full range of sensoria (Mitchell 2005). Film maker David MacDougall has written that "we see with our bodies, and any image we make carries the imprint of our bodies" (MacDougall 2006: 3). A complementary way of thinking about this is that images see us, projecting themselves over the screens of our bodies, the fleshy, dense surfaces that actively respond when, to use Roland Barthes' provocative idea, an image punctures or pricks us with what he called its *punctum* (Barthes 1981: 27). Such instructive studies suggest that what Socrates and many others may find dangerous about images is precisely the way they insinuate the body and its felt ways of knowing, its sensuous forms of cognition, into the linguistic and rational spaces of controlled discourse— theology, catechism, preaching, evangelism, teaching, philosophizing, and scholarship.

Understanding the importance of images in modern media culture (and in any historical epoch) means examining the fear of images, the practices of their use, and notions of their power. Doing so will allow us to discern various ways in which images have been situated within accounts of human cognition as well as the construction of human values. The task is to recover the embodied nature of seeing in the history of thought and practice regarding mediation. In what follows, I attempt a sketch of the themes and something of the historiography that might belong to such a project.

Moral policing and the power of images

Western philosophical and theological reflection on images has been preoccupied with their truth and falsehood, which are expressed in Judaism, Christianity, and Islam in terms of the singularly negative category of the idol. In practice, it is very important to point out, each of these religions has often departed sharply from the rigid theological standards that many of its authorities and intellectuals have upheld as strictly representative of all "true" practitioners of each faith. A great deal of recent scholarship in religious visual culture on these three religions, especially Protestant Christianity and Shi'ite Islam, has demonstrated an extensive and varied use of images and visual practices. So pervasive are images in religions, and so common is their denial by purists, that art historian David Freedberg has referred to the "myth of aniconism" (Freedberg 1989: 54). Many religionists insist that their faith is free of images but may do so only by turning a blind eye to the plethora of pictures crowding their altars or homes (Morgan 1998).

Why the denial? To begin with Socrates, the problem with images and any form of artistic representation—poetry, drama, music, or the visual arts—is that they project themselves deeply into the soul. This is a problem because the wrong sort of representations readily take seat there and exert a powerful influence over the person. "Imitations practiced from youth become part of nature and settle into habits of gesture, voice, and thought," Socrates asserted, and argued that the training of the Greek elite should be strictly controlled in their imitation of dramatic roles. Those who were "self-controlled, pious, and free," Socrates reasoned—that is, the Athenian upper crust—"mustn't be clever at doing or imitating slavish or shameful actions, lest from enjoying the imitation, they come to enjoy the reality" (Plato 1992: 71–2).

It may seem puritanical at first glance, but parents, religious organizations, and Congress members commonly make the same point about the effect of portrayals of violence and sex in television programming, films, and video games. For example, in a policy statement of 1993, the National Council of Churches flatly asserted that film and television

> increase an appetite and tolerance for entertainment with a violent content, since the more violence an audience sees, the more violence it will want. This appetite for violence entails an increased callousness to people who may be hurting or in need.
>
> (NCC 1993: 10)

A 1999 Senate Committee report on "Children, Violence, and the Media," prepared "for parents and policy makers," echoed the belief, claiming that it "identifies and begins to redress one of the principal causes of youth violence: media violence" (Senate 1999: 1). The report attributed violence in media as "a principal cause" of youth violence, citing studies which showed that eighty-seven percent of American households included more than one television set, that almost half of American children have televisions in their bedrooms, and that more than eighty-eight percent of homes with children "have home video game equipment, a personal computer, or both" (Senate 1999: 2). Socrates would have agreed with the report's lament that media expose children to fictional scenes that exert a negative effect on their behavior. "By age 18 an American child will have seen 16,000 simulated murders and 200,000 acts of violence." If, as Socrates averred, the danger of representations is that we become like them, the report's conclusion would serve as confirmation of the fear that "television alone is responsible for 10% of youth violence" (Senate 1999: 2, 5).

Yet the stark difference between the high rate of exposure to simulated violence and the low rate of violent acts perpetrated by young people suggests, at best, a complicated and indirect account of causation. More persuasive, however, was a longitudinal study conducted by psychologists, which showed that exposure of children to television violence increased their risk of aggressive and violent behavior as young adults (Huesmann et al. 2003). Even if the link is not strongly determinative, Socrates' antagonism toward images corresponds to the modern fear of media, especially new media, suggesting that media are dangerous in part because there is a long tradition of believing they are dangerous. In both instances, ancient and modern, the anxiety is premised on the direct appeal of representations to domains of the mind or body that obviate reason or moral scruple, which is often another way of saying the influence of moral or social authority.

Pictures and children

If modern children participate in too many violent games, the fear of parents and moralists is that they may be irrationally inclined to imitate art in real life—to commit violent acts in school or on the playground. The menace of art, according to moral authorities ancient and modern, is its ability to invert its relationship with reality. Images have a way of coming to life. The danger of images is that we become like them—we imitate them, rather than simply the reverse. Sunday school teachers, parents, and reform-minded congressional investigators have sounded a similar alarm. During the nineteenth century, promoters of religious instruction became enthusiastic about the power of images as a kind of moral technology. They celebrated the power of illustrations in the newspapers, books, and tracts that they published to rivet the attention of children. Engravings and lithographs were joined to stories, primers, and catechisms to exert an almost magnetic pull on young readers and to aid in the memorization of texts but most often to facilitate the internalization of a lesson in indelible, felt terms. Most of the images were deployed in one of several affective, embodied circumstances: to enhance the humor, fear, curiosity, pity, or revulsion of viewers, especially children. The power of an emotional association between image and viewer colored a text and made it memorable (Morgan 1999: 223–4). The success and appeal of images became so quickly evident to religious publishers by mid-century that the process of illustrating publications was soon image-driven. Writers were sent engravings to use as prompts to generate corresponding stories (Morgan 2007: 21).

In the visually driven publications of children's religious literature, modern editors updated Pope Gregory's widely invoked maxim that images were the books of the illiterate. Young children were said to read the language of pictures before they were able to read words. Asa Bullard, a leader in Sunday school initiatives, published his *Children's Album of Pictures and Stories* on the premise that

> Even the 'little ones', before they know a letter, can *read* the pictures; and they will be entertained, or will entertain themselves, for hours at a time, with such a book. Neither the pictures nor the stories ever weary. Such a book becomes the children's daily companion, till it is literally *worn out* with use.
>
> (Bullard 1866: 196)

In 1861, *The Well-Spring*, a weekly newspaper for children issued by the Massachusetts Sabbath School Society and edited by Bullard, published a small engraving of a boy discovering a dead horse (Figure 1). The image was accompanied by two short paragraphs of description and moralizing comment, which drove home an emotionally charged message about death and the afterlife that pitted soul against body, using the image's somatic appeal to instill a spiritual disposition:

> It is a sad sight to see the poor, faithful horse, that had so long served the [boy's] family, with her tongue out of her mouth, lying dead.
>
> But how different our feelings at the death of a horse and that of a person! This is the last of the poor horse. There is no soul to live hereafter…But when a person dies, it is only the body that, like the body of the beast, turns to the dust again.
>
> (Anon. 1861: 27)

The expired horse evokes a certain revulsion, while the large-eyed colt in the background presses viewers toward pity and sadness. The pathetic death of a familiar animal was used to strike a chord of solemn reflection in young viewers: "Beyond the grave there is a life that never dies," the short piece ended. "Oh, may that eternity be one of bliss to all our dear readers!"

Though Protestant and Catholic literature aimed at both children and adults in the nineteenth century could often dwell on the morbid or grim to direct readers and viewers to the grave topic of their eternal welfare, some readers of *The Well-Spring* took offense at the engraving of the dead

THE WELL-SPRING.

POOR DEAD HORSE.

Figure 1   "Poor Dead Horse," *The Well-Spring*, vol. 18, no. 7, February 15, 1861, p. 27. Courtesy of Billy Graham Center Museum.

horse. One reader who wrote to the editor claimed to be quoting "a knot of children who had just then gathered round the little paper and were reading and looking at it." Their response alarmed the correspondent: "It is a nasty looking thing, a miserable concern...What is the use of putting such things into this darling Well-Spring?" The writer agreed with the children:

> The picture is a vulgar thing. Not one redeeming quality in it. The moral attempted to be drawn from it is lost totally. The picture nauseates and unfits the mind for receiving any good moral impression from the reflections which are printed under it.
>
> (Anon. 1861a: 60)

Bullard replied to the letter, countering that, in his view, the illustration was "in the main, an accurate and very life-like representation of the scene, the dead horse and all." He asked readers to reexamine the picture in order that "they may judge of the correctness of the above criticisms?" (Anon. 1861a: 60).

Letters followed Bullard's request. One objected to the children calling the picture "by such ugly names" and insisted that the image was well executed. However, the writer then turned to criticize the newspaper for publishing two other offensive images, one of them depicting "a crocodile with a little black child dangling between its jaws, just ready to be swallowed by the voracious reptile" (Anon. 1861b: 86). The picture in question likely resembled the one reproduced here, which was used in other Evangelical publications at the time (*My Picture-Book*, Anon. 1863: 46). The writer complained that the images exerted a negative effect, threatening to "haunt them in their night visions." The problem with images was that they turned the mind into a brain, a body, a tissue whose surface received the material impress of the image, and forgot the immaterial soul in the process:

> There is a sort of fascination about such things in the impressible minds of children. They like to hear bear stories and see crocodile pictures, and yet will be afraid afterwards to go down cellar alone, or go to bed in the dark. Therefore, we say keep away from the vivid imaginations of children whatever tends to terrify them, or to harden their sensitive natures.
>
> (Anon. 1861b: 86)

However, others argued for the utility of such images. Medical missionary Dr. John Scudder wrote in his *Tales for Little Readers, About the Heathen* that a girl had been galvanized in her decision to become a missionary to Africa by the sight of "a picture of a heathen mother throwing her child into the mouth of a crocodile" (Scudder 1853: 201). The image played to

THE HEATHEN MOTHER.

Figure 2   "The Heathen Mother," *The Picture-Book*, New York: American Tract Society, 1863, p. 46. Courtesy of Billy Graham Center Museum.

a child's desperate horror at its mother's diabolical betrayal. Figure 2 also portrays a light-skinned child (the better to invite the self-identification of white children viewing the image) abandoned by a dark-skinned mother. In contrast to the letter writer, Scudder and Bullard felt that the fear generated by such an image could be put to effective use.

What was the value of portraying the dead horse? The grimly expired animal embodies the Protestant belief in soul, a metaphysical substance that merely inhabited the material body, and departed at death. The pathos evoked by the horse's grisly corpse was linked by *The Well-Spring* to the horse's utter loss at death. Child readers were urged in a strongly embodied way to believe in soul over the temporal, putrefying body. If this emotional connection to the paper's young clientele were not enough, the large-eyed, cutely diminutive colt, which has survived its parent's demise and gazes directly at the viewer, establishes a viscerally sympathetic relation with viewers. None of the letters mentioned the colt, but it is difficult to imagine that any child would have missed it or failed to identify with it. The two may operate in a coupled fashion, pairing pity for the colt with sadness at the mare's humiliation. The one incites revulsion at the decaying body, while the other engenders hope in the survival of the soul—the child's own. Children needed to be taught that they had souls and that souls were not to be confused with bodies. The illustration drove that home in no uncertain terms. Images such as those in Figures 1 and 2 instrumentalized the body as an imperfect, finite receptacle for something ontologically superior, and they charged the child's imagination with a sharp jolt to reinforce the distinction. Fear, revulsion, and pity put the body and soul in a characteristic relation to one another.

Visual epistemologies

The exchange of letters in the pages of *The Well-Spring*, simple and informal as they are in one respect, nevertheless reveals the outlines of tectonic shifts in the American understanding of children, education, the body, and the operation of the mind, all of which had enormous implications for the new mass media of religion and instruction. Images appealed to the imaginations of children and contributed directly to the formation of their taste and moral feeling, using feelings and the senses to discipline the body. Taste was itself a faculty of discernment that Protestants since the eighteenth century had recognized as a mark of distinction and moral sensibility. Imagination had gone from the frivolous and untrustworthy nature of mere fancy to the status of an epistemological faculty, which charged images with greater purpose and recognized in them a concomitant risk. Images had become in the Idealist philosophies of Immanuel Kant and others and in Romanticism a medium of cognition and had therefore to be taken seriously for the influence they exerted. According to Kant, for example, the mind assembles a visual norm from particulars. The imagination is able, he wrote in his *Critique of Judgment* (1790), to "let one image glide into another; and thus, by the concurrence of several of the same kind, come by an average, which serves as the common measure of all" (Kant 1951: 70). The idea of a beautiful human figure, he asserted, is not deduced from rules but compiled from a thousand figures by the intuitive powers of the imagination.

Though it is often said that Protestantism exercised no patience for images, regarding them uniformly as idolatrous in the domain of religion, matters varied considerably among different Protestant groups. Both Martin Luther and John Calvin taught that images acted as a medium for human cognition. In response to those who insisted that images must be forcibly removed from churches and destroyed, Luther countered that he was unable to hear of the

Passion of Jesus and not form mental images of it (Luther 1958: 99). John Calvin regarded images as the traffic of the mind but drew very different conclusions. Whereas Luther urged his contemporaries to recognize the value of images for teaching religious stories and precepts, Calvin claimed that images were unable to teach anything true about the Gospel (Calvin 1989: 90–103). According to Calvin, images are not in the least inclined to tell the truth because they are the product of the human imagination, a faculty dedicated to dissimulation. The human mind, he wrote, is a "perpetual forge of idols" (Calvin 1989: 97): by imagining the divine, the mind gives it a body the size of an image. The human propensity to lie was an epistemological issue, residing in the unholy linkage of rebellious will and creaturely cognition but sloshed over into the messy domain of bodies. To think was to appropriate the world to one's interests, carnal and selfish, and therefore inevitably to limit the inherently transcendent and infinitely sovereign stature of the divine. If one wishes to know God, Calvin claimed, one has no choice but to rely faithfully on the medium by which the deity reveals itself: the Bible. Images were unlike words because they serviced the human will. The words of the Bible corresponded to those spoken by God himself, and were therefore privileged to convey divine truth.

Romanticism and the Idealist philosophy that it embraced turned a sharp corner on Calvinism. Sociologist Colin Campbell has argued in an insightful study of the broad impact of Romanticism that modern consumerism was shaped by a hedonism that directed Europeans toward an imaginative pleasure-seeking (Campbell 1987). Yet Puritanism had also accorded a vital place to feelings, or affections, as theologians such as Jonathan Edwards referred to them. Affections, properly evaluated, could be evidence of the movement of the Holy Spirit—or of a sham undertaken by the wiles of Satan or the deceiving individual (Edwards 1959). The cultivation of feeling, directed by the faculty of taste, was Romanticism's answer to the Calvinist evaluation of feelings. The legacy of the Puritan doctrine of the affections is evident in the nineteenth-century evocation of emotions in illustrated children's publications. If Edwards debated with his parishioners whether a revived person's panting or swooning were an index of spiritual awakening, Victorian Protestants disagreed over the effects of illustrations as moving or repulsive, compelling a solemn spirit or causing nightmares. The shift noted by Colin Campbell was toward the pivotal role of the imagination and the pleasure of feelings in the consumption of mass-produced goods. Accordingly, religion was not the victim of modern disenchantment but negotiated the transition to capitalism and consumption to great advantage. The explosion of mass print among Protestants and Catholics in the United States and Europe and among Christian missionaries and colonial governments throughout Asia and Africa during the nineteenth century and the aggressive use of imagery of all kinds—from illustrated tracts to panoramas, lithographs, lantern slides, and early film—demonstrates a highly mediated, market-friendly Christianity that saw little reason to indulge in other-worldly asceticism.

Public opinion and visual persuasion

The ubiquity and mass appeal of modern visual media such as film and the widely shared notion that images constituted a medium of thought informed the pivotal work of Walter Lippmann, *Public Opinion* (1922), which James Carey rightly considered "the founding book in American media studies" (Carey 1989: 75). Having seen the use and effect of propaganda during the First World War, Lippmann was deeply concerned about the prospect of democracy faltering in mass-mediated society (Steel 1980: 171). He agreed with Socrates that the human mind relies on images to think, and at its own peril. However, modernity had plunged human society into an even more precarious epistemological condition.

> Modern life [Lippmann wrote] is hurried and multifarious....There is neither time nor opportunity for intimate acquaintance. Instead we notice a trait which marks a well known type, and fill in the rest of the picture by means of the stereotypes we carry about in our heads.
>
> (Lippmann 1922: 89)

Stereotypes, like the common opinions (*doxa*) that Socrates incessantly targeted for overturning in his argumentative quest for genuine knowledge (*episteme*), are the traffic of daily thought and the basis of public opinion. Stereotypes are mental pictures distributed with ceremonial observance in schools, churches, films, and newspapers, and they form the body of sacred symbols, images, and devotions that constitute nationality, "without which," Lippmann asserted, the individual "is unthinkable to himself" (Lippmann 1922: 235).

Modern public opinion consists of the mass-mediated circulation of stereotypes that simplified the real world, reducing it to easily transmitted and assimilated formulae that appealed to people by exercising their minds in familiar plots such as good versus evil. Modern citizens were impelled to consume films in passionate identification with characters (Lippmann 1922: 95, 163). The large audiences of modern society, he judged, "are more interested in themselves than in anything in the world. The selves in which they are interested are the selves that have been revealed by schools and by tradition" (Lippmann 1922: 168). These institutions and ideological formations were the culture that supplied the mass-mediated language that predetermined what people saw. And what they saw was directly related to how they behaved—as consumers, voters, and citizens. The link was imagination: "The way in which the world is imagined determines at any particular moment what men will do" (Lippmann 1922: 25). That is where the menace of propaganda arose: as "the effort to alter the picture to which men respond [in order] to substitute one social pattern for another" (Lippmann 1922: 26). Visual media such as posters and film provided pictures that were internalized as the mental medium of shared thinking, images that occluded social circumstances to convince people en masse that matters were otherwise.

Like Socrates, Lippmann argued that the power of images resided in their inexorable tendency to become what they only referred to, picturing a world "to which we are adapted…We feel at home there…it fits as snugly as an old shoe" (Lippmann 1922: 95). However, Lippmann the social analyst, like Socrates the wily philosopher, did not intend to leave the public in the comfort of familiar foot-ware. Just as Socrates would induce lovers of wisdom to abandon the shackles of delusion in the allegorical cave of ignorance, relying on the dialectic of philosophical reasoning to move them from mere opinion to true knowledge, Lippmann argued that scientific thinking used *hypotheses* instead of stereotypes—provisional images readily admitting falsification by actual data and critical analysis. Stereotypes forming public opinion were fictions "accepted without question," myths demanding belief under the force of authority as conveyed by tradition and powerful social institutions like church and school (Lippmann 1922: 123).

Lippmann's critique of public opinion was enthusiastically taken up by Daniel Boorstin in his excoriating attack on the American desertion of Puritan self-restraint and ideals for self-indulgence in an image-culture. As a criticism of postmodernism avant la lettre, Boorstin's widely read book, *The Image: A Guide to Pseudo-Events in America*, was a kind of secular jeremiad in which he lamented the American loss of ideals, which he defined in Platonist terms as ideas or forms for which people ought to strive but never reach.[1] A copy is never equal to its prototype. Americans must seek perfection without expecting to achieve it.

Hyperreality: the continuing menace of images

Lippmann hoped that the stereotypical features of the cookie-cutter plot and characters of mass entertainment might be discarded and that the medium of film would be used "to enlarge and to refine, to verify and criticize the repertory of images with which our imaginations work" (Lippmann 1922: 166). One imagines Lippmann would have been encouraged by the rise of documentary and experimental film in the second half of the twentieth century, not to mention other screen media and alternative media outlets such as Internet and video. Whatever Lippmann might have thought of these new media and their countercultural uses, his Platonist hackles would surely have been raised by the postmodern delight in the surface, screen, and simulacrum.

Jean Baudrillard contended that the relation of sign and signified bore an inherent movement from the regime of representation to the regime of simulation, marked out as "successive phases of the image" (Baudrillard 2001: 173). The first is the image as a faithful or trustworthy reflection of a fundamental reality. Viewers believe the image delivers reality to them, undistorted and true. When difference between the two becomes apparent, such as in the conflict between rival images, one version is vilified as perverse and said to mask or hide the truth. The next phase of the image unfolds when it is determined that neither representation may lay claim to validity because the very notion of representing reality itself is impossible. The truth is absent from all representations, whose real purpose is to mask that absence, to make people think they have access to something they do not. This is the juncture at which simulation becomes a possibility, because the sign plays as a surface, covering nothing but the absence of what was once assumed to be accessible in the sign. The last step in this cascade of deconstruction is the complete detachment of the sign or image as surface from any putative depth. There is nothing behind it and therefore no need to regard it as referring to anything but itself. The result is the simulacrum, the final moment in Baudrillard's evolution of the sign. The simulacrum is not a representation—it does not refer to something behind, above, or ontologically superior (more real) to itself. Indeed, he says that the simulacrum precedes the thing that it used to follow: a map that no longer refers to actual terrain but generates endless maps. The simulacrum is what Boorstin meant by a pseudo-event—a sign that was its own referent and therefore lacked foundation in the metaphysical substance of God. The diagnosis of the postmodern condition for both writers turned on the absence of a bedrock reality. In what Baudrillard called the "hyperreal," images endlessly generate other images.[2]

Some writers like to compare this process of simulation to *The Matrix* (1999), which featured a computer-generated simulacrum in the place of reality. However, the film doubles back to endorse a regime of representation when Neo and fellow rebels infiltrate the digital world, attempting to liberate its captives from the illusion and to destroy the hyperreal. Perhaps a better instance of what Baudrillard has in mind is the film *Blade Runner* (1982), in which a replicant destroys its maker and humans hunt replicants with lethal force in order to bolster the compromised distinction between human and artificial human. The hero who executes renegade replicants changes his view of them when he falls in love with a replicant and abandons an ontology of the real as endorsed by Platonic metaphysics.

Baudrillard does not accept the simulacrum on its own terms but describes it to deploy it in a critique of the unscrupulous deceptions of capitalism. "Capital" emerges as a raving beast, "a monstrous unprincipled undertaking, nothing more" (Baudrillard 2001: 176). One wishes that his account of the evolution or, better, devolution of the image were not so strongly driven by an internal logic because it fails to do justice to the far richer and much less tidy historical record of images and visual practices. Nevertheless, Baudrillard's critical intuition diagnoses a keen loss of the image as face in consumerism. The body to which advertising images refer is not the viewer-consumer's body or anyone else's but a digital concoction designed to trigger a fantasy body that exists in a capitalist gaze of envious desire.

Though parents, politicians, and moralists will continue to lament the visual allure of sex and violence, it is important to recognize the power of film and television to return the body to the image, to make the screen an interface, a countenance or thick surface in which the senses may command a substantive role in the construction of the felt world. Implicit in the fear of images are notions of their power, of their relation to the structure of thought and feeling, and of the subtle but compelling linkage of human bodies to one another and to social bodies of various kinds. One task for the study of images in religion and media is to make visible the network of submerged assumptions that do so much to make seeing what it is and, very commonly, what it is not.

Notes

1   Boorstin 1992. The book originally appeared in 1961 under the title *The Image, or What Happened to the American Dream*.
2   Boorstin parallels this judgment: "Pseudo-events spawn other pseudo-events in geometric progression" (1992: 33).

8

Media

Peter Horsfield

Media as culture
Media as industries
Media as text
Media as technologies

The term *media* in the study of media and religion may be understood in either a focused and specific way or a more expansive and discursive way.[1] Understanding this difference is important in making sense of the development of the study of media and religion and also of the different perspectives that become apparent in approaches to writing and research in the area. Both have particular strengths and limitations.

The interest in media as an area of study can be traced back to the United States in the 1920s, when the relatively new mass communication technologies of newspapers, film, and radio were assembling large audiences, giving them the potential to influence social behavior on a mass scale that was not possible in previous times. Anecdotal evidence about the effects of Nazi propaganda in Europe and the desire to understand how these new media could be harnessed for political and commercial purposes led to an interest in more accurate information about media uses and effects. The dominant methodologies of research for these investigations were the relatively new but influential social and behavioral sciences.

In line with the scientific preference for clear definition, media in this paradigm were understood primarily as the recognized utilities of mass communication, such as newspapers, magazines, film, radio, and later television. Reflecting the scientific concerns to understand phenomena in terms primarily of causes and effects, media communication was understood as a linear process: a sender constructed a message, that message was fed into media technologies that multiplied and distributed it to a widely scattered mass audience, where it worked its effect. Research was directed primarily toward isolating and measuring the particular contribution made by each stage of that process to the final outcome. Whether the communication was effective was evaluated according to whether the effects intended by the communicator were achieved (such as change in attitudes, voting for a particular politician, or buying a particular product).

This narrowly focused view of media and the communication process has been and continues to be an influential one, for a number of reasons. It corresponds to a common pragmatic way of thinking about how the world works and our part in it: things that happen are caused by something that makes them happen—in turn, we can make things happen by finding out what causes them to happen and doing that ourselves. The perception of scientific methodologies as objective lent an aura of impartiality to research findings around media effect that belied their particular focus and limitations. The approach also has an adaptable simplicity. Forget about complex media theory: communication is simply a process, media are just tools—learn how they work, adopt the right techniques, and you can make things work to your own advantage. Studying media by focusing on individual media as instruments of effect also avoided involving researchers and institutions in the politically loaded critical issues of things like media power, ownership, and social functions.

Though many aspects and limitations of the approach have been questioned in recent decades, the hermeneutical power and practical applications of this focused way of thinking about media have made it an enduring way of thinking about media, particularly in areas such as policy making and strategic media planning to the present time, leading Denis McQuail to call it "the dominant paradigm" in media theory (McQuail 1994).

This approach has been the most common framework for scholarly research into media and religion until recently, particularly in the United States. That research has focused on a number of main issues: describing and tracking religious interactions with media; critical comparisons of media content and values from the perspective of religious content and values; and studies of the effects of religious uses of media, looking at such things as audiences of religious programs, uses of religious programs by audiences, effectiveness of religious programs in such things as evangelism and attitude change, and strategies of various religious uses of media.

These studies into media and religion reflect a number of unquestioned assumptions about what media are, what religion is, and how the two are related. Religion is seen as a separate domain of human experience from that of media and the media world. Religious meaning was generated and governed primarily by religious people according to their own distinctive religious criteria and principles. Media were simply instruments or channels for carrying this religiously determined message to the intended audience. Whether a religious communication was effective was evaluated by the extent to which the changes in behavior intended by the communicator happened or not.

This focused way of thinking about media as instruments began to change in the latter part of the twentieth century, for a number of reasons. Sustained and unresolved debate about the relationship between viewed media violence and social violence in the United States in the 1960s and 1970s created a skepticism, even disillusionment in some, about the capacity of scientific research alone to fully resolve and predict media effects, and many researchers went looking for alternative ways of thinking about media and human behavior. There was a growing appreciation of the fact that the recognized mass media were just one part of a much wider process of social mediation within which all humans are nurtured and the need for thinking about media to include a broader understanding of mediated communication became apparent. There was a growing awareness that media were not just neutral channels for carrying information and messages but had their own character that infused the message along with the overt content—media had effects apart from those intended by the communicator that needed consideration. Within this ferment, approaches in European media studies, with a focus on such things as text and meaning, media and ideology, media audiences and media as agents of cultural construction began to be taken up across the Atlantic. This convergence of factors led to a broadening of the concept of media that began to change how the relationship between media and religion was understood.

This more cultural view moves away from a focus on specific effects of individual media toward a view of the entire society or culture as a mediated phenomenon to which all forms of media contributed. Within this view, thinking about media and religion moves away from a narrowly focused concern with how religious organizations use specific media and the effects they achieve, to looking more broadly at religion as a mediated phenomenon within the context of the wider culture of mediation.

The cultural approach is undergirded by a quite different worldview than the modernist, scientific view. It sees various descriptions of reality not as objective reflections of what exists but as constructed, mediated views that carry with them the particular interests of those who hold them and that contend with other constructions for social recognition and access to social resourcing. Media are now understood not as individual instruments to be studied on their own but as part of the dynamic of society itself, a mediated reality comprising not just technological media of mass communication but the total process of mediation of life. Given the interrelatedness of these cultural processes, media should be understood not as instruments carrying a fixed message but as sites where construction, negotiation, and reconstruction of cultural meaning takes place in an ongoing process of maintenance and change of cultural structures, relationships, meanings, and values.

In recent years, therefore, scholarly interest in media and religion has shifted away from understanding how religious groups use media, how media represent religion, or how the values of media and religious bodies intersect to questions of religion as a mediated phenomenon. The theological view of religion as a separate realm of knowledge and practice governed by its own criteria, or the institutional view of religion defined by authorized religious bodies, are challenged by this approach. Religion is more accurately understood as a social construction that originates, develops, and adapts itself through the same mediated processes of creation, conflict, and negotiation within itself and in relation to its wider environment that all of life participates in. The study of media and religion, therefore, needs to be broadened to include the messy, diverse, and at times contradictory individual and group practices of mediated daily life to which religious meanings are ascribed.

Key questions now become not how does religion use media but how are media and religion interrelated? How is what we know as religion constructed, shaped, practiced, and transformed by the different media practices within which it is embodied? Though the dominant agents of religion within any society—such as religious leaders, religious institutions, and organized belief and practice systems—are important to study, the more discursive view sees these identifiable manifestations of religion as just some of the players in a much broader game of social religious mediation that includes many other players, playing to quite different sets of rules that need to be deciphered and correlated.

This is not to say that the instrumental paradigm is no longer used in research on media and religion. As with other areas of media study, particularly in marketing and advertising applications, the view of media as instruments for carrying particular messages and the testing and measurement of the effectiveness of specific uses of media to achieve particular outcomes in religious marketing, promotion, and institution building are still widely used.

The strength of the discursive way of thinking about media and religion, however, is that it more realistically considers the complexity of religious practice and mediation processes within any social or cultural situation and how such media uses construct the character of religion as religion adapts itself to them. The weakness is that with such a broad view of social mediation and of religion, its rich description can be so diffuse as to be of little strategic or policy value. In practice, however, one can see a number of key tropes of media reoccurring in this approach.

Media as culture

The trope of media as culture presents the understanding of medium as the ecology within which organisms grow. We become who we are through nurture within a mediated social environment that provides us not only with the practical necessities for physical survival and growth but with resources of symbols and practices for building insight, meaning, and coherence in human understanding. We are not simply autonomous, independent individuals—we are first and foremost mediated beings. Our physical, social, and verbal environments are inseparable.

Significant development in rethinking media as culture took place within Britain during the 1960s and 1970s, particularly through the work of Stuart Hall. Hall broke from the established understandings of culture as the epitome of elite Enlightenment civilization and began looking at culture as people's everyday lives, redressing earlier elite views with studies of the cultures of the working classes. Influenced by the critical perspectives of Marxism, Hall conceptualized the dynamics of culture as conflicts or struggles between forces of domination and subordination. Other cultural approaches have emphasized more the dynamics of consensus and how groups who share a similar language and interests work together to build meaning within the larger system. In the United States, James Carey, for instance, argued for approaching the study of media from the perspective of how media serve as ritual performances for maintaining the integration of culture (Carey 1989).

Approaches to thinking about media as culture depart from earlier anthropological understandings of culture as something relatively fixed, identifiable, and stable that is simply handed down and reproduced from one generation to the next. Rather, human cultures are seen as diverse, relatively fluid, dynamic associations that are constantly being modified and reconstructed through ongoing challenge, contest, and negotiation between different power centers that form and reform in institutions, groups, subgroups, and individuals. Patterns of mediation can be important markers in the formation and identity of cultural and subcultural groups, providing the cultural web or framework on which interaction occurs.

The concept of media as culture likewise challenges the view of religious cultures as stable, reified structures of meaning embodied in hierarchies or structures that have evolved in a "natural" or ordained process of development. The coherence of religious cultures and subcultures is constantly being negotiated and built through communicative, cultural, material, and political interests that work in an ongoing movement toward both stabilization and change.

The view of media as culture also challenges the perception that the nature of religiosity in a society is best understood through the lens of its authorized expressions. The opinions of the institutional religious elite are seen as just one opinion among many, gaining greater power in many cases through their domination of the processes of mediation within the religion or through correspondence of their religious media preferences with the dominant cultures of mediation within the broader culture. The structure of theological education that evolved in Western Christianity during the Modern period, for example, is more than just a functional way of preparing people for the practicalities of pastoral work. The cultural practices of theological education—the adoption of university classroom practices (lectures and seminars, for example), linking pastoral education with extensive libraries, the testing of people for pastoral ministry by requiring them to read books and write academic essays, the awarding of degrees—all positioned the leadership of modern Christianity within a literate, book-based culture that was aligned with the elite literate culture of developed Western nations but often at odds with the practical daily culture of lay Christians. That media culture of Christian leadership is being significantly challenged by the media culture of digital technologies within which the new generations are nurtured. Thinking about media from a cultural perspective prompts a number of questions. What are the authorized and unauthorized views within any religious tradition and in what ways are those views associated with or embodied in particular media practices? In what ways are established power structures and practices within a religion challenged by their adaptation into other cultures of mediation? In what ways do people within or outside particular religious traditions adapt aspects of the mediated religious language, practices, or symbols in their own processes of religious meaning making?

Media as industries

The most common use of the term *media* today is as a collective term for the constellation of institutions, practices, economic structures, and aesthetic styles of social utilities such as newspapers, movies, radio, book publishers, television, and the related creative industries (such as advertising, marketing, and graphic design) that service them.

Because every form of mediated communication is a social activity, every medium requires a supporting social infrastructure to function. You cannot write and send a letter to someone, for example, unless you have materials to write with, unless there is a way for the letter to get there, and unless the person you are writing to knows how to read or has access to someone who does. Every new medium, therefore, must develop a supporting social infrastructure or industry before it can function as an effective social medium. This industrial infrastructure includes a common language, language forms or literacies appropriate to the new medium; a means of education or induction to pass on those literacies to new generations; a steady and reliable supply of materials and technologies needed by the medium (e.g., sheepskin, marsh reeds, cotton or wood pulp paper for writing; printing presses, ink and plenty of paper, roads for distribution, and sellers for selling for mass print, and the like); a framework of protocols, legal regulations, and policy structures for managing the integration of the new practices and new centers of power into existing societies.

Without these industrial factors, no medium will become established as a sustainable form of communication within a society. Once established, however, the industry becomes a new center of power. Its new literacies challenge established epistemologies, structures of language, and ways of seeing the world. New communication practices challenge and change existing social networks and structures built around old practices. Its new leaders can displace old leaders whose power was based in old media practices. Investigation into how media are organized and function as industries has been an important area of study over the past five decades because of the significant power that media have come to exercise in modern states.

The character of media as industries has significant implications for how media and religion are conceptualized and studied. The ability of religious bodies to communicate their message and perspectives to the wider society is influenced significantly by the extent to which they can translate the language and practices of the religion, constructed within particular media-cultural contexts, into the required languages, industrial demands, and cultures of the dominant media industries. Conversely, the development of new languages and practices of new media can generate new expressions and practices of religion.

The ability of religious bodies to adapt their message or practices to form mutually beneficial relationships or economic alignments with developing media industries has been a significant factor in some key shifts within religion. As writers such as Edwards and Eisenstein have demonstrated, a key factor in the development and impact of Martin Luther's Reformation within European Christianity in the early sixteenth century was Luther's alignment with the commercial printers of his time and his ability to construct and communicate his reformed view of the Christian faith in a way that corresponded to the commerce and production processes of publishing (Edwards 1994, Eisenstein 1979). A similar case has been made for the more recent ability of evangelical Christianity to adapt more readily to the dramatic, commodified marketing requirements of electronic media (Clark 2007b, Horsfield 1984, Moore 1994). Part of this impact may include ways in which changes in media industries affect social structures by changing the preferences of social mediation in a way that privileges particular expressions of religion rather than others.

Thinking of media as industries prompts a number of other questions in the study of media and religion. In what ways do the signifying systems of particular media industries serve particular ideologies that may support or challenge religious ideologies? In what ways do the economic structures and requirements of media industries require religious institutions to restructure to participate in them? How do the professional ideologies and work practices of those who work in the media affect other social institutions and practices that engage with them, such as religion? How have sociopolitical factors such as ownership of media technologies, access to media, and power centers created by media industries shaped the culture and distribution of power within religious institutions?

Media as text

According to the trope of media as text, the only way we can make sense of the world is through the use of language, and language can operate only through texts of mediation. A major approach to thinking about media, therefore, has been through the theorization and study of texts and textual practice. In a discursive approach, this involves more than just deciphering overt content. In its broadest use, a media text is any signifying structure that uses cultural signs and codes to convey or evoke shared meaning. In these broader terms, religious understanding and practice can be sustained only in texts, so an important aspect of understanding the relationship of media and religion involves the study of texts and textual practices in the construction and communication of religious meaning. This meaning is not an objective thing waiting to be discovered and explained. It is constructed socially through the agency of signs, not in an arbitrary or naturalistic way but within traditions of textual practice involving groups and individuals cooperating and competing to build shared and divergent understanding. This process is a constantly moving one, involving the full gamut of textual practice such as codes, myths, discourses, genres, intertextuality, symbolic capital,[2] and the life of the text in circulation.

Though the instrumental view of media emphasized the power that the medium gives to the producer or the one who controls the instrument, the textual approach views media power in a more distributive way. Understandings, positions, and relationships in a media situation are neither fixed nor simple. Studies of how audiences receive and use media within the textual tradition see audiences as active agents in the process of communication and in the construction of meaning, not just as passive recipients. For some, this more fluid view of communication as a negotiated outcome between production and reception means that we have to change our concept of "media" away from just the physical artefact (such as a book, radio, or television) and see media instead as the physical and mental space of interaction between the person producing the message within a particular media form, the media form itself, and what the person who receives the communication does with it. This new individual "reading" generated by the individual then becomes a new text itself (Lewis 2005).

Looking at media and religion in this way significantly challenges the idea of religious authority that is assumed in the instrumentalist approach, where media texts are seen as powerful tools that enhance the power of those who have the resources to produce them. In the textual approach, media still have power, and those who have control over their production and distribution have their power enhanced, but that power is not absolute. Power arises from a complex cultural interaction and negotiation between producers of messages, the texts of the messages, and those who receive and use the messages. The power of communication and of religious leadership is not as an absolute power to impose one's meanings on others. Religious authority arises from effective interaction and negotiation of ideas and meaning between producers and users of texts.

The metaphor of media as text has been an influential one within Christianity. Christianity is a text-based religion with a strong sense that its defining beliefs and values are to be found in historically mediated texts. There are, however, diverse and conflicting opinions about what those "texts" are and how the correct ideas and meanings are to be derived from those texts. The opinions range across a continuum, from a narrow fundamentalist textual objectivity, which sees particular written scriptural documents (now printed) as culturally unconditioned writings dictated by God and true in all areas of knowledge for all time. In some views, religious texts such as the Bible are seen as having power within themselves to effect changes on people, either through the content of the text or even the material object itself and to mistreat the text is tantamount to abusing God. Against this view is an extreme poststructuralist approach, which sees written Christian texts as de-authored, ideology-saturated, historical documents that need radical critical deconstruction and creative reconstruction.

The rise of the empirical sciences in the late nineteenth and early twentieth centuries created an impetus among some thinkers within Christian churches to apply scientific methods to establish objectively the historical reliability of Christianity's founding texts, particularly the texts of scripture. This concern with text, however, was limited to particular concerns. As Gamble noted in the early 1990s, the huge research effort of the nineteenth and twentieth centuries in Biblical studies was largely directed to establishing "the contents of documents, their chronological and theological matrices, and similar questions" (Gamble 1995: ix, 42). Broader issues of text from a media perspective, such as questions of production, sponsorship, circulation, ownership, and use of books, he suggests, have been significantly neglected.

Changed perspectives on the nature of text and textual practice open a range of new possibilities for rethinking the interaction of media and religion. How do texts function and exercise power in the construction and mediation of religious ideas, practices, and institutional life; how do texts function in the creation or restriction of diversity in religious ideas and experience; how do texts and textual practice contribute to the building of religious coherence and identity; where does authority lie in the interpretation of texts and what are the implications of reader reception theory for religious authority; how are religious texts performed and in what ways is their performance part of their meaning construction?

Media as technologies

The concept of media as technologies looks at media technologies, not just as neutral carriers of content but as having particular physical, social, and technological characteristics that become an integral part of the communication. One of the earliest to propose this perspective was the Canadian economist, Harold Innis, in the late 1940s and early 1950s (Innis 1950; 1951). Innis's ideas were developed and popularized by his colleague at the University of Toronto, Marshall McLuhan.

The focus on media as technologies challenged the dominant instrumental thinking of the time which, it was argued, missed the vital issue of the technological and sensory characteristics of the medium and the way the medium itself structured communication and influenced the society. The form of a medium massages the communication by favoring particular kinds of messages over others and by adding particular sensory preferences to the content. All communication, therefore, needs to be understood as "content-in-form" and, when push comes to shove, McLuhan argued, the form of a communication is of greater importance than the content, summed up in his adage, "the medium is the message" (McLuhan 1964).

McLuhan proposed that technologies of communication work by addressing and extending particular human senses and functions. In the process, the perceptions and understandings that are linked to those senses are affected. When new technologies are developed and adopted within a society, therefore, they create broad new sensory experiences and consciousness, in the process changing the existing balance of sensory use and experience. These changes are subtle ones—changes in perceptual habits and ways of thinking brought by new forms of communication are massaged into a culture rather than dramatically imposed. The consequence, though, is that different mediations of phenomena create different perceptions of those phenomena within people, without the people necessarily being aware that their perceptions are different.

There are many criticisms, even scorn, of this approach to thinking about media. However, the trope of media as technologies has been important in breaking the dominance of the instrumentalist view for thinking about media. Its insights have been developed through more extended and nuanced explorations into the interaction of technology and society and the materiality of communication practice. Meyrowitz, for example, develops the concept of medium theory further by examining how different media lead to social changes on a macroscale by constructing fundamentally different patterns in the formation of group identity, socialization and social hierarchy (Meyrowitz 1994).

Without falling into a simple deterministic mindset, the trope provokes different questions in thinking about media and religion. Compare three religious contexts: exchanging religious ideas on an Internet-based network; participating in a megachurch with flashing lights, loud amplified music, and multiple visual projections; and sitting in a small rural church where voice is unamplified and singing is accompanied by a small organ or piano. In what ways do the presence and availability of particular media forms stimulate particular types of religious perception and practice compared to differently mediated religion, and what are the social consequences of that? In what ways do the sensory characteristics of the media by which communication takes place shape perception and legitimize particular religious forms over others, and what are the social and political consequences of that? In what ways do particular media stimulate or require particular forms of social relationships and structures to be established or changed, and what are the consequences for religion of that? What are the relative contributions made in the construction of meaning by the content of a communication and the form of its mediation? David Morgan, for example, suggests there is a difference between those types of media or forms of communication in which the content of the communication and the form of the communication are clearly distinguishable and others wherein the distinction between the two is blurred or deliberately blended. He argues that any mediation that makes one aware of its material nature transforms the mode of representation from a discursive one to a figurative one, engaging different tools of analysis. "When the medium materializes, when it begins to perform rather than defer, we become aware of it rather than through it...Meaning is 'in, with and under' the physical elements of the medium" (Morgan 1998a: 4–5). In what ways do particular media forms establish organizational patterns or hierarchies in the social ordering of religious phenomena and perceptions of religious power and authority?

Notes

1   The term *media* is used variously in different places now as either a singular or plural term. When the term *media* is used as a singular, it is most commonly as a collective term for all different media that together are seen as impacting on societies. This use has the implicit ideological assumption that all media, though different, are basically one in the combined role they play in contemporary societies. I consider that the differences between different media are as significant as their commonality in understanding the nuanced way in which media function within any society. For that reason, I use the *media* as a plural term to preserve that distinction. The term *medium* will be used when referring to an individual medium.

2   *Codes* are wider systems of meaning held by a society or group that are incorporated within language, often as a subtext of the communication, and accessed or triggered through different verbal or visual cues. *Myths* are integrated narratives that organize and interpret reality for particular communities or groups. Along with conceptual theories, myths provide a mechanism for constructing and carrying a world-overview that integrates individual episodes and experiences in people's or groups' lives. *Discourses* are characteristic patterns of statements, conventions or language use that construct representation in a way that reinforces the power interests of particular groups over others by enforcing particular "regimes of truth." *Genres* are particular types of structured discourse or narrative that circulate within cultures. A genre generates particular expectations of a style of narrative or argument that become part of the construction of meaning through the process of consumption. *Inter-textuality* refers to the process of incorporating within a particular text references or allusions to other texts that contribute to its meaning. Being able to detect or read the inter-textual references is one of the skills of cultural literacy—knowing how to read the culture—and can divide the audience into in-groups and out-groups. *Symbolic capital* is the status or prestige ascribed to a person or persons by a group that gives them power to name the meaning "the power to name (activities, groups), the power to represent commonsense and above all the power to create the 'official' version of the social world" (Mahar et al. 1990).

9

Narrative

Jolyon Mitchell

Repetition of narratives
Amplifications of narratives
Elaborations of narratives
Reverberations of narratives

In Manila, at 7:03 AM on December 30, 1896, a Filipino writer, poet, sculptor, and eye doctor by the name of Jose Rizal was shot dead by Filipino soldiers. A line of Spanish troops stood behind them to ensure that they carried out the execution. As he was shot, Rizal is said to have twisted around so that he fell on his back, staring up to the sky. The band played on. As soon as he had fallen, some Spanish bystanders clapped, others even cheered: "*Viva Espana.*" The story of Jose Rizal's death at Bagumbayan Field soon transformed into an act of martyrdom, becoming a foundational narrative for the emerging nation of the Philippines. With the help of a range of different media, Rizal became a national hero, a unifying point for the evolving "imagined community" of the Philippines (Anderson 1991).

I am using the example of Rizal to consider the place of narrative in relation to the study of media and religion. Over the last thirty years, narrative has become a hotly debated topic, with scholars from a wide range of disciplines speaking of a "narrative turn." The nature of this turn has been mapped in detail elsewhere (Herman 2007: 4). It is useful in the context of my discussion, however, to note how several scholars have drawn on the work of Vladimir Propp, who identified common plot functions (narratemes) in Russian folk tales, emphasizing the significance of "disruptive events" (Propp 1928) in driving a narrative forward. Hearing news of Rizal's execution undoubtedly upset the equilibrium for many of his followers, but his story, far from terminating with his death, was soon transformed into a pivotal moment in the evolving national narrative. And as we shall see, this disruptive event became the subject of novels, dramas, and films. There are already extensive discussions of how best to analyze a narrative's plot, characters, dialogue, language, genre, or structure (Herman 2007: 39–123). For example, scholars such as Roger Silverstone identified what he described as the mythic structure of narratives on television (1981: 181). My aim is to go beyond the investigation of the apparently closed world of the story to consider the different ways in which narratives take on a life of their own and are shaped through four recurrent processes: repetition, amplification, elaboration, and reverberation.

To consider these processes in greater detail in this chapter, I analyze the many different kinds of narratives that have clustered around Rizal's life and death. Narratives are rarely static, constantly moving, circulating, and adapting. They invariably take on a life of their own, reappearing in unexpected places. The narratives connected with Rizal are a mere drop in the never-ending "sea of stories" (Rushdie 1991). As we shall see, Rizal's story morphs into many different forms and is expressed through a range of materials. There are, in the words of Roland Barthes, "numberless" narratives appearing in "infinite forms" throughout human history (Barthes 1989a: 89). I choose this particular narrative rather than the billions of other stories I could have selected partly because of my own recent experience. My story briefly intersected with traces of Rizal's far more famous narrative. I found myself literally following in his footsteps from his small prison cell in Fort Santiago, Manila. There are brass footprints imprinted into the road leading out from the fort of his final incarceration toward the place where he was shot. A small group of us followed this route, walking through the old walled city, *intramuros*, passing many cars, crammed minibuses, and horse-drawn carriages touting for tourists to the actual spot of his execution. Being there helped bring this narrative to life in surprising ways, but so also did engaging with the numerous accounts of his life and death alongside reading Rizal's own writing. Immersing myself in the stories that have attached themselves like barnacles to his death and life has highlighted some of the ways in which narratives can function. The fact that his death was almost immediately framed as a martyrdom with cultural, political, and religious significance makes this a valuable example for those reflecting on the interactions between media, religion, and culture.

Repetition of narratives

Using the narratives connected with Rizal as a central case study, my aim is to explore the creation, production, and reception of narratives. More precisely, I analyze how these narratives repeat, amplify, elaborate, and reverberate in a wide range of settings. This example will be a useful reminder of how narratives evolve in countless ways: a process that can be accelerated by what Michel de Certeau describes as the "interminable recitation of stories" (de Certeau 1984: 186). Since his execution, stories about Rizal have been regularly recited in the Philippines and beyond. As I have already suggested,

Rizal's death was rapidly transformed into a martyrdom, which in turn became for many Filipinos a lens for reinterpreting not only his death but his life and work. At the outset, it is important to make clear that the sequence of repetitions, amplifications, elaborations and, finally, reverberations is by no means set in stone. In other words, repetitions or elaborations of a narrative may well happen before amplifications, for example, or simultaneously with reverberations. Repetition and amplification can happen together, as can all four processes. As I also consider repetition within the three other processes, I have kept this first section the briefest.

The story of Rizal's execution was reiterated textually, visually, and materially. In the *London Times*, the story of his execution received only a few lines, whereas in Spain, his death was a lead story on the front page of several Spanish newspapers. For example, both *Todas Las Noches* and *Una Información* devoted almost their entire front page to the news, including a realistic-looking picture of the execution in the former and a large photograph of Rizal himself in the latter. Such extensive coverage in Spain is not surprising given that at that time the Philippines was a Spanish colony. The rapid transmission, repetition, and amplification of the story relied on a comparatively new form of communication: the telegraph. Within two years, the Philippines were no longer governed by the Spanish, and Rizal's bones were exhumed, placed in an ivory casket and, as we shall see, later given a state burial at "an expressly designed" monument. The result was that the story of Rizal's life and death was repeated again and again, especially annually on Rizal Day (December 30). The story of Rizal is firmly embedded within the Filipino educational system, with teachers regularly retelling the story of Rizal to school children. Through this repeated iteration of the narrative of his death, his memory has been preserved, revivified, and disseminated. Both repetition and amplification revivify in their own particular ways and sometimes do in tandem with each other. These repetitions have contributed to the story of his death and life being amplified, and amplified in many different ways. It is to amplification that we now turn to consider in greater detail.

Amplifications of narratives

A microphone amplifies a voice, making it louder and bringing it closer. There is a sense in which amplification creates a certain kind of intimacy between a speaker and a listener. A poor amplification system can do the opposite, distorting the sound and distancing listeners from the original sound. Obviously, even the very best systems can compress, condense, and change the tone and pitch of a voice. Narratives are both literally and metaphorically amplified through an entire host of modern media. When an amplifier works well, the central story is not simply repeated but enlarged, isolated, clarified, or underscored. It is possible to hear or see the story more clearly as a result of effective amplification.

How then was news of Rizal's death amplified? And how far did the amplification bring the narrative closer to audiences or distance them from his death? First, within a few decades there were different kinds of *material amplifications*. Several statues and other monuments were built; a plaque marking the place he actually fell was commissioned, and stamps, banknotes, coins, and postcards were produced, all with his figure or face being given pride of place. Material amplification continues to this day. Just as in Lebanon it is now possible to buy mementoes of recent local martyrs, so in modern-day Manila you can purchase mugs, t-shirts, and posters with Rizal's face emblazoned on them. These material amplifications do not always remain static and are constantly being renewed and refreshed to speak to new generations of Filipinos. One of the objectives of such revivifications is to preserve and reinvigorate the memory of Rizal's life and death.[1] Consider, for example, the annual Rizal Day events, which included the publication of a *Rizal Day Souvenir Programme*. This was retitled in 1951 as *Rizaliana*, which included tributes to Rizal, stories about Rizal, and quotations by the man himself. Here was something concrete to buy, to read, to look at, to talk about, and to collect.

Closely connected to material amplification is a process that I will describe as *rhetorical amplification* through narratives. Many of the material amplifications discussed above are used rhetorically, with the intention of encouraging audiences to remember their national hero and follow Rizal's footsteps. In other words, Rizal's story is used to persuade people of the value not only of celebrating his wisdom but of acting in certain ways. Several examples will suffice to illustrate this claim. In *Rizaliana,* we find one page full of Rizal quotes celebrating the "Freedom of the Press," such as: "A government cannot do away with the freedom of the press by which it can feel the beatings of a people's pulse." At the bottom are a few lines that connect the sponsor with the theme of the page: "Your paper manufacturers, in supplying the press with a vital commodity, are giving a priceless contribution to the preservation of a very important freedom." In another edition, we find an advertisement where Rizal's name and figure are used in detailed prose to endorse the only university in the Philippines exclusively for women. It is almost as if Rizal has been transformed into an ideal type. This can be seen even more clearly in *Rizaliana* marking the sixty-first anniversary of his death, where he is commended not only as a patriot but as the ideal citizen. On this particular page, Rizal's figure and face have been replaced by a mother holding the arms of a smiling toddler while a muscular man, presumably the father, looks on. In a brief few lines "the Filipino people" are exhorted to recall and "seek inspiration" from his example. Taken together, these three examples illustrate how Rizal's words and depictions of his face or entire body are used to encourage readers to value a free press, a rigorous education, and commitment to the nation, while also encouraging them to support a local university or paper manufacturer.

In ways reminiscent of how John Foxe's *Book of Martyrs* (1563) was used in England to promote different causes from the sixteenth to as recent as the nineteenth century, so Rizal's life and death become a rhetorical resource to promote anything from social decorum to locally manufactured paper. Take the page in *Rizaliana* where Rizal is held up as a model of good manners "with all his dealings with the fair sex": the "perfect gentlemen." An artist brings this claim to life by depicting Rizal sitting beside his "sweetheart," Leonor Rivera, but with at least forty centimeters safely separating them. The commentary beneath the image goes on to claim that "our present day youth have much to learn from Rizal in this respect." The fact that he was romantically involved with at least thirteen women is not mentioned.

As we have seen, Rizal's death also became a rhetorical resource for advertisers. It is worth reflecting on this process a little more closely. At first sight in several editions of *Rizaliana*, the image and text combine to celebrate Rizal's heroic example. For instance, beside the flamboyantly inscribed headline "Rizal's Immortality" is the assertion "The immortality of the Jose Rizal lies not alone in his death as a martyr. His greatness lies in the sublime philosophy of his writings." Beneath this claim is a picture of the cover of his best known book, *Noli Me Tangere,* which we return to discuss in a few moments. Looking carefully, one can see how both the story *of* Rizal and stories *by* Rizal are used once again to promote Menzi and Co., a paper manufacturer who "suppl[ies] the vital commodity on which are immortalised the sublime thoughts" of the likes of Rizal. Here is one example of how the narratives connected with Rizal were used to help to endorse a commodity. Paper was not the only commodity associated with Rizal's life and death. For instance, one picture puts the Rizal memorial in the background with a large picture of a bottle in the foreground accompanied by "For a Bigger and Better Rizal Day celebration serve: Pepsi."

One finds the rhetorical purpose of amplification at work even in Rizal's own fictional writing and its continuing reception. Rizal's novels, first *Noli Me Tangere* (1887) and subsequently *El Filibusterismo* (1891), are often described as one of the main causes of his arrest, trial, and execution. Initially they were banned and burnt, but later they would become almost canonical. The words *Noli Me Tangere* are taken from John 20.17, where the risen Christ tells Mary Magdalene "don't touch me." Curiously, there is no direct reference in the novel to this incident. However, in a letter to a friend,

Felix Resurrection Hidalgo, about *Noli Me Tangere*, Rizal reveals the taboo-breaking sense he had in mind:

> The book contains things which no one has spoken about until the present—things so delicate that they cannot be touched upon by anyone. I have tried to do what no one has ever wanted to do.
>
> (Bantug with Ventura 1997: 69–70)

Through a satirical novel, Rizal dares to touch matters such as the hypocrisy, infighting, and oppression of the Spanish Friars in the Philippines. The characters from *Noli* and *Fili*, as they are commonly known today, regularly reappeared in novels, films, and plays throughout the twentieth century. The once-banned book has been translated into numerous foreign languages, is sold worldwide, and appears in the core syllabus of many schools in the Philippines.

Part of the power of these two books is the way in which their narratives resonate with the experience of Filipinos in the late nineteenth and early twentieth century. Through ironic characterizations, these stories subvert the status quo. Rizal ridicules many of the friars, and some of the collaborating politicians, who then controlled so much of life in the Philippines. Though the excesses of the Spanish regime were the original target, the fact that Filipinos would endure colonization by the United States for nearly half a century and a brief occupation by the Japanese during the Second World War, made these subversive narratives even more attractive to locals in search of an independent national identity.

There is considerable debate as to whether the central protagonist in *Noli*, Ibarra, should be interpreted as Rizal himself. There are clearly similarities between the peripatetic life of this fictional character and Rizal. It is ambiguous who actually dies at the end of the novel, either Ibarra or his bold friend Elias. So the last words, "whispered as if in prayer" come from an "unknown":

> Nothing will remain of me... I die without seeing the sun rise on my country. You who are to see the dawn, welcome it, and do not forget those who fell during the night!
>
> (Rizal 2004: 371)

These words are regularly quoted, often out of their original narrative context, as if an actual prophetic insight of Rizal about his own martyrdom, dying before he would see the Philippines gain its brief independence in 1898, which did not become permanent until 1946. As with many fictional narratives, they are appropriated and put to work in nonfictional settings.

The process by which the communicative impact of a narrative is *amplified* through different media *and* by different members of the audience. In *Folk Devils and Moral Panics* (1972), Stanley Cohen made famous use of amplification theory, suggesting in his study of youth subcultures (mods and rockers) in the late 1960s that social deviance could be amplified through a downward spiral of mediated publicity. My argument here inverts his observation, suggesting that it is also possible to have an upward spiral, not of deviance but rather amplification of heroic qualities. In this case, Rizal is made a purer figure and, as we shall see, believed by some to be worthy of devotion and even worship.

Elaborations of narratives

The narratives associated with Rizal's life and death were not only iterated and amplified, they were elaborated. This happened in several different ways. First, there was what could be described as *devotional elaboration*. There is a sense in which Rizal was celebrated as both a secular and religious saint, with sites of devotion created in several spaces around the country. Successive governments have invested in preserving his memory as a "national hero," with considerable care being devoted to his reburial on December 30, 1912. Rizal's remains were transported by an artillery caisson drawn by six horses to the actual site of his martyrdom. Only a few steps away, the urn was then carefully placed at the base of where a monument, entitled *Motto Stella*, was built during the following year. More than forty designers from around the world had competed for their elaborate designs to be chosen. The winner was Richard Kissling, who had sculpted the Swiss people's monument to their national hero and freedom fighter William Tell. The Rizal monument is still guarded by an honorary guard and remains a focal point in Rizal Park in Manila and especially at the annual Rizal Day celebrations.

The monument has been the venue for many eulogies elaborating Rizal's life and death. For instance, a local dignitary by the name of Camilos Osias gave an address in 1953 entitled, "Rizal, Martyr to Human Liberty," wherein he asserted that:

> Rizal was a martyr in fact and in truth. In infancy, in youth, and in manhood he witnessed the martyrdom of his people and bitter anguish was brought home to his family. He himself was the victim. He was ridiculed and maligned. He was persecuted and exiled. He was imprisoned and tried on trumped up charges. He was tortured, sentenced to death, and done to death. His influence continues. His spirit is immortal. Rizal was not born to die… Rizal, the patriot, the hero, the martyr lives. He will never die.
>
> (April 27, 1953)

The allusions to a first-century figure in Palestine are hard to miss and illustrate how Rizal's sacrifice was sometimes paralleled with Jesus' sacrificial death and at other times to the early Christian martyrs. Notice how a contemporary narrative is given greater significance by its association with an ancient narrative, which has an even longer history of repetition, amplification, and elaboration.

In the same year as Osias' speech, a modern museum was built at Fort Santiago in Manila to house some of the memorabilia from Jose Rizal's life and death. As part of the centennial celebration of Rizal's martyrdom and the Philippine Revolution, the shrine was renovated in 1996. Apart from the replica cell, there are numerous objects preserved in glass cases, such as an original copy of *Noli*, sculptures by Rizal and, perhaps more poignantly, a "secular relic," which is a bone of Rizal's bearing a bullet wound and enshrined in a glass urn (Maria 1996: 261). Thousands of "pilgrims" and tourists pay different kinds of visual homage to both this shrine and the monument in the park every year.

Several different Filipino groups went even further in their devotion to Rizal, weaving complex theological narratives around his life and death. The so-called *Rizalistas* hold belief systems that have Rizal as their focal point. Their beliefs and practices are far from homogeneous, with some regarding Rizal as divine, as the embodied power of the Holy Spirit, as a second Christ, or as a new messiah who will return (as in the Banner of the Race Church— *Watwat ng Lahi*). One of the best known groups is the Philippine Church or *Adarnistas*, which was named after their founder, Mother Adarna, who believe that Rizal was "not executed but lives as true God and man" (Bowker 2005: 489). In some cases, Rizal is prayed to in worship services for healing or help, in the same way in which Catholic saints are invoked for assistance. Those outside these religious movements regard most of these elaborate stories told about Rizal in these contexts as apocryphal and point to the fact that many of the Rizalista churches have declined over the last three decades. Nevertheless, even though many of these groups may be shrinking, their histories of loyal following attest to the power of these elaborate narratives to encourage devotion.

Alongside devotional elaborations are *artistic elaborations* of Rizal's life and death. Both devotional and artistic elaborations were deeply engaged in hagiography, that is, adding to the life of Rizal the narrative motifs and structures of martyrdom and sainthood. Some artistic elaborations have become sites of devotion. His execution is the subject of several artistic interpretations. For example, the national artist known as "Botong," Carlos V. Francisco, portrayed the moment of Rizal's execution, in which the neatly dressed figure of Rizal dominates the picture while his executioners stand in the background. As his hat tumbles off his head, the look on his face is a mixture of pain, self-control, and even ecstasy. Suffering is given an *ecstatic* quality in many Baroque Catholic depictions of saints and, in this tradition, it was often less about pain and more about holy suffering. This portrait of Rizal resonates with Catholic visual piety, which the Spaniards brought to the Philippines and is still visible among the devotional iconography in the Church of St. Augustine, Intramuros, Manila. Botong's image is far from the traditional Man of Sorrows and closer to a man embracing his fate, his holy suffering. The central figure dominates even more than the victim in Francisco de Goya's *The Third of May 1808* (1814) or in Edouard Manet's five versions of the *Execution of Maximilian* (1867–1869). Though Francisco may well have been influenced by such earlier depictions of execution scenes, he is elaborating the narrative of Rizal's death in a particular way. Unlike Goya and Manet, Francisco shows almost all the soldiers' faces, gazing toward Rizal as they fire. The figure of Rizal himself is thrust forward and upward toward the viewer, almost inviting watchers to lean forward and catch him before he crumples to the ground. The invitation goes further. The viewer is invited to witness the event almost like the creation of a martyr, so Botong transforms the execution into a spiritual event, an epiphany. Rizal floats in ecstasy. He is portrayed not as Jesus but as the leading saint of Philippine nationalistic civil religion.

Francisco's artistic elaboration is far more dramatic than the picture that is commonly claimed to be the only existing photographic record of his execution. The black and white photograph contains the diminutive and smartly dressed figure of Rizal with his back turned away from the firing squad. Ranks of soldiers and bystanders, out of focus, appear to observe the soldiers as they raise their rifles to fire. Commentary on the photograph often implies far more about the interpreter than the image itself, with one commentator claiming that "the hero's serenity is visible. So is his love of country and great expectation that the nobleness of humanness would triumph" (Maria 1996: 250). More recently, the authenticity of the photograph has been questioned, with some even suggesting it was taken from one of the early screen versions of Rizal's life (Deocampo 2007: 61).

The moment of Rizal's execution has also undergone a number of *cinematic elaborations*. The scene is usually placed within the wider canvas of his life and death. Albert Yearsley's *The Life and Death of the Great Filipino Martyr, Dr Jose Rizal* (1912) and Edward Meyer Gross's *The Life of Dr Jose Rizal* (1912) released within a day of each other, competed for public attention, attracting considerable audiences. Such early cinematic elaborations were not, however, without their contemporary critics. In 1913, one local magazine writer was highly critical of these American-made films:

A few months back, there were local screenings of some films based on the life and death of [Dr. Jose] Rizal. Despite the grandiose advertising about the excellence of the film, we frankly think they are the most dismal works that we have ever seen. Furthermore, we think that such films should never be shown, much less allowed to be screened because they are badly done and because they insult the sacred memory of the glorious Martyr of Bagumbayan.

(Deocampo 2007: 244)

Elaborations of the founding tales of nations, or semi-sacred narratives, commonly become sites of controversy. The stories are contested, with many different voices claiming control over the authentic and original narrative.

Among a number of other more recent cinematic elaborations, including *The Life and Loves of Rizal* (1956; Gerardo de Leon), *Rizal in Dapitan* (1997; Amable Tikoy Aguiluz), it is *Jose Rizal* (1998; Marilou Diaz-Abaya), starring Cesar Montano, which has received the greatest critical acclaim, winning a large number of international awards. The most expensive Philippine movie ever made, it also proved popular at the local box office. Two of the producers of the film, Butch Jimenez and Jimmy Duavit, claimed that their objective was to reinvigorate the traditional Rizal narrative: "We want to bring Jose Rizal down from the monument and into people's hearts... Our desire is to humanize him, to give a new generation an opportunity to be better acquainted with him." This can be seen in a number of scenes in this epic of three hours plus. For instance, Rizal's execution is portrayed in a dramatic though restrained fashion reminiscent of Francisco's painting and the "original" photograph referred to above. In many ways, this is a comparatively cautious cinematic elaboration that draws on previous artistic elaborations without sliding into an entirely hagiographic narrative.

More daring are the cinematic elaborations now easily found on *YouTube*. There are several dramatic though not lavish music videos reflecting aspects of his romantic involvements or his execution. For example, a group of Filippino students were set a task of creating a short film about Rizal in the autumn of 2006.[2] They did this, putting the scenes to music and reenacting his last hours. The result is a somewhat melodramatic but memorable rendition of his final hours. It brings together many of the best known moments in the Rizal passion narrative. To this point, more than 11,000 people have visited this virtual narrative, which is set to local popular music. In his book on *Narration in the Fiction Film*, David Bordwell examines the process of narrative comprehension of film (1985). What he describes as "cognitive schemata" allow viewers to create a narrative in their imaginations. Bordwell is drawing on insights from cognitive science to outline how viewers are able to put together, and perhaps also elaborate on, the story that they watch.

Watch many of these amateur or semi-amateur productions and one is struck by how often the film makers rely on the audience to elaborate on what they see, so creating for themselves a meaningful narrative.

Reverberations of narratives

I now consider the reverberations of Rizal's narratives. By "reverberations" I mean the echoing or forming of stories that refer to the core narrative, serving both to draw meaning from it and to infuse it with thematic relevance. Reverberation is a very important cultural operation because it forms the new on the old but also refreshes the old, changing it however slightly or dramatically in the process. These are intermeshed in such a way that it will be more helpful to consider different kinds of reverberation alongside one another. The controversial photo that has become so firmly embedded in the collective Filipino memory of Rizal's story reverberates in several dramatic contexts. For example, it is brought to life in one of more than sixty dioramas, which are small illuminated scenes with model figures and dramatic backdrops or scenery. The set of dioramas is found at the Ayala museum in Manila, and they trace the history of the Philippines. The fact that Rizal is given two separate scenes, one of him writing *Noli Me Tangere* and the other of his execution, underlies his perceived importance in this dramatic account of the formation of the modern-day Philippines. Thousands of Filipino school children are taken around this display every year, with the diorama being a particular favorite for both the organizers of the school trips and the children themselves.

The narrative of Rizal reverberates in other dramatic settings. Every night, currently at 8 PM, in Rizal Park there is a sound and light display reenacting his life and death. Music, lights, and a commentary help to bring the eight-foot-high metallic sculptures to life. Most of these lifelike figures are portrayed in the moment of Rizal's execution. There is a heroic quality to Rizal's figure, which is reminiscent of Francisco's portrayal. There is also something ironic in that a man who stood little more than five feet in real life is turned into an eight-foot giant, towering over any visitor walking round the site during the day or any viewer watching the show in the evening. The daily recalling of his life and death has a ritualistic quality, which is even clearer throughout the country on Rizal Day, December 30, the annual commemoration of his martyrdom. Flags fly at half-staff, masses and services are held, floral offerings are made, bells are rung, his last and most famous poem *My Final Farewell (Mi Ultimo Adiós)* is recited, with processions, speeches, and meals all marking the day as noteworthy. There is a participative quality to these rituals, which ensures than his story resonates at more levels of Filipino society. Notice how civil rituals are brought together with religious services, as a predominantly Catholic country reflects on its own birth story and passion narratives.

The story of Rizal's execution reverberated particularly powerfully after the assassination of Benigno Aquino on August 21, 1983 just a few minutes after he had arrived at what was then known as Manila International National. As with Rizal, public spaces were transformed or changed to mark his death. The airport was later renamed as Ninony Aquino International Airport in his honor. On the plane back from his three-year exile in the United States, he admitted to the accompanying journalists that "My feeling is we all have to die sometime and if it's my fate to die by an assassin's bullet, so be it." Aquino personally linked his own story with Rizal's story, who had likewise returned home from exile to face death. After his assassination, many other commentators did the same. It was later pointed out that just as Rizal's death marked the beginning of the end for Spanish rule, so Aquino's death marked the beginning of the end of Ferdinand Marcos' twenty-year autocratic rule over his own people.

These parallel narratives are told and woven together in many places. Increasingly, the Internet has become a site for Rizal's story to reverberate around the world. The official web site is maintained by the Jose Rizal University and offers surfers extensive details about his life and death.[3] There are a few signs of the contested elements of Rizal's narrative, though the materials provided about his last hour "retraction" of some of his anti–Catholic Church views are particularly useful, allowing the reader to engage with different biographers who offer conflicting accounts of whether Rizal ever made such a retraction. The fact that so much ink has been spilled over this question illustrates the importance attached to preserving, correcting, and owning his narrative. The web allows for the diversity of views to be easily available in the public domain and provides a setting for the reverberations of the debate to be considered and then added to by participants.

Conclusion

In the previous sections, I have analyzed four related processes in the formation, circulation, and reception of one set of narratives related to the life and death of Jose Rizal. Canadian composer John Cage was well known for developing the "prepared piano," which involved elaborating on the design of the original instrument by adding rubber, stone, screws, and wood between the strings of the piano. The result was to transform the way the amplified piano sounded, changing the musical repetitions and reverberations that emanated from its body. This was used to memorable effect with his music designed to evoke the sounds of Asia, in particular Bali. My argument is that audiences and media producers have done and are continuing to do something similar to the Rizal story, adding new materials onto or between the original stories. This is a dynamic, rapid, and ever-changing process.

The case study of Rizal provides a valuable insight into the ways in which narrative can work. Narratives do not remain still and are never owned by only one individual, community, or institution. They are iterated and amplified in many different forms for numerous ends. I suggested that there are times when amplification can both bring a narrative close to audiences and yet distance them from the original story. Narratives are also creatively elaborated on, becoming sites of devotion, celebration, commemoration, persuasion, and contest. Narratives are transformed as they are adapted or translated into a new media. The 1961 cinematic version of *Noli* represents a different kind of narrative from the original text penned by Rizal and published in 1887. Finally, the dramatic reenactment of narratives contributes to the ways in which stories reverberate across distinct historical, cultural, and religious settings. Nevertheless, in the midst of this sea of stories, the words from Rizal's account have a habit of resurfacing. However rich and thought-provoking his surviving words and stories are, when brought together, even these are incomplete, a collection of fragments and narrative strands that have continued to be constructed long after his execution. Knowing some of the many ways in which Rizal's story is repeated, amplified, and elaborated not only sheds light on how narratives work but facilitates some of Rizal's original words to reverberate across generations and cultures: "Nobody can say how he [or she] will die. But everybody must decide how and for what he [or she] shall live."

Notes

1   See David Morgan's discussion of memory and recognition in the experience of popular religious imagery (Morgan 1998: 34–43).
2   See: http://www.youtube.com/watch?v=DjE7zEfT1N8. For another example, see http://www.youtube.com/watch?v=-BL8oS19PDo
3   (http://www.joserizal.ph/in01.html)

10

Practice

Pamela E. Klassen

"Everyday" uses of the notion of practice
A brief genealogy of the concept of practice
The effects of practice

As an object of study, the intersection of religion and media offers a never-ending supply of primary sources, whether niche-market Bibles, televised depictions of Hindu epics, or Internet sites selling online ritual services. Even the more traditional textual sources that have long been the focus of religious studies—canonical and extra-canonical scriptures, spiritual diaries, law codes—are themselves excellent sources for the study of how religion is "mediated" or conveyed. Despite this plethora of sources, scholars have only relatively recently considered texts and images of religious communication as something more than containers of doctrine, debate, or other kinds of data. Spurred in part by a reinvigorated interdisciplinary interest in book history and print culture, scholars of Christianity, for example, have begun to study not only competing interpretations of biblical texts but how Christians have cultivated reading itself as virtuous and profitable (in both spiritual and financial senses) (Brown 2004; Coleman 2006; Cressy 1986; Gutjahr 2001; Hall 1989; Johns 1996; Klassen 2006; Nord 2004; Peters 1999). A common denominator in the shift from the study of the theological or intellectual meanings of texts and images to the investigation of their production, consumption, and physicality is the theoretical concept of practice.

In his study of "visual piety," David Morgan clarifies the utility of "practice" for the study of how particular media—in his study, religious images—are made, sold, bought, and used:

> practice...is helpful here because it stresses that thinking, wanting, deciding, speaking, and looking, as well as ritual performance and gift-giving, are all part of the concrete world-making activities that constitute social behaviour. These are not mindless actions but embodied forms of cognition and collective memory that reside in the concrete conditions of social life.

> (Morgan 1998: 4)

In this chapter, my task is to situate practice—a theoretical concept that roots the analysis of ideas, social relations, and technologies in human practical activity—as a concept that has shaped the scholarly study of religion and media. To do so, I first consider everyday uses of the word *practice* and sketch out four ways that the concept of practice has reoriented the study of religion and media. Second, I provide a selective genealogy of the theoretical concept of practice. I then discuss some of the most fruitful practice-oriented theoretical and methodological approaches to the study of religion and media. Finally, in the spirit of what Marx called "praxis," I consider how scholarly activity itself has been transformed by thinking with practice and what transformations are yet to come.

"Everyday" uses of the notion of practice

Practice is a concept that attempts to bring together thought and action—both how people think about the world they live in and what they do in it. At the level of ordinary speech, two meanings of the word *practice* are frequently employed when talking of religion. The first takes practice as a synonym for customary activity, or action. Practices of prayer, meditation, or preaching are all examples of activities that share some common characteristics across religions. Though not all prayer looks or sounds the same, for example, it can be categorized for the purposes of analysis as a communicative form usually directed to a deity or spirit. In a second meaning, practice is repetitive action undertaken to become better at something, whether playing piano or being a compassionate human being. In this case, practice has a forward-looking, ameliorative sense, implying commitment on the part of the practitioner. Conventionally speaking, a "practicing" Christian, Buddhist, or Jew is one who cultivates her or his religious identity not only as a question of intellectual assent or accident of birth but in daily or weekly customary actions such as going to church, meditation, or observing holy days. Interestingly, however, we rarely speak of "practiced" Christians, Buddhists, or Jews as we would of a "practiced liar," implying that the job of cultivating religious identity is never done.

The ceaseless job of scholars of religion, by contrast, is to utilize, theorize, and critique concepts such as practice (and religion), recognizing how particular concepts help us to understand complex cultural phenomena while also being attentive to what certain concepts might prevent us from seeing. Practice has brought into the purview of religious studies a multitude of ways of "being religious" that have previously been largely ignored; for example, scholarly attention to practice has brought to prominence the religious lives of women and marginalized peoples, the role of religion in seemingly "nonreligious" spheres, and the messiness and creativity of religious borrowing, appropriation, and hybridity (Griffith 1997; Bender 2003; McNally 2000).

In the case of religion and media, the concept of practice has facilitated a shift from focusing purely on the message of a text, image, or sound to considering the medium in its many dimensions: how it works and who controls it, to what range of human senses a particular medium appeals, what people do with both messages and the media that transmit them, and how ritual, theologies, and religious dispositions are constituted and transformed by different kinds of media. Thinking with the help of practice situates a particular medium (e.g., scrolls, books, icons, television) in at least four ways: (1) as a pathway for communicative discourse, (2) as a product that requires both human labor and resources for its creation, (3) as a pliable form that calls forth a range of embodied and imaginative responses from its consumers, and (4) as a communicative form that is given religious meaning in and of itself. Radio, for example, is at once (1) a wave medium that allows for the transmission of sound across great distance, (2) something that has been regulated by state legislation and requires training and costly equipment, and (3) an entity that religious groups have used very effectively to transmit their messages to listeners who hear and react to these messages while in their homes, cars, and workplaces (Hangen 2002; Hilmes 1997). At a fourth level, radio is a medium that some have considered to be a vibrational force tuned to a spiritual frequency, parallel to the way in which some religions consider text to be a medium of divine communication. Anglican clergyman Frederick Du Vernet, for example, argued in the 1920s that "spiritual radio" transmitted the healing power of God (Klassen 2007; see also Schmidt 2000; Peters 1999).

Whether via radios, Bibles, sutras, amulets, or video games, religion is created and mediated through a variety of communicative forms that depend on physical, technological, and cultural production and the reception and response of audiences. As Colleen McDannell suggests: "Religious practices are 'multimedia events,' where speech, vision, gesture, touch, and sound combine" (McDannell 2001: 4). The concept of practice helps scholars of religion and media to pay attention to how people think and how they act in a range of sensory modes and to the material conditions, structures of authority, and relations of power that make such action possible.

A brief genealogy of the concept of practice

The concept of practice became especially important to scholars of religion in the 1980s and 1990s as the field became increasingly interested in the role of religion in people's everyday lives, including those people not represented in traditional scholarship based as it was on textual sources mostly authored by literate men. Coining such phrases as "lived religion" (Hall 1997) and "domestic religion" (Sered), scholars of a wide variety of religions have gravitated to the concept of practice as a tool for not simply developing a new analytic approach to their data, but for instigating an intervention that would reshape what counted as legitimate sources, methodologies, and topics in the study of religion more generally (Lopez 1999; Maffly-Kipp et al. 2006; Hoover and Clark 2002).

An early contributor to the concept of practice was Karl Marx, whose notion of "praxis" sought to bring together thought and action at two levels.[1] Defining practice as "sensuous, human activity" (McLellan 1977: 156) that was the ground of thought, social relations, and change, Marx argued that any analysis of human activity needed to place it in the context of social relations that were deeply conditioned not just by ideas but by material conditions. Under capitalism, Marx argued, whichever group of people (or class) controlled the making and selling of commodities had substantial power over those who did not have such resources (or capital). At the same time, the dominated classes maintained some power based in their own labor—or more broadly, their own practices. Arguing against an intellectualist view of history that saw ideas as the primary motor of social change, Marx asserted that "social productive forces are produced not only in the form of knowledge but also as the direct organs of *social practice; of the real life process*" (McLellan 1977: 381; italics added). Religion, according to Marx, grew out of and mirrored the social practices of human beings: "All social life is essentially practical. All mysteries which lead theory to mysticism find their rational solution in human practice and in the comprehension of this practice" (157). Practice—sensuous human activity—was the starting point of all critical analysis for Marx and, more specifically, the starting point for critically analyzing religion in particular.[2]

Marx argued that praxis was not simply a conceptual tool meant to clarify the social world around us, and he charged social critics with their own fusion of thought and action—"the philosophers have only interpreted the world, in various ways; the point is to change it" (McLellan 1977: 158). The prescriptive, activist flavor to Marx's praxis shaped the later concept of practice, which held the promise of bringing to scholarly attention the lives of those ignored by traditional scholarship and thereby contributing to the transformation of the social structures and practices that colluded in their oppression. In media studies, the legacy of Marx's practice has been especially fruitful for scholars analyzing the ways in which various forms of media—whether advertising, entertainment, or state-run broadcasting—have shaped and been shaped by the material conditions of capitalism (e.g. Lears 1994; McClintock 1995). Taking a page from these studies, analyses of religion and media could benefit from more attention to the material conditions of capital, colonialism, and state regulation that have made possible media production in religious arenas.

Drawing from Marx's critiques of class domination without fully acceding to Marxist historical determinism, cultural historians of early modern Europe were particularly innovative in drawing together religion, media, and practice. Searching for a way to make the study of popular culture and everyday life a viable field brought cultural historians face to face with the constraining effects of media upon their sources—texts written by the literate, dominant classes were largely the only media durable enough to last for 400 years (cf. Goody 2000). What could texts from an inquisition really tell one about a peasant tried for witchcraft? When studying largely oral cultures, via what media could a scholar access her sources? Instead of abandoning the study of "ordinary" people, historians such as Carlo Ginsburg read against the grain of such texts as records of Catholic inquisitions to find the beginnings of a path for the study of the largely "undocumented" people of early modern Europe. Ginsburg was particularly reflexive about his sources as media:

> The almanacs, the songsters, the books of piety, the lives of the saints, the entire pamphlet literature that constituted the book trade, today appear static, inert, and unchanging to us. But how were they read by the public of the day? To what extent did the prevalently oral culture of those readers interject itself in the use of the text, modifying it, reworking it, perhaps to the point of changing its very essence?
>
> (Ginsburg 1980: xxii)

While Ginsburg and other historians were finding ways to critically and creatively tease submerged practices out of the media—the texts and images—on which their scholarship depended, sociologist Pierre Bourdieu was emerging with a theory of practice stemming from his ethnographic work in colonial (and revolutionary) Algeria. Bourdieu articulated a dense theory of practice that grappled with the theoretical significance of the habits and minutiae of daily life. Bourdieu's definition of practice had none of the precision of Marx's "human sensuous activity." Instead, he argued that practice could largely be understood only negatively, by what it was not. Practice could not be abstracted outside of the pace and physicality of lived time, as scientific reasoning might be; practice could not be pinned down by academic analysis, because once it was recognized, it would lose its defining characteristics as a taken-for-granted, habitual common sense (Bourdieu 1990a: 82–3).

For Bourdieu, the concept of practice was intimately tied to his understanding of habitus, the taken-for-granted aspects of being an embodied person who can operate according to the "rules of the game" in a particular culture. Drawing especially from Marcel Mauss, who analyzed "techniques of the body" across cultures and religions, Bourdieu's notion of habitus also echoed Marx's contention that practice is a "state of the body" (Bourdieu 1990a: 68). For Bourdieu, the "common sense" of being a body in practice in a particular culture was not natural; instead, the "feel for the game" that was *practice* was "social necessity turned into nature" and thus obscured (Bourdieu 1990a: 69). Not natural but naturalized, practice contained within it both cultural competency and cultural domination.

Bourdieu understood practices to make sense in particular cultural "fields," such as education, art, or religion. The ways in which actors related to each other in these fields had much to do with their different levels of not only economic but cultural and symbolic capital; the knowingness and authority that one commands in a boxing ring, for example, is based on different kinds of capital than those operative in a lecture hall. In its demonstration that particular kinds of practices make sense in one field and not another and its analysis of conflict within fields, Bourdieu's theory of fields of cultural production was particularly useful for bringing together his theory of practice with the study of media (Bourdieu 1984; 1993; cf. Peterson and Anand 2004). Bourdieu's own attention to religion in particular was more sporadic, but his theories of practice, habitus, and symbolic capital have deeply influenced the study of religion (e.g., Bell 1992).

Another strong current among practice theory was the work of the French historian Michel de Certeau, who argued that Bourdieu's "logic of practice" sacrificed the embodied knowingness of practices for benefit of constructing his theory: "Scrupulously examining practices and their logic—in a way that surely has had no equivalent since Mauss—[Bourdieu's] texts finally reduce them to a mystical reality, the *habitus*, which is to bring them under the law of reproduction" (de Certeau 1984: 59). Most troubling for de Certeau was Bourdieu's insistence that practice was defined by the unknowingness of its actors—once an actor reflected on her actions as a "practice" it was no longer naturalized or common sense, and thus no longer a practice. De Certeau, by contrast, thought of practice as a more knowing disposition, made up of both "strategies" and "tactics." For de Certeau, strategies were practices calculated by those individuals, organizations, or bodies of expertise that had power over others and that were able to claim a space of their own—for example, armies, businesses, and scientific institutions. A tactic, by contrast, was a calculated practice of the "weak" or those who did not have a protected place from which to operate and who were forced to act within the territory of those who held the bulk of the (violent) power (de Certeau 1984). His articulation of strategies and tactics allowed de Certeau to make space for resistance or for practices that were knowingly counter to dominant views, though he could not be considered entirely optimistic about the possibilities of tactics in the face of strategies. This was clear in his discussion of the continuum of religious belief and media manipulation. Arguing that "advertising has become evangelical," de Certeau went further to say that media had assumed the place of religion in organizing the everyday:

> Captured by the radio (the voice is the law) as soon as he awakens, the listener walks all day long through the forest of narrativities from journalism, advertising, and television, narrativities that still find time, as he is getting ready for bed, to slip a few final messages under the portals of sleep. Even more than the God told about by the theologians of earlier days, these stories have a providential and predestining function: they organize in advance our work, our celebrations, and even our dreams.
>
> (de Certeau 1984: 186)

According to de Certeau, scholars themselves are both agents and subjects of this all-encompassing narrativity, as they engage in the "modern mythical practice" of creating theories and writing texts to explain their world (de Certeau 1984).

Despite this bleak view of media manipulation, de Certeau's notion of tactics left some room for the possibility of what historian Henri Lefebvre called "inventive praxis." For Lefebvre, Marx's notion of praxis was based both in the material conditions of human existence and the (sometimes) metaphysical speculation that humans engaged in to think of their worlds: "praxis encompasses both material production and 'spiritual' production" (Lefebvre 1966: 25; 2002: 237). Inventive praxis, according to Lefebvre, was based on the repetitive, habitual kinds of practice (akin to Bourdieu's notion) but led to creative transformations of "human relations (including their ethical dimensions)" (Lefebvre 2002: 242).[3] Despite his attention to inventive praxis, Lefebvre's analysis of media fell largely within the "mass media as propaganda" approach of many twentieth-century critics.[4] Similarly to de Certeau, Lefebvre saw mass media as taking over the propagandizing role previously performed by religious institutions (namely churches; Lefebvre 2002: 84). In their fatalistic critiques of the overweening power of mass media (which for them was constituted largely of the press, television, films, and radio), these master theoreticians of practice seemed to have closed their eyes to the wedge that practice could open for understanding how women and men reading, seeing, or hearing media images and narratives might have creatively reinterpreted or even resisted them.

Practice, then, is a concept with much invested in it. Scholars and critics have turned to it as a category that can house the reflective and the habituated body, the strategic powerful and the tactical weak. It has played an important role as a concept that called scholars away from doctrinal and official discourses of religions, states, and elites, and toward the "everyday" actions, movements, and sensations of "ordinary" people. This reorientation from a focus on large-scale social, economic, and political structures or superstructures to the action and agency of people living within (or against) those structures has done much to transform what scholars of religion take to be legitimate, or even viable, topics of study. However, the optimistic democratization of sources and stories promised by practice theory also calls for caution, as anthropologist Sherry Ortner has suggested: "To say that society and history are products of human action is true, but only in a certain ironic sense. They are rarely the products the actors themselves set out to make" (Ortner 1994: 401; see also Asad 1993). Analyses of religion and media underscore Ortner's point, especially when considering the rapid and often unintended social and political transformations that media technologies have effected in the past century; who knew in Marx's day that in 2007 taking communion, being wed, and attending a Bible study in an Anglican cathedral would all be possible as an "avatar" in Second Life, a virtual world accessed only by computer? (http://slangcath.wordpress.com/).

The effects of practice

Many twentieth-century theories of practice were particularly attentive to textual practices, both in terms of those groups they studied and their own practices as scholars making use of sources. More recent approaches to the study of media and religion have had to come to terms with an even wider array of communicative possibilities, as digital media continually transform the ways in which people engage with one another and the "real" and "virtual" worlds around them, while older media, such as books and radio, hang on as popular modes of communication. Practice theories have led scholars to pay attention to the kinds of communication made possible *and* circumvented by particular forms of technology while keeping them from thinking of communication technologies as only a matter of scientific innovation (e.g., Hilmes 1997: xiii). As a mode of analysis concerned both with the conditions of material production and with the social relations and cultural contexts in which mediated communication happens, practice opens up a very fruitful path for thinking about conundrums of religion and media. For example, why have almost all the cinemas in Accra, Ghana been bought by Pentecostal churches, which now hold their services on their stages and show their own, in-house films on their screens? (Meyer and Moors 2006).

One of the most promising directions in the practice-oriented analysis of religion and media is Birgit Meyer's articulation of "sensational forms" that encompassed both the "official" paths to religious experience and those routes that are less orthodox:

> Sensational forms, in my understanding, are relatively fixed, authorized modes of invoking, and organizing access to the transcendental, thereby creating and sustaining links between religious practitioners in the context of particular religious organizations...the notion of 'sensational form' can also be applied to the ways in which material religious objects—such as images, books, or buildings—address and involve beholders. Thus, reciting a holy book as the Quran, praying in front of an icon, or dancing around the manifestation of a spirit are also sensational forms through which religious practitioners are made to experience the presence and power of the transcendental.
>
> (Meyer 2006: 9)

Meyer asserts that religion itself is "a *practice of mediation* that organizes the relationship between experiencing subjects and the transcendental via particular sensational forms" (Meyer 2006: 18; italics added). As a practice, religion as mediation must be situated both in the embodied lives of its practitioners and in the wider networks of power and authority—from local evangelists to capitalist systems—that structure their lives.

Rooting her analysis in attention to feelings, aesthetics, and power, Meyer argues that while sensational forms sacralize certain kinds of media—in her Ghanaian Pentecostal example she discusses "televised miracle sessions"— they also "mediate, and thus produce, the transcendental and make it sense-able" (Meyer 2006: 14). Meyer wants the concept of sensational forms to draw scholars' attention to the ways in which particular media are given authority in particular traditions to mediate what practitioners experience as the transcendental. She thus wants her concept to bring out the way in which media—whether books, videos, radio, email—are given particular kinds of spiritual virtuosity as paths of divine transmission in particular traditions but also to situate how power, authority, and aesthetics shape the experience (and practices) of people engaged in religious traditions.

Meyer's concept of religion as a "practice of mediation" effected through sensational forms is aptly reflected in Leigh Schmidt's discussion of the role of *hearing* or "practices of listening" in Enlightenment debates about religious experience (see also Hirschkind 2006). Venturing through stories of Enlightenment debunkers of religious oracles to the testimonies of spiritualist mediums who conveyed the voices of the spirits through levitating trumpets, Schmidt argued that new technologies made possible both of these approaches to "hearing". Enlightenment debunkers used acoustic technology as "a useful means of exposing the absences in the oracular. Twisted around, [for spiritualists] mechanical mediation became instead a vehicle of presences, a salvific force alive with vibrational and telegraphic connections" (Schmidt 2000: 239). Schmidt's careful attention to a wide variety of listening practices—those of both religion's detractors and its enthusiasts—challenged the premise that mediated religion equals manipulation and the equally problematic view that mediated religion offers the possibility of a transparent devotional practice. Religion, he argued, is mediated both as spectacular entertainment and contemplative exercise (Schmidt 2000: 245).

Another example of mediation via sensational forms is Lisa Gitelman's discussion of the ways that nineteenth-century American spiritualist practices of "automatic writing" were imagined through the new media of telegraphy—the disembodied communication of words across great distances. Gitelman gives detailed attention to the laws, technologies, and gendered divisions of labor that arose with the development of "writing machines," arguing that technological innovations of the late nineteenth century made possible new practices of textuality and inscription that had not only communicative but cultural and religious effects (Gitelman 1999; see also Mràzek 1997). Arguing for an expansive approach to the "data of culture" provided by the study of media, Gitelman insists that studying the effect of "new" media on religious imaginations and practices requires close attention to historical context (Gitelman 2006; 2003). Scholars must imagine social worlds without the telephone, for example, while also acknowledging the possibilities that were afforded by now obsolete technologies, whether the speaking trumpet or the telegraph.

Just as Gitelman calls scholars to re-imagine what counts as "new media," so too does John Durham Peters ask for a reconsideration of a concept at the heart of media studies: "communication." In a lyrical book that finds its sources everywhere from New Testament scriptures to recent attempts to contact extraterrestrials, Peters traces "the history of the idea of communication" by way of early Christian theologians, angelology, Enlightenment philosophers, and later theorists including Hegel, Marx, Durkheim, and Adorno. Peters argues against a narrative of communication that depicts technological innovation as necessarily leading to better forms of interaction (1999: 10). As does Meyer, Peters places the body at the center of practices of communication, considering it neither a barrier to true, "unmediated" contact nor somehow expendable in the midst of new techniques of drawing together human messages across distance: "If success in communication was once the art of reaching across the intervening bodies to touch another's spirit, in the age of electronic media it has become the art of reaching across the intervening spirits to touch another's body" (Peters 1999: 224–5). Focused not so much on "lived religion" as on the communicative practices of theorists of communication, Peters' book demonstrates the profound significance of religious traditions and spiritual inquiries for the very concepts of communication and mediation themselves.

Conclusion

Practice is a concept that can help to ground the study of religion and media in social interactions, in the interplay of thought and action, and in economic, political, legal, and historical contexts that foster certain kinds of mediation and not others. Practice is also a concept that invites reflexivity, making space for scholars to interrogate their own assumptions about what counts as "mediated religion" or how attitudes of suspicion toward manipulation, propaganda, and mass culture may inflect a scholar's analysis. Applying this reflexivity to the sketch I have provided above, it becomes clear to me that I have drawn my examples largely from Christian or what might be called "post-Christian" (e.g., spiritualist) contexts. Though this is partly because these areas are what I know best as a scholar of religion, John Durham Peters' book leads me to speculate that there might be more going on. In Peters' book and in the work of most of the theorists and scholars I discuss here, Christianity is the primary religion used to think with: whether formulating a theory of practice via a critique of Feuerbach's *The Essence of Christianity* (Marx 1970); comparing the calendrical and narrative dominance of the Church and that of radio and newspapers (de Certeau 1984); or drawing parallels between the propaganda of the Church and that of the magazine industry (Lefebvre 2002; see also Hall 1997; Morgan and Promey 2001). Peters thinks with Christianity in a very explicit manner, in that he traces a genealogy of communication focused on questions of spirit and body as found in critical theorists such as Adorno and Benjamin, and Christian thinkers such as Augustine, Kierkegaard, and Ernest Hocking. Whether implicit or explicit, however, the practice of thinking about religion and media primarily through the category and history of Christianity is necessarily limiting (cf. Hoover and Clark 2002; Meyer and Moors 2006; Hirschkind 2006; Whitehouse 2000). The virtues of practice, then, are that it both opens an approach to the study of religion and media that can account for "everyday life" and larger structures of social organization and calls for a persistent reassessment of what counts as sources for religion, media, and the everyday within the practices of scholars.

Notes

1   Writing in German, Marx used *praxis*, but English translations of his work alternate between "praxis" and "practice." Praxis seems more fully inflected by

Marx's contention that thought and action were necessarily interrelated, even in the act of cultural and political criticism itself.

2 Marx discussed praxis primarily in his earlier "philosophical" writings. A predominant strain of later Marxist theory, which often relegated culture, religion, and other forms of human expression to a "superstructural" or secondary position in relation to the primary importance of economic forces, did not draw primarily from this notion of praxis. Many scholars who have revived its use in cultural studies continue to relegate religion to a superstructural role or ignore it altogether (see Hall 1980).

3 Inventive praxis could be helpfully paired with Judith Butler's analysis of performance (Butler 1993).

4 See Benjamin 1999; Collingwood 2005. For analysis of this trend, see Peters 1999.

11

Public

Joyce Smith

It is a scene familiar to anyone living in an urban center. Imagine two friends agreeing to meet at a local coffee shop:

> As he waits for Monica, Hanif sips his FirstMate coffee, leafing through *The Economist* he picked up from the next-door newsagent. On the cover is a photo of a hooded Abu Ghraib prisoner.
>
> Hanif is looking forward to discussing this with Monica. They've agreed to meet here this week to continue their online chat on the nature of religion and the public sphere.

It is no accident that this chapter begins here. Coffee houses are among the settings for Jürgen Habermas's nascent public sphere (Habermas 1991). Basking in Enlightenment liberties, individuals could discuss issues of common purpose and good, free from church and state fetters.

Habermas himself insisted that the specific context of eighteenth-century Europe was important to understanding his theories about the public sphere. My exploration of religious publics, their construction, production, and use of media sources will also revolve around the coffee shop but in its twentieth-century form.

Most communities have at least one physical public square and, if not, people will gather at the coffee shop or the various wells in the global village. The use of physical space to conceive of the public sphere spawns universally appropriate metaphors. But it needs some definition to discuss the way in which the idea of the public intersects with the nature of religion in a mediated society.

The Habermasian coffee shop is not a government building, nor is it a church. People are free to congregate here, regardless of their station in life, and they will come not only for the coffee but also for the promise of discussion with other customers. The coffee shop itself is not the public sphere but rather the container for the space in which people meet and discuss. It is the brick and mortar demarcation of the zone wherein certain types of behavior are not only fair game but expected.

The public sphere can be described as

> a mode of interaction in which mutually dependent private individuals seek to build enabling interpretations of their shared circumstances and call for a general response to collectively significant needs and dissatisfactions…It designates a political process in which common cause is built through the search for solutions to problems initially encountered as private concerns.
>
> (Johnson 2006: 1)

In other words, the public sphere exists within the rules of engagement allowing individuals to find solidarity.

Monica is a Seventh Day Adventist, so only decaffeinated no-fat latte for her.

Before enjoying her coffee, she asks for the key to the toilet. Though FirstMate is open to the public, only paying customers can use the washroom, and there is an often-unnoticed sign warning that there is to be no soliciting and that FirstMate's management can ask people to leave.

Worth noting is that though the public sphere is potentially open to everyone, in practice there are restrictions. FirstMate is happy to offer itself as a place to meet (and even relieve oneself) but only for a price.

In eighteenth-century Europe, Monica might not have passed through the coffee house door, not because of her religion's avoidance of caffeine (the first Seventh Day conference took place only in 1861) but more probably because of her gender. The private home would have been the "habitat" of a young woman, and a salon would have been Monica's space in which to interact. Indeed, women hosted many of the most popular salons. Definition of the public sphere was one of the first debated by feminists of the late 1960s and 1970s, many of whom asserted that "the personal is the political."

Though the place of meeting is important, so too is the host medium, particularly as communities grow and diversify and the physical bricks and mortar of the meeting place become virtual. In discussing the American case, Martin Marty notes that

> The *the* public in the writings of John Dewey and Walter Lippmann…gave voice to and found expression in premier agencies of publicness as it was then conceived and experienced. These include national newsmagazines and other popular journals, metropolitan newspapers, mainstream church body leadership, network radio and early network television.
>
> (Marty 1999: 9)

Before going further, you will note the italicized "the" in Marty's description. It does not take long, even in the eighteenth-century case, to realize that the public is in fact constructed of sub-publics, collectivities that may have as their common thread gender, religion, socioeconomic class, or ethnic identity. Marty's the *the* public is the collection of all American sub-publics. He has noted that it is often only when there is a debate over "public opinion" that people become aware that they are conceived as being part of the *the* public (Marty 1999:1). And chief among the recognition of a general public as well as its subdivisions is the press.

How are publics put together (and subdivided) with the help or even manipulation of the media?

> Karl is down the street from FirstMate at the fair-trade coffee shop. He refuses to buy anything but equitably produced food. But he likes the engaged atmosphere of this shop, where local media have placed alternative newspapers at the front door. Above them is a corkboard where ads for bicycles and notices of anti-globalization rallies are posted.
>
> The shop originated as a socially-active Christian church initiative, but there are no obvious signs of this genesis. Karl's grandparents belonged to the founding church, but this isn't why he likes this spot, and his grandparents never darkened the coffee house's door.
>
> Karl takes a lot of flack because he totes a reusable coffee mug. He wouldn't identify himself as a 'granola cruncher' any more than he would describe himself as a Mennonite.

Can one opt out of a public? No, because one cannot opt in. But one can be part of a public nonetheless. Though Karl refuses to adopt the labels of "granola cruncher" or Mennonite, to many in his community he is a member of both publics, because of his consuming decisions and the nature of his surname.

The gap between Karl and his grandparents speaks to the difference between local religious publics as communities of belief and practice and those that might more easily be identified as consumer communities. At the most basic level, this consumption is material; hence, Karl and his insistence on fair-trade coffee. But it also makes it attractive to the researcher to begin to relate the idea of a religious public to the selection and consumption of cultural products and symbols. Karl might not self-identify as a "granola cruncher," but his choice of food, clothing, and media combine to suggest membership in such a public.

I will explore the relationship between media and publics via four interactions: religious publics exerting influence on the *the* public; media products and processes influencing publics and subpublics; governments attempting to influence the *the* public and religious publics; and finally, religious publics attempting to use the secular media to influence themselves.

Religious groups have struggled with how to engage with those outside their number; for all but those in monastic separation, there is a quest to be *in* but not *of* the world.[1] Phillip Hammond has argued that in the United States, religions can be religious in public up until the point where their actions impinge on the larger whole (Hammond 1999). If they wish to be taken seriously in public debate, they must translate their beliefs into claims that can be understood and argued apart from a specific, theological framework. They can continue to speak their own language but should not expect everyone else to learn the language to engage with them.

Religious publics have in the past succeeded to some extent in influencing the *the* public without too much translation. Often this has been in communities where a religious public is synonymous with the membership of a nation's citizens, for example, the Roman Catholic Church's ability to enforce the *Index Librorum Prohibitorum* in Ireland well into the 1960s. To be Irish was almost always to be Catholic, so *nihil obstat* needed no translation (the phrase denotes that a publication is in accordance with Catholic teaching, so "nothing stands in the way" of reading it).

Even in a minority situation, a religious public may be able to exercise its influence over the larger public vis-à-vis mass media. The Production Code—largely influenced by the Catholic Legion of Decency—served as a means of self-censorship for Hollywood producers. The 1930 Code restricted language, nudity, sex, and violence in the name not just of the American but the global public:

> Motion picture producers recognize the high trust and confidence which have been placed in them by the people of the world and which have made motion pictures a universal form of entertainment...They know that the motion picture within its own field of entertainment may be directly responsible for spiritual or moral progress, for higher types of social life, and for much correct thinking.
>
> (Hayes 2007)

However, the age of the Index and the Code has passed, at least in the North. It would be difficult to imagine the claim above eliciting anything but guffaws in a contemporary movie theater.

The second type of interaction is driven from the media end of things: pkroducers attempt to influence the public and religious publics, sometimes for "good" but also for greedy reasons.

Dismayed by young Indians' ignorance of their own culture, Anant Pai in 1967 created what became *Amar Chitra Katha* (immortal illustrated story), a series of comic books telling epic stories from various religious and eventually secular traditions. The series begins with Krishna but includes everyone from Sai Baba to Kalpana Chawla, who died aboard the space shuttle Columbia.

Pai chose to educate the young of post-independence India by translating "5,000 years of India's mythology, history, legend—the very soul of Indian culture—packed into volumes of 32 colourful pages" (India Book House as cited by Pritchett; Pritchett 1995: 81). But he also maintained a policy of "*satyam bruyāt priyam bruyāt*": loosely, tell the truth but only the positive elements (Hawley 1995: 115). Following the gore of Partition, it is not surprising that Pai should want to integrate religious publics, which according to Hawley he does in ways both obvious (depicting historically impossible meetings between the saints [Hawley 1995: 115]) and subtle (illustrations can suggest one tradition, while text communicates another [Hawley 1995: 128]). However, with success came increased tension: "sales versus educational values; scholarly accuracy versus the need to appease particular interest groups; a commitment to Indian history versus a commitment to national integration" (Pritchett 1995: 81).

Some stories are proposed by community representatives eager to have their tales join the *Amar Chitra Katha* canon. With this interaction, Hawley suggests that the comic books become "a quasi-public institution" (Hawley 1995: 129). "The March to Freedom" series, created after a request by the Indian National Congress, is perhaps the most remarkable (Hawley 1995: 130).

Sometimes it is journalists who attempt to neutralize differences between religious publics in the professed interest of the *the* public. In Canadian reporting, there is a curious prevalence of Canadians of Indian ethnicity being described as "Indo-Canadian" at some points and "Sikh" or "Hindu" at others. I suggest the Indo-Canadian (and occasionally South Asian) label is applied when a journalist is fearful of equating a specific religious public with a particularly unsavory event. Headlines such as "Indo-Canadian mother killed in Surrey" (CBC News 2007) continued to appear after three women of Sikh descent were killed and another shot in the face in a space of four months in British Columbia. It would appear that the hyphenated ethnic identity is seen as being more acceptable than a religious one (i.e., Sikh-Canadian). This could well be in response to claims of anti-Sikh coverage leveled at news sources over the coverage of the 1985 Air India Flight 182 bombing and subsequent trial.

Patricia Spyer describes reporting in post-Suharto Indonesia wherein the identification of victims and aggressors as Muslim or Christian was suppressed by journalists in hopes of diminishing revenge attacks. Spyer suggests that instead of helping to end the violence, this dislocation of the identifiable religious publics from the reality of corpses piling up made it easier for violence to be perceived (and enacted) as mysterious and anonymous (Spyer 2006: 160).

With the best will in the world, media homogenization of religious publics for the good of the larger public can backfire. However, the best will in the world is seldom the only one in play: While encouraging national unity, *Amar Chitra Katha* makes money, and sanitizing the sometimes violent history of India almost certainly results in more sales. John Bowen suggests that French media have found it lucrative to publicize the threat of *Islamisme*:

> The viewing and reading public encountered one exposé after another about the breakdown of ... mutual respect in schools, hospitals, and towns. The shock value of these exposés helped increase magazine sales and television audiences, and made a few books instant best-sellers.
>
> (Bowen 2007: 163)

Bowen writes that former President Jacques Chirac read one of these bestsellers, *The Lost Territories*, and that it influenced his advocacy of the law banning scarves in schools (Bowen 2007: 164).

Through state broadcasters, governments can be directly involved in the maintenance (if not creation) of religious publics. In countries where the official policy is to recognize religious diversity (for example, post-apartheid South Africa), there is a struggle to give all religious publics state airtime (in this case, the SABC) as well as dealing with a citizenry that may object to having taxes support any form of religious communication (cf. Hackett 2006).

Sometimes these struggles take place behind the scenes. Bowen reports that after watching a 1999 broadcast of *Vivre Islam* (on state television France 2), the French interior minister reacted to seeing an eloquent young woman wearing a headscarf. Concerned that it would encourage other women to adopt the veil, he "'called the director of the program and suggested they not do that.'" Bowen writes that as a result "Islam appears on *Vivre Islam* as a faith, but people do not 'look Muslim' unless they are shot in other countries. There women 'look Muslim,' but not here in France" (Bowen 2007: 206).

Some viewers also complained that stories about the headscarf debate were often placed just before or after segments about violent Algerian Islamists in newscasts (Bowen 2007: 207). This sequential linking of foreign fanaticism and the domestic veil was perceived as unfair. Bowen suggests that this linkage is not circumstantial, because

Islamism (*islamisme*) has become a usefully ambiguous term for some French social scientists and journalists. It is used to refer to movements that advocate creating Islamic states as well as to those that merely promote public manifestations of Islam. What both references share is a negative feature, the denial of a European notion that religion properly belongs in the private sphere. The ambiguity permits writers to draw on fears of totalitarian Islamist regimes abroad in order to condemn French Muslim associations that advocate a public presence for Islam in France.

(Bowen 2007: 156)

Later, Bowen makes the problem of defining the public clear: "Islamism is global and transnational, and thus particularly ill-equipped to become *citoyen*" (Bowen 2007: 188).

One gets the sense from Bowen that other publics exist only to define and defend the Republic (the French version of Marty's the *the* public). Arguments that succeeded in extricating the Catholic church from the public sphere (especially in terms of women's liberation) are now employed in the *Islamisme* debate (Bowen 2007: 221). Particularly in periods of the (re) establishment of national identity, a government may use religious publics to legitimize and popularize their regime (cf. Chen 2007: 183). Much of this is done via symbols made visible in mass media: for example, a broadcast of Russian president Vladimir Putin attending a service at St. Basil's Cathedral. The visual element of a newscast (especially if only a backdrop to commentary) does not require the actor to provide a justification for his actions. The fact that the secular leader is doing something (lighting a candle during a Russian Orthodox service) is enough to suggest approval from the religious public and, in turn, grants the religious public legitimacy in the *the* public (The Associated Press 2004).

Finally, religious publics have been known to conduct their internal soul searching not only *in* but *through* the press. Consider the recognition of homosexuals by Anglican provinces. The differences in opinion between members of the global Anglican public play out in news media (notably the struggles between African and American bishops), but so too do the rifts within local communities, as evidenced by "sniping" via letters to the editor rather than, as Nicholas Adams puts it, "debat(ing) patiently and charitably in synod" (Adams 2006: 21). The group most ably translating its argument for the public sphere may gain enough support from the *the* public to prevail, regardless of the merits of its theological case.

Occasionally the search for a solution to an internal religious problem finds its way back into the *the* public. James Kelly traces the phrase "common ground" to its origins in a piece published December 26, 1989 in the St. Louis Dispatch titled: "Common Ground on Abortion." In it, Andrew Puzder, a pro-life attorney (and now CEO of a restaurant chain) suggested that pro-choice and pro-life advocates could agree that impoverished women and children needed help and, from this, the factions could work together.

Kelly writes that the phrase *common ground* was quickly adopted by Catholics and by the *the* public, including a 1992 *New York Times* headline: "In Bitter Abortion Debate, Opponents Learn to Reach for Common Ground" (Kelly 1999: 121). The religious sub-publics used the *the* public to connect and, in turn, had their phrase co-opted for unrelated discussion in the larger sphere, as Kelly gives examples of the phrase being used by others (including Bill Clinton) to suggest flexibility without admitting compromise.

But speaking of grounds, what is going on at the coffee house?

While Monica waits for Hanif to arrive, she starts up her laptop, taking advantage of FirstMate's wireless Internet connection. She chats with her friend Rachel, who's spending a year in Thailand. Rachel is in a FirstMate in Phuket, sipping her own latte.

The introduction of Internet access has often taken place in cafes, giving those without private access the chance to join the network society (Eickelman and Anderson 2003: xii). It is not quite the way in which Habermas's Enlightenment coffee houses functioned, but there is a parallel. Even where private access is prevalent, Internet cafes persist, often located near bus and train stations. (The online sphere as a transitional space has been discussed elsewhere, for example, by Mia Lövheim [Lövheim 2006].) Here, the coffee house engagement is not with members of the local public but with the (religious) public "back home."

New media technologies allow not only the bridging of space and time but what Lawrence Babb has described as "social bottlenecks," whether these are of caste, gender, or socioeconomic status (Babb and Wadley 1995: 3). In a Muslim public, Eickelman and Anderson suggest that new media allow those who would otherwise be left out of theological discussions an opportunity to offer the *ummah* their take on teachings (Eickelman and Anderson 2003: 10–13).

The old media were easier to circumscribe. Governments could control the spread of the mass-mediated message by means of everything from postal subsidies for home-grown magazines to the registration of journalists. The simultaneity of transnational technologies and transnational religions begs the question: do religious publics still exist, and if so, how can they be studied?

Monica packs up her laptop, throws away her cup and leaves, angry that Hanif has stood her up.

Once outside, Monica realizes that there is another FirstMate kitty-corner to the one where she's been all along. How was she to know? This one looks just like the one where Hanif has been waiting for the past hour, caught up in his *Economist*. She blushes and hurries home.

In a world of transnational retailers, a main street in Vancouver may have more in common with a Manchester high street than with a small town in northern British Columbia. However, the loss of locality is not the only difficulty facing those dealing with the concept of publics.

What if religious publics are only fictional? Consider Melyvn Bragg's description of the British series *Vicar of Dibley*. Despite having its central character portrayed by a female comic (Dawn French), Dibley is

> somehow a believable C of E, deeply satisfying and relevant... This village church in England is pastoral, fallible and warm at heart. It is still, for many viewers, the epitome of the Church of England. It is hugely popular and much loved. Perhaps it is craved for. It is also fiction.
>
> (Bragg 2006: 62)

Mediated wish fulfillment may demarcate an otherwise impossible public.

Could a media organization or product itself become a religious public? Al Jazeera English describes itself as

> the English-language channel of reference for Middle Eastern events balancing the current typical information flow by reporting from the developing world back to the West and from the southern to the northern hemisphere.
>
> (Al Jazeera 2006)

It could be argued that particularly in its English form, Al Jazeera is the face of the transnational Muslim public.

Are the basic units of a given public the consumer? The citizen? Or is it the family? Rhys Williams writes that the American liberal assumption that the social building block is the individual may not hold true: "What if families, genders, or religious groups—and not autonomous individuals—are considered the basic social formation?" (Williams 2007: 53). The intersection of religious and media publics in this sense has been studied by Hoover et al. in the home (Hoover et al. 2004). The desire among some Western Muslims to have *shari'a* law govern family affairs has made this emphasis concrete.

More than one critic suggests that Habermas's public sphere existed only in Enlightenment Europe. Without taking care to evolve the concept, the public sphere will remain particularly Christian, and the ensuing discussion will be relevant only with respect to this very specific time and religious and cultural context (Adams 2006).

It would be foolish to let the idea of statehood remain static in our thinking about the *the* public. The evolution of trading associations and continental organizations such as the European Union are changing the definition of these boundaries. In discussing public space as occasioned by the European Parliament, Fossum reworks the phrase as a "sphere of publics" (Fossum and Schlesinger 2007: 283). National churches in both legislative and de facto terms are being challenged not only by the presence of other religious publics but by those who would prefer governance in Europe to be reimagined in purely secular terms (Fossum and Schlesinger 2007: 283–4; Adams 2006: 4).

Despite these challenges, I would submit that the *the* public and religious publics do continue. And I would suggest the concept of social sin as providing an iterative sense of what constitutes the new *the* public as created by media. In Catholic teaching, social sin stems from individual actions that eventually make others "accomplices" and so create "structures of sin" (Catholic Church 1999: 1869; cf. *Justice in the World* 1971).

Muslims and non-Muslims were generally outraged by photos published in 2004 showing the abuse of prisoners in Abu Ghraib. It did not matter much how individuals saw the photos, whether online at a site created by and for Muslims or via an issue of *The New Yorker*. I would argue that the most important fact was that the photos became the water cooler–water well conversation throughout the global village. The visceral reaction was that no human being should suffer at the hands of another in this way.

I would further suggest that the story entered the realm of the global public because of widespread recognition that this was particularly horrible because of the Islamic emphasis on modesty. Whether this realization came because one had heard the headscarf debates or had seen something about Muslim sexual mores in a film or, indeed, because one was a member of the *ummah*, the response is the same. No one in the global public—but *particularly* no one from a religious public that sets such store on modesty—should be treated this way.

The reaction to protests led by Buddhist monks in Burma during 2007 is similar. Though there would be general agreement that people deserve to live free from military repression, the particular fact that demonstrations led by men in saffron robes ended in violence is important (cf. *The Economist* 2007). Whether the conviction comes from watching Brad Pitt in *Seven Years in Tibet* or because there's a temple down the street is inconsequential. That anyone in the global public should be assaulted in this way is wrong, but the fact that these are men who embody nonviolence makes this *particularly* so.

The solidarity felt is simultaneously rooted in the recognition of what is common to the human condition, as well as that which is specific to a given public. Here I lean on news judgment, the hallmark of journalism: Why will I care about *this* story? The answer lies in how relevant it is to my life (a requirement of utility and empathy) and yet, how different it is from the everyday world I inhabit (the need for novelty).

Unfortunately, much of the discussion in the global public is the result of conflict, at least as it appears in the news. As Adams notes, it matters whether the public sphere is "described as a place of hospitality or a war zone" (Adams 2006: 19). However, here religion and news have something in common.

> Religion is significant for Habermas precisely because it is the realm where the hyperbolic is identical with the everyday; it is where traditional aspects of human life, including commitments to peace and practices of hope, are most intensely expressed.
>
> (Adams 2006: 19)

Eickelman and Anderson are among those who suggest that by decreasing the gap between producer and consumer, new media create new public space. This may be true, but if the space is perceived to be only the size of a phone box (regardless of its interior spaciousness), it does not make much of an impact on the global public.[2] And as they themselves acknowledge, publicness does not necessarily translate directly into participation in the *the* public (Eickelman and Anderson 2003: 6). The globally broadcast Live Earth Concert of July 7, 2007 was exceptionally public, but its ability to generate action was disappointing.

To return to the concept of social sin, once the sin is known to exist, it becomes a further sin not to confront it. And this failing is shared by all those in the know, not just by the originators. So once brought to screens worldwide, Darfur and Rwanda become responsibilities of the global public, not only the scourge of the religious, local publics.

> Monica and Hanif do eventually meet again, but online, where she admits to being in the wrong FirstMate, and Hanif apologizes for getting so wrapped up in *The Economist* that he didn't look for her. But they do chat about the Burmese protests, and Monica fills him in on what Rachel in Thailand has heard. Hanif suggests that the next time they try meeting at a new coffee shop his friend Karl recommends…

Notes

1 See John 17:14–15 for a New Testament parallel.
2 Here I am thinking of the time machine employed by the fictional Doctor Who, which masquerades as a police phone box, while being spacious inside.

12

Religion

Sarah M. Pike

Druids and witches in the virtual world
Altars and shrines as heterotopia writ small
The sacred geography of back yards and roadsides
Slam dancing and chanting for God

In 1997, a television news reporter called me to set up an interview about the Heaven's Gate suicides that had occurred in San Diego the previous week. Scholars of religion are often given the task of explaining what seems inexplicable: why educated and economically comfortable men and women would decide to die by their own hand to catch a ride on an alien ship they thought was behind the Hale-Bopp comet, why dedicated Muslims would destroy innocent people on September 11, 2001, or how Catholic priests could justify molesting boys under their spiritual guidance. These and other examples of religious people's incomprehensibility to outsiders are a typical occasion on which religion scholars speak to the news media.

I had taken to heart Susan Sontag's dictum that the task of the intellectual is "to promote dialogue, support the right of a multiplicity of voices to be heard, strengthen skepticism about received opinion," and so I wanted to educate television viewers about the difference between a "cult" and a "new religious movement" (Sontag 2001: 296). "Cults," according to received opinion, are not real religions, and the news media's stereotypes of Heaven's Gate's "deluded" followers did not represent a multiplicity of voices. During our half-hour interview, I suggested that most religions begin as "cults" or small groups gathered around charismatic leaders. I also pointed out that mainstream religions include all the "bad" things that are commonly attached to "cults," including substance abuse and child molestation. The reporter nodded with understanding and asked me several questions about local religious groups in Chico, including religions that recruit on campus, none of which I had encountered. However, the next night, when I sat down to watch the news program, I was startled by the title: "Vampire Cults in Chico." The ten-minute report consisted of my comments taken out of context and spliced in between rumors about a "blood-drinking cult" recruiting on college campuses, so that I seemed to be warning parents to protect their children from dangerous cults. In the few minutes allotted to Heaven's Gate, the program portrayed its leaders as evil and manipulative and their followers mentally unstable, guaranteeing their incomprehensibility.

The deep need to categorize some religions as normal and others as deviant has distorted both academic study and popular understandings of religion. Anthropologist Johannes Fabian accuses the field of anthropology of "intellectual imperialism" because its "claim to power" originated in the uses of time to construct its own object, "the savage, the primitive, the Other" (Fabian 1983: 1). What is true for anthropology may be even more to the point for religious studies. Talal Asad and others have argued that the concept of religion is inextricably bound to its colonial past (Asad 1993). Or, as Robert A. Orsi puts it,

> the discipline was constructed by means of exclusion—in fact and in theory—of these other ways of living between heaven and earth, which were relegated to the world of sects, cults, fundamentalisms, popular piety, ritualism, magic, primitive religion, millennialism, anything but 'religion'.
>
> (Orsi 2005: 188)

In the history of the study of religion, excluded practices have been identified with the "primitive" past and natural world, seen as overly focused on the body and located in "other" or profane spaces. It is these excluded "other ways of living between heaven and earth" that I want to move front and center (Beal 2005).

By starting at the edges rather than at the center and by paying attention to the margins where alternative religious cultures take shape, one brings important issues sharply into view. From these often-excluded vantage points, we might more readily see how alternative and marginalized religious communities contest or invert dominant ritual patterns, lifestyles, practices of the self, political involvement, and communal structures. What happens when we invert the opposition between religion and its other and look for the source of religious creativity in otherness, including the body, teenage television fan online discussions, alternative music subcultures, new religious movements, festivals, and other unlikely sites? These places are akin to what Michel Foucault calls "heterotopias" that function as "counter sites, a kind of effectively enacted utopia in which…all the other real sites that can be found within the culture, are simultaneously represented, contested, and inverted" (Foucault 1986: 23). Heterotopias are interesting in their own right and for what they reveal about more traditional religious sites that they implicitly or explicitly call into question. There are, of course, many possible "other" sites to explore. The ones I have chosen are particularly clear examples of the dissolution of boundaries between sacred and profane, religion and popular media, dominant and alternative religions. These "other spaces" exemplify the shifting focus of the study of religion: (1) alternative religions on the Internet, (2) shrines and altars in unexpected places, (3) backyard and roadside religion, and (4) music subcultures and festivals.

Druids and witches in the virtual world

Religious heterotopias tend to push at the boundary between sacred and secular. This is particularly true for religious communities on the Internet that allow individuals to move back and forth between real and virtual identities and practices. In the 1990s, at the same time that online religious communities first emerged, I began researching Neopaganism, a new religious movement of men and women recreating ancient nature religions. In his 1995 article on "Technopagans" in *Wired* magazine, Erik Davis observed that online Neopagans "keep one foot in the emerging technosphere and one foot in the wild and woolly world of Paganism" (Davis 1995). Even though many Neopagans prioritize intimacy with nature, Neopaganism was among the first religions to appropriate the Internet to build online communities and promote online rituals. As an "other" space in the 1990s, the Internet provided a creative forge in which these religious outsiders could construct and express their identities together. "Archdruid" Isaac Bonewits sent out an announcement for a large-scale ritual on July 4, 1995, encouraging "Pagans, as well as Ceremonial Magicians, New Agers, and all others concerned with freedom in our country—especially religious freedom—to cast spells this July 4th" (Pike 2004: 126). This July 4 ritual is one of many examples of electronically mediated communities making ritual participation possible on an international scale, thus connecting participants in small religious movements such as Neopaganism, who would otherwise be isolated from each other. Ritual requires what ritual theorist Ronald Grimes has called "founded places" that are set aside for ritual (Grimes 1995: 72). Internet rituals happen over virtually founded places that are created by the intentions of participants and the physical actions involved with casting spells.

Though relatively comfortable on the Internet, Neopagans have been ambivalent about popular media. Though Neopagans criticize popular stereotypes of their religion, witches advised the makers of the film "The Craft" and have created fan communities for "Buffy the Vampire Slayer." In 2001, anthropologist Kathryn Rountree noticed the increasingly widespread appearance of "the contemporary appetite for magic" in various forms of media:

Titles including "magic" spill from New Age bookshelves, while Xena, Sabrina and the sisters from *Charmed* enchant prime-time television audiences...and children the world over punch computer keys to undertake vicarious magical quests offered in role-playing games.

(Rountree 2006: 190)

No teenagers approach Neopaganism today without being familiar with Harry Potter's magical world. Twenty-first century witches, one of the largest groups under the Neopagan umbrella, are more likely than their parents' generation to locate their beliefs and practices in relation to popular films and television shows than ancient Greek and Celtic mythology.

Teenage Witchcraft, for instance, has been on the rise since the 1990s, facilitated in part by television series such as "Charmed," "Sabrina the Teenage Witch," and "Buffy" (Berger and Ezzy 2007). Many young Witches are uncomfortable expressing their religious identities at school and home because they are harassed for wearing pentacles and black clothes, so they immerse themselves in online communities. In her doctoral research, Hannah Saunders surveyed teenage Buffy fans over the Internet and discovered an interwoven world of books, television, and real-life practice. Besides discussing Buffy, asking about free Web sites for spells, and reviewing books for each other, these teenage Witches shared serious health problems and described ritual experiences, bringing their bodies into the online world (Saunders 2005). Teenage Witches exemplify the ways in which religions dwell in (to borrow Thomas Tweed's idea of religions as "dwelling") electronic as well as real spaces (Tweed 2006). Neopagans move back and forth between online and physical selves, popular culture and ancient traditions, fringe and mainstream, blurring the boundaries of these oppositions.

Altars and shrines as heterotopia writ small

The Internet is the obvious religious frontier of the twenty-first century, but so are public sites of mourning that increasingly inscribe the landscape with personal and national narratives of tragedy and loss. Shrines and altars appear on streets and roadsides and in parks, creating a sacred landscape unattached to any particular religious tradition (Doss 2006; Santino 2006). I was enjoying my customary run through the park on September 12, 2007 when I came across a bench covered with flowers and messages remembering twenty-one-year-old Nicole Miller, who died when the hijacked United Flight 93 crashed in Pennsylvania on September 11, 2001. Public expressions of grief around September 11 are a recent example of how altars and shrines have become a common American vernacular or, as media scholar Stewart Hoover puts it, a "new civil religion of commemoration and mourning"

(Hoover 2006: 10). Other expressions of the new civil religion appeared after the Oklahoma City bombings, in Colorado after the Columbine High School shootings, and in New Orleans after the devastation of Hurricane Katrina. These events provided opportunities for personalized expressions of national solidarity in spontaneous altars and shrines. In so doing, they called into question the adequacy of traditional religious sites to meet the needs of grieving Americans.

The Columbine shootings in 1999 were an occasion for public memorializing that has involved ongoing controversy. Conflicts over how to remember the teenagers who died began almost immediately after the tragedy when Greg Zanis, a Christian carpenter from Illinois, erected fifteen crosses on a hill in a public park near the school. Each cross was marked with the name of the person who died and was intended by Zanis as a way to extend love to all the grieving families, including the families of the two shooters, Eric Harris and Dylan Klebold. What art historian Erika Doss has called the "material culture of grief" was immediately under way as the crosses became pilgrimage sites where people left stuffed animals and flowers and wrote messages on the crosses themselves, as Zanis had intended (he left pens at each cross) (Doss 2006). The victims' crosses were covered with messages of love and loss, while writings on Harris' and Klebold's crosses ranged from sympathetic messages to "murderers, burn in hell," written by Brian Rohrbough, the father of one of the victims (Zoba 2000: 47). Ten days after the shootings, Rohrbough and the family of another murdered student tore down Eric's and Dylan's crosses. Rohrbough was quick to justify their actions: "We don't build a monument to Adolf Hitler and put it in a Holocaust museum—and it's not going to happen here" (Zoba 2000: 49). When they extended the space of mourning beyond churches and funeral services into the landscape, the memorial crosses became a focus for public debate over the meaning of Columbine.

Because the Columbine killers were excluded from public mourning and memorializing, their friends and sympathizers created online shrines and memorials. High school students also turned to these online memorials to talk about the relationship between popular media and youth violence. "Michael," who created a Columbine memorial site, explained his motivations: "I'm not a Nazi, neither am I Hitler's fan. Indeed I'm a Nine Inch Nails fan, but I don't think it has something to do with the Colorado shootings." Michael's Web site included icons of burning fires and photos of Eric and Dylan. Text under the photos read, "They tore down your crosses—great! You don't need them" (Michael 2000). Many messages archived on Michael's site called the media to task. "Foxtrot" asked, "Why does the media try to hide the reality of this tragedy? One word 'entertainment.' Open your eyes world, it's going on in every school around the world and don't bother with the "facts" from mainstream media, believe what you see, what you hear, and above all, what you know. RIP eternal Eric and Dylan" (Foxtrot 2000). On these online memorials, teenagers who felt marginalized by the public discourse on Columbine challenged the news media's representations of the shootings and constructed their own narratives.

Another site for excluded discourses and the material culture of grief is the Burning Man festival, a week-long art festival in the Nevada desert that attracted more than 40,000 participants in 2007. Though news reports often focus on the secular side of Burning Man, every year since 2000 a large memorial temple that is burned at the end of the gathering has been one of the most popular festival draws. Ritualizing at Burning Man, like online rituals and park bench memorials, challenges any attempt to draw a clear boundary between the secular and the religious. In 2003, the Burning Man memorial temple was called "the Temple of Tears" or "Mausoleum" and was dedicated to suicides. By the end of the week, the temple was covered with thousands of hand-written messages, photographs, and offerings for the dead, many of them focused on the central altar, dedicated to suicides. "They can be honored here," temple designer David Best told me. He wanted to create a space for remembering suicides because he saw them ignored and silenced by most religions (Pike 2005). Heterotopias writ small such as Eric's and Dylan's memorial Web site and the Burning Man suicide altar allow for personalized interactions with the dead unavailable elsewhere. Like other forms of the civil religion of commemoration, the temple provided a space for everyone to engage with religious forms (temple and altar) without being committed to any particular religion.

Intimate bodily practices such as writing on the Mausoleum walls and leaving flowers on crosses for the Columbine shooters become ways to express religious aesthetics, attitudes and values that may conflict with those of the dominant society. However, bodies themselves can also become living memorials for the dead, testaments of faith or, as David Chidester sees them, "the basic global ground for religion" (Chidester 2005: 5). Religious images of the dead can be both worn and materialized in memorial shrines. As John Berger reminds us in *Ways of Seeing*, though we explain the world with words, "Seeing comes before words... It is seeing which establishes our place in the surrounding world (Berger 1972: 7). Images of faith and grief are in plain sight on bodies at gang funerals and inner-city high schools, and these images serve as reminders of youth violence. Photographer Aswad Hayes prints "R.I.P." photographs on T-shirts for high school students in Oakland, California who want to remember friends and relatives who died violently: "It's a way to show sympathy, mourning and grief... It's immortalizing them on a T-shirt" (May 2004). Attendees at a wake in New Orleans in 2004 wore R.I.P. shirts that promised, under a photo of the deceased, "I'll see you on the other side" (Young 2004). Like the offerings on the park bench I came across during my morning run, R.I.P. T-shirts are personal testimonies of faith expressed in public space. As Elizabeth Arweck and William Keenan put it in their introduction to a recent book on material religion, "the idea of religion itself is largely unintelligible outside its incarnation in material expressions" (Arweck and Keenan 2006). Wearing symbols and religious images can be important forms of religious observance that take place in everyday life at home, school, the mall, and in the streets. The park bench memorial, Columbine crosses, Burning Man temple, and memorial T-shirts are contemporary examples that suggest one need not go to places publicly marked as "religious" to find men and women doing religious work.

The sacred geography of back yards and roadsides

Sacred geographies are all around us: in homes, back yards, parking lots, and roadsides. Immigrant communities exemplify the crossing and dwelling that Thomas Tweed argues characterize religions in the form of "sacroscapes" (Tweed 2006). Immigrants cross oceans and mountains and learn to dwell in their new homes while keeping traditional beliefs and practices alive. Hmong war refugees from Laos provide one of many examples of the conflicts between immigrant religious cultures and modern Western expectations about the nature of religion that extend into physical space. Not long after I moved to northern California, I noticed a large gathering of Hmong families under a tent in the tiny back yard of a house I passed on my way to work. Though crowded in close to their neighbors, they kept chickens and brewed exotic-smelling stews outside in a large kettle. Three days later, they were still there for what I learned was a funeral gathering. Funerals and other traditional rituals have attracted trouble for the Hmong, especially when they include animal sacrifices in public places such as parking lots (Chow 2004). For the Hmong in California, the troubles that come from transposing one way of life onto another that is entirely different have been most visible at sites where important life passages take place, such as hospitals and funeral homes (Fadiman 1997).

"Shaman rituals are almost never performed in a hospital or a public setting for an individual person, unless it is when there has been an accident at an area and the shaman goes there to raise the spirit of the person who experienced it," argued an anonymous Hmong posting in response to a blog about a "Grey's Anatomy" episode in 2005 ("Racial Pro-File" 2005). In one of the episode's story lines, a young, Westernized Hmong woman refuses to have life-saving surgery because her parents tell her that a shaman first needs to call her soul back. Though the doctors and nurses are initially intolerant, they eventually agree to fly in a shaman by helicopter to perform the ritual

(Barrett 2005). After the show aired, Hmong viewers debated the accuracy and likelihood of the shamanic hospital ritual on blogs and discussion groups ("Yellow Content" 2005). Another anonymous viewer thought the conflict was overemphasized. Her family, she explained, respected both Western and traditional healing practices, even though many of her male relatives were physicians and her mother was a shaman ("Racial Pro-File" 2005). These Internet discussions bring together the life-worlds of young Hmong television consumers and convey the kind of negotiation that the Hmong have engaged in to bring their ritual healing practices into hospitals and Western medicine into their communities. At about the same time as the episode aired, Hmong shamans in Merced, California were wearing hospital badges and performing animal sacrifices in hospital parking lots (Udesky 2006). The Hmong have transposed the sacred landscape of their villages in the mountains of Laos onto American parking lots and back yards.

There is much diversity in Hmong-American communities, as evidenced by the wide-ranging discussion about "Grey's Anatomy." In response to postmodern and postcolonial theorizing about grand narratives, scholars have begun to pay more attention to difference both within and between cultures. Wendy Doniger advises looking for "the particular flash of difference" in the context of sameness that can illuminate comparative work (Doniger 2000: 72). The Hmong are in conflict not only with Western institutions but with their own families who want to suppress traditional practices. In contrast to the anonymous Hmong posting, a Hmong student told me about the tensions that arose in her family because her mother was a traditional healer and her uncle was a born-again Christian who denounced shamanistic healing as the devil's work. Conflicts within families suggest that religions do not always "dwell" comfortably. They often coexist in tension with one another, in this case challenging both American Christian and Hmong traditional ways of being religious.

Slam dancing and chanting for God

Though I have been pointing to religious activity in unexpected places, such as park benches and hospital parking lots, popular film and music can be found unexpectedly in places that are explicitly religious. Every summer since 1983, the sounds of Cornerstone Christian music festival have been heard on the remote back roads near the small town of Bushnell, Illinois. In 2004, journalist Andrew Beaujon was strolling through the exhibition tents at Cornerstone in the midst of 20,000 other festival-goers. He was surprised that not all the festival-goers looked the part of conservative Christian youth. Beaujon noticed, for instance, that a popular "Rock for Life" booth displaying T-shirts that said "STOP KILLING MY GENERATION" was staffed by a young man "sporting a ceiling-scraping Mohawk and a leather jacket festooned with patches from punk bands who'd probably have had coronaries if they saw where he was working" (Beaujon 2006). When it comes to Christian youth music and style, common stereotypes simply do not fit. A Florida mother, Jackie Roberts, drove a carload of kids to Cornerstone in 2003 but, she said on her blog, it "wasn't the contemporary Christian music scene they expected...as they passed lines of hippies, punks, Goths, brightly-colored Mohawks, and lots of tattoos" (Hertz 2003). They had driven into the heart of the Christian youth music counterculture. Cornerstone has made a name for itself by inviting Bible believers to investigate diverse forms of popular culture.

Cornerstone is very much like Burning Man in that thousands of participants undertake a kind of pilgrimage and expect to have their hearts and minds transformed at the festival. Though one might assume they would be at opposite ends of the festival spectrum, both Burning Man and Cornerstone offer a range of music and dance and religious services, altars, and shrines. The hundreds of bands that play at Cornerstone cover all genres from punk to world beat, with only two criteria: they have to be good, and they have to be saved. The biblically-based messages, pro-life slogans, abstinence from drinking, and sex policies of Cornerstone, for example, make it clear that this is not the Woodstock of the 1960s even though it has been called "Jesus' Woodstock" by Christian journalist Todd Hertz (Hertz 2003).

Nevertheless, Cornerstone is a striking case of the Christianizing of alternative cultures and popular media. The Imaginarium is the site at Cornerstone that goes farthest in inviting festival participants to encounter popular culture and make it their own. One of the Imaginarium's programmers describes activities at the tent as "a cross between a Star Trek convention and the Micky Mouse Club" (Hertenstein 2006). Festival-goer Kathleen Lundquist puts it this way:

> It's the place where Christians of all stripes meet to study, dissect, and celebrate popular culture—everything from Godzilla to Flannery O'Connor to the X-Files to Lord of the Rings to Frankenstein to Jason and the Argonauts to Jules Verne to Buffy the Vampire Slayer.
>
> (Lundquist 2006)

Each year the Imaginarium sponsors a theme around which its programmers organize events, films, speakers, and workshops. The themes tend to focus on the margins and extremes of popular culture: Marilyn Manson instead of Paris Hilton, cult films instead of Hollywood blockbusters.

Stories about Cornerstone suggest that the appropriation of alternative music and style is on the rise in Christian youth outreach. The Web site

Christiangoth.com features articles, testimonials, and a link to a Washington D.C.–Maryland area organization called "Hope for the Rejected," which ministers to Christian subcultures. Loyal T., a "Youth for Christ evangelist since 1998" runs Hope for the Rejected with the goal "to establish unity and fellowship in the underground scene as a whole…to not only bring together but unify the three largest underground subcultures: the Punk, Goth, and Hardcore communities" ("Hope for the Rejected" 2007). Christian music festivals such as Cornerstone and organizations such as Hope for the Rejected work hard to blend traditional ritual such as prayer and Bible study with American youth subcultures.

However, Christian rock musicians are often caught in a tension between the lure of the mainstream and the needs of the Christian communities that they largely serve. Christian stores refused to carry "The Fundamental Elements of Southtown" by hard rock band P.O.D., a popular act at Cornerstone, because its cover depicted "a figure sitting cross-legged with open cavities in his head and body (one stores the sacred heart of Jesus, and a dove is dropping a symbol of the Trinity into another)." P.O.D. changed the artwork for the Christian market to a "black cover with a small square showing only the seated figure's face" (Beaujon 2006: 29). Like an earlier generation of evangelicals that utilized television and radio to spread its message, young twenty-first century Christians—journalist Lauren Sandler calls them the "Disciple Generation"—have appropriated the Internet and popular music to gather in their peers (Sandler 2006: 121). Like Christian Goths negotiating between the larger Gothic subculture and conservative Christian values, Christian rock musicians are making their way in a contested terrain between evangelical Christianity and mainstream commercial success.

Many conservative Christians are uncomfortable with the appropriation of subcultural style and popular media. "Donnie Darko" played to a packed room of Imaginarium participants, many of them identifiably Goth. Tim, one of the audience members, complained in his blog that he could not help but hear a protest group "just outside the tent singing songs like 'Light of the World' and 'Jesus is the Light' over and over" (Tim 2006). Protester Dwayna Litz described her "covert mission trip" to Cornerstone 2006 in her blog on "Days of the Dead at Cornerstone 'Christian' Youth Camp": "Skulls and pictures were also placed to remember Mr. Rogers. However, it was not a beautiful day in the neighborhood! It was a satanic night in the 'Days of the Dead.'" Litz worried that young people were not learning appropriate Christian beliefs and practices concerning the dead:

> There were the pictures in the glowing dead shrine of everyone from Rosa Parks to Mr. Rogers…Many would speak to the dead people saying, 'I just want to thank ___ for all he/she has taught me,' as if the person's spirit

was in the place to hear. (No clarification was made on how we should not speak to the dead according to the Bible, of course).

(Litz 2006)

Litz's blog on Cornerstone 2006 set off a lively blogging battle and a spirited defense in Jesus People USA's *Cornerstone* magazine (Trott 2006). Controversy about Cornerstone reveals rifts among conservative evangelicals over the proper attitude toward popular media and youth subcultures.

The emergence of music festivals all over the country, the presence of bands and their friends on MySpace, and the ease of downloading music have enabled music and religion to negotiate new relationships in the "other spaces" of alternative clubs, music festivals and online communities. Christian Goths, Hare Krishna hard-core fans, and Muslim hip-hop followers, to name just a few examples, have created spaces for themselves in a larger corporate mediated music culture. The punk and hard-core scenes, often typecast as radically secular and anarchistic, include Christian and Muslim punk and Hare Krishna hard-core. Hare Krishna hard-core is a far cry from Krishna devotees chanting in airports, and yet there is overlap between them, for instance, when hard-core band 108 chants "Hare Krishna, Hare Rama" between songs at their live shows and includes band member Rasaraja's personal testimony on their MySpace site (Dasa 2007). Religion, popular music, and politics converge in unexpected ways at festivals and music shows.

From devotional chanting in punk clubs to Black Muslim rap, music is an important medium for expressing and shaping religious belief and practice. In "Enemy," Ice Cube raps, "Master Fard Muhammad [founder of the Nation of Islam] comin' like a comet/when they see him, they all start to vomit" (Knight 2006). The Five Percent Nation, an offshoot of the Nation of Islam, blend rap and the teachings of N.O.I. prophet Elijah Muhammad. Five Percenters have included Queen Latifah, Erykah Badu, and members of the Wu-Tang Clan as past or present members. Like hard-core Hare Krishna youth and Christian Goths, most Five Percenters practice clean-living and vegan lifestyles. Subcultural Christians, hip-hop Muslims, and Hare Krishna hard-core bands have created spaces for themselves in popular culture and within their religious traditions that subvert norms and challenge stereotypes.

Judging from the popularity of supermarket tabloids, the reading public and obliging reporters love stories of the evil other. Vampires preying on innocent college students make better headlines than my attempts to humanize the members of Heaven's Gate. To restore agency to the objects of earlier studies of religion and to correct the colonial history of religion and its Other, we might, as Johannes Fabian recommends, strive to achieve "coevelness" that recognizes "cotemporality as the condition for truly dialectical confrontations between persons as well as societies" (Fabian 1983: 164). Formal theories of religion tend to hinder the study of religion from the ground up. They often make us more distant from than intimate with the subjects we study.

Examples of religious people literally doing their work on the ground, such as Hmong shamans in hospital parking lots and Christian Goths in dusty festival campsites, are new hybrid forms of religious expression. Religious heterotopia—these other and unexpected places—are a new religious frontier: festivals, teenage Internet communities, city streets, hospital parking lots, roadside shrines, home altars, and bodily practices. Scholars are not only looking in different places for religion but religious men and women today are likely to carry on with their beliefs and practices in their homes and back yards as well as in churches and temples. Muslim punks pulling out their prayer rugs, Days of the Dead altars, chants of "Hare Krishna" on stage, and roadside shrines are not the primitive relics of obsolete religions. Like online teenage witches, they are ancient traditions adapting to and shaping an Internet generation. By bringing together Christian right-to-life Goths, Krishna hard-core animal rights activists, and Muslim rappers, I want to challenge assumptions about religion and popular media. Important religious trends begin at the margins, in other spaces, and in larger, more recognizable religious institutions. Clearly, expressions of religious commitment and religious questioning are evident in daily life and bodily practice, including the production and consumption of music, television, material culture, and the news. Attention to lived religion, religion in the streets, and material religion requires first looking around in ordinary and unexpected places to recognize the plural religious landscape and the importance of what is happening out there.

13

Soundscape

Dorothea E. Schulz

Sound sensation and religious mediation
Muslim soundscapes
Soundscape: origins and uses of the term
Soundscape and/as religious mediation
Soundscape and religious mediation:
authenticating authority and religious experience
in Muslim West Africa

Sound sensation and religious mediation

Most scholarship on sound sensation and religious practice has focused on the role of music, however diversely defined, in mediating spiritual experience. Left out from these scholarly accounts of religious music are other forms and "genres" of sound that feed into the complex topography of sensually mediated religious experience, a topography that forms the backdrop against which spiritual leadership and community are performed and validated. Still, an important insight of conventional scholarly accounts of sacred music is that religious traditions differ substantially in how they conceptualize "sacred sound," that is, sound that mediates divine presence.

Only in some traditions does music constitute a legitimate modality of sacred mediation. Other religious traditions sanction only a few, selected aural and oral modes of religious mediation and oppose them to music, its mundane character, and sites of performance.

In Hindu religious traditions, for instance, esoteric notions of sacred sound form a cornerstone of devotional practice and of disciplinary techniques aiming at higher spiritual awareness. Music is believed to have divine origins and is explicitly acknowledged as being instrumental to generating and validating genuine spiritual experience. Accordingly, institutions of sacred music production and performance are deeply engrained in the social-organizational setup of Hindu religious practice. In sacred sound, orality is intertwined with melodic-rhythmic sonic forms. That is, ritual hymns and incantations depend on their power as intoned speech to gain effectiveness

(Beck 1993; 2006). In Sikhism, conversely, music as sacred sound is not only integral to devotional experience but constitutes the foundations of religious community and spiritual leadership. Central to the powers of the historical founder of this religious tradition were his extraordinary skills in devotional chanting, skills that not only singled him out as chosen leader but allowed him to call on and bind together believers in shared devotional practice (Singh 2006). Chant and music also played an eminent role in the early transmission of scripture.

Though the existing literature on religion and sacred sound pays primary attention to music (e.g. Beck 2006), there are strong reasons why phenomenological approaches to the study of religious mediation should open up the terms of analysis and use the concept of soundscape to elucidate these processes of sensuous mediation. For one, the category of "sacred music" does not correspond to any equivalent conception or "emic category" in certain cultural and religious contexts. Sound, as a category encompassing a wide variety of aural perception, is more useful to make sense of the diversity of ways in which relations between the oral, aural, and transcendent are conceptualized and practiced.

Second, the spatial metaphor implied in soundscape pinpoints the intricate connection between a patterned form of sonic expression (involving metric, melodic patterning) and religious practice and their emplacement in time and space. Seen from this analytical angle, sound production and sound perception combine to form a site for religious experience, for an experience of transcendental immanence, and thus for any human communication with the divine. Finally, because sound constitutes an essential mode of embodiment and of bodily engagement, it yields powerful capacities to move the believer's heart and mind, to inscribe particular sensibilities, and thus to "tune" particular religious subjectivities. Yet, the particular significance it has for the making of religious subjects varies not only with particular religious tradition and regional conventions but across history.

Muslim soundscapes

Taking sound and aural perception, rather than music, as an analytical starting point is particularly apposite in the context of Muslim religious and mundane practice. Not only do Muslims consider Qur'anic recitation, as a principal and unique sonic form of Muslim religious practice and experience (whether in its simple style [*murattal*] or melodically more elaborate version [*mujawwad*]), to be conceptually distinct from "music"; the question of whether music should be performed and enjoyed at all in Muslim societies has remained a thorny and unresolved object of debate among Muslim scholars. This does not preclude the spiritual, aesthetic, and affective richness of sound practices in Muslim societies. After all, aurality and orality are foundational to Muslim religious practice and experience. According to Muslims, God's ultimate revelation, the Qur'an (literally, recitation) was made accessible to human understanding not through vision, inspiration, or writing but through sound and, more specifically, the sound of the word. Because God cannot be heard or seen, his message was rendered audible by the archangel Gabriel, who admonished the Prophet Mohammad to "recite" and thereby acquaint humankind with God's will (Qureshi 2006: 89f). Accordingly, the Muslim art of recitation, conceived as the sonic form of rendering God's recited word, and the attendant "science" of correct articulation (based on the precise memorization of both word and melodic-rhythmic pattern) both emphasize the uniqueness of the Qur'an. They also establish the fundamental distinctiveness of Qur'anic recitation from other sonic and "musical" forms, be they rendered vocally or instrumentally.

The soundscape that forms the backdrop to Muslim mundane and religious experience is produced not only by the conventional and all-pervasive presence of Qur'anic recitation; *adhan*, the call to prayer, varying from simple intonation to elaborate melodic patterning, adds to it as much as sermons delivered to believers during Friday congregational worship in and around the mosque (Tayob 1999). The melodiously murmuring chant of children engaged in memorizing the Qur'an constitutes another building block of the topography of sound sensation that, in its combination with other forms of sensation, impresses "the sound of the divine" on Muslim everyday experience (Nelson 1993; 2001[1985]), in and beyond the ritual sphere. All these sound "bites" of divine presence have a strongly community-generating dimension. They are evaluated according to their emotional and ethical efficaciousness: a faithful rendition of God's words and a truthful sermon should have the effect of moving a believer's heart to tears and to ethical action. Touch through sound, and the experience of feeling touched by sound, are thus central to the ways in which believers assess and validate a compelling, truthful performance.

Similar understandings of the "moving" capacities of the sound and of the spoken word inform the expressive ("poetry") and sonic performances that aim to enhance mystical forms (*tasawwuf*) of experiencing God's presence and to facilitate believers' striving for a state of ecstatic communion with God and his all-encompassing love.

Numerous Muslim societies cultivate additional expressive traditions that are devotional—rather than liturgical—in nature and that combine poetic texts with melodic-rhythmically patterned chants. Among them are "hymns" (Arabic, *inshad*) that articulate devotion to the Prophet and his family and sometimes take on the form of personal supplication (*du'a*). Similar to recitation, they are conceptually distinct from other "musical" genres. Certain chants serve a similar devotional purpose but are explicitly acknowledged to form "music" in the proper sense of the term. In some Sufi contexts, praise songs may also be directed at particular local "saints" (sing. *wali*: literally "friend of God"). To a greater extent than the different styles of Qur'anic recitation, all these chants and hymns draw on the musical and oral-expressive repertoire and stylistic conventions of particular Muslim societies.

In some regional contexts, women have historically played an important role in composing and performing these forms of sonic devotion and in organizing the religious celebrations (such as the Prophet's birthday, *mawlid al-nabi*) of which the chants are a foundational element (e.g., Mack and Boyd 2004).

The all-encompassing nature of this sound architectonics is currently reinvigorated by new, mostly aural recording technologies. These technologies move practices and experiences related to the aural perception of spiritual presence into new arenas of daily life, beyond the immediate sphere of ritual action to which these aural forms of spiritual experience used to be restricted. Along with these changes, they generate new sites for the assertion, validation, but also contestation of religious authority. For instance, in many Muslim majority settings, the advent of new audio and visual recording technologies creates new opportunities for women to excel in their conventional "musical" and expressive performances at a new scale; simultaneously, however, these developments yield very equivocal effects for women. Rather than helping women to simply "carve out" new spaces of moral authority and religious leadership, they also expose women to the criticism of the religious establishment and of other critics.

In most Muslim majority settings, audio and visual recording technologies interlock with an expanding market of consumer culture and mass-mediated forms of entertainment. They thereby facilitate a blurring of the conventional divide of Qur'anic recitation and its attendant strict rules regulating the correct oral rendering of the Qur'an (*tajwid*; Nelson 2001, ch. 2) on one side, and music and other aurally and vocally mediated spiritual engagements on the other. Not only does the figure of the reciter or "musician," as the mediator of religious experience, receive new attention and generate new debate and disagreement within the Muslim scholarly community; the recitation and sermonizing traditions absorb stylistic conventions and expectations of the entertainment industry and thus make preachers and reciters accountable to the same requirements of an aesthetically compelling performance to which other types of public performers need to submit. These various aural forms thus generate new spaces for experience, practice, and forms of authenticating spiritual leadership and new modes of attention, media engagement, and debate (Nelson 2001, ch. 7; Hirschkind 2006, ch. 4; Schulz 2004, ch. 9; 2006).

How can the concept of soundscape help to elucidate the complex and dynamic process of religious mediation and of making religious subjectivities in Muslim contexts and beyond?

Soundscape: origins and uses of the term

The origins of "soundscape," sometimes used interchangeably with "acoustic space," can be traced back to three fields of scholarly debate since the 1950s. The first field of scholarly debate in which it gained currency is represented by the journal *Explorations* (1953–9) created by McLuhan and Carpenter, who, in their endeavor to counter predominant scholarly assumptions about the hegemony of vision as principal mode of perception in modernity, introduced the notion of acoustic space. Their University of Toronto Center for Culture and Technology project focused on media transformations and sought to reinterpret a Western history of orality and literacy from the vantage point of twentieth-century electronic communications. Though both authors shared an interest in relating studies of perception to transformations brought about by new media technologies, they pursued distinct analytical trajectories. Whereas McLuhan in his later work tended to contrast different sensual forms of perception and thereby risked to replace visualism with a similarly fallacious "audi-centrism," Carpenter came to emphasize the interrelationship between these perceptual modes. His article on acoustic space (1960) explored the cultural implications of the "earpoint," whereas in later publications, he looked at the interplay between the visual and the auditory as combined forms of perception.

In the mid-1950s, the term *auditory space* also gained currency in scholarship reflecting on new developments in music studies. Here, it was introduced by the music philosopher Zuckerkand (1956) who, while drawing on Heidegger and Bergson, coined the term to emphasize the interpenetration of auditory space and time. Other authors, among them Murray Schafer, used the term to pinpoint the artificial nature of the distinction between "music," "sound," and "noise" and to argue that what was commonly referred to as "music" should be appreciated by reference to its location in a wider, culturally and historically specific topography (or "scape") of sound forms. Influenced by the anthropologist Carpenter, Schafer was instrumental in organizing the World Soundscape Project centering on an exploration of the complexities of the "soundscape design" and "acoustic ecology" of Western society and synthesized in Schafer's "The Tuning of the World" (1977; also see Attali 1977; Russolo 1986). Developments in installation arts similarly focused on explorations of soundscapes by emphasizing the synaesthetic and "full-bodied" nature of sound perception and linking sound sensation to spatial orientation and movement (e.g. McCartney 2004).

The concept of soundscape also became central to anthropological and ethnomusicological studies of "acoustemology," which took the concept into different analytical directions. Rather than exploring the "acoustic ecology" of particular social environments, anthropological studies of soundscape focused mostly on how people imagine, respond to, hear places as sensually sonic (see Feld 1996: 96). Though most authors employed the term primarily in reaction to the ocularcentrism of conventional scientific discourse and to the presumed primacy of vision to Western epistemology, the conclusions (and agendas) they drew from this heuristic perspective were actually very different. Authors such as Ong posited (and essentialized) vision as being the characteristic perceptual mode of Western modernity and contrasted it to the alleged centrality of smell, taste, sound in non-Western societies (Ong 1981 [1967]; also see Burrows 1990; Classen 1993; Beck 2006). Other authors, in contrast, criticized the McLuhanite tendency to think along, and reify, a visual-auditory great divide and its underlying assumption that "seeing is analytic and reflective, sound is active and generative" (Schafer 1985: 96). They warned against countering "commonsensical" assumptions of the centrality of visualism in Western analytic discourse by erecting an anti-visualism (e.g., Gouk 1991; Schmidt 2000). Instead, they emphasized the need to analyze all registers of sensual perception in their interplay. To them, thinking about sound and soundscape formed part of a larger anthropological exploration of the senses. Accordingly, they considered soundscape as a domain in which aural sensation interacts with other perceptual modes, conveys a sense of orientation (e.g., Idhe 1976; Howes 1991, 2004; Bull and Back 2003), and serves to inhabit memory (Casey 1987[1976]; Corbin 1998; Smith 1999). Rather than ontologizing "culturally specific" orders of sensual perception, they emphasized that modes of sensory dominance change contextually with bodily emplacement (e.g., Feld 1991; 1996).

Soundscape and/as religious mediation

How, then, can these scholarly approaches to the study of soundscape be brought to bear on explorations of the relationship between sound sensation and religious mediation, of sound sensation as a form of religious mediation? Practices and technologies related to the aural-oral mediation of religious experience illustrate that "religion" itself should be understood as a form of mediation (de Vries and Weber 2001; Stolow 2005). Similar to "communication," religion refers to the act of establishing contact, of binding together two different entities or realities; in short, of mediating (between) them. By its very nature, religion renders palpable and perceptible that which eludes human cognition and thus mediates between what can be physically and sensually known and verified on one side and the meta-physical on the other. In this sense, religion always entails a range of materials and techniques to which we refer as *media* and relies on specialists holding authority in questions relating to the proper use of technologies of mediation. Religious traditions, to persist, need to be constantly translated or "trans-mediated" into new material form and practice (Plate 2003; Meyer and Moors 2006: 7). It is therefore useful to explore from a historical angle how individual media intervene as means in processes of communication, how they help to reproduce or rework existing "channels," by generating opportunities for religious practitioners to engage in spiritual and religious experience. Rather than assuming that the adoption of new media effect clear-cut shifts from one mode of religious mediation to another, their repercussions should be seen as being more fragmentary and unsystematic in nature, affecting particular messages and practices and engendering new conflicts over authority, proper religious practice and experience (Meyer and Moors 2006; Schulz 2006, 2007).

Depending on what venues of communication with the transcendental a particular religious tradition privileges, its teachings and objectives are often articulated and promoted through the interlocking of various media and media practices. Some religious traditions privilege media that are external to the body. In others, the body itself becomes the primary means of mediating the world of the transcendental. Yet most religious traditions encompass and embrace a combination of different media, techniques, and understandings of communicating with the transcendent world.

Religious traditions importantly shape the ways in which media are represented and acknowledged as actual "channels" of conveying a message, experience, or mediating between this world and the realm of the transcendental (Meyer 2005). This is evident, for instance, in how religious traditions define what modes of sound production and sensation generate genuine or "true" religious experience and how these modes relate to, and possibly interlock with, other modes of sensation. In Islam, reciting and listening to God's word has conventionally constituted the orthopractic form of submitting to God's will (Larkin 2001), defined among other things by its complementary relationship to reading and writing as modalities of worship. In Christian history, there has been a stronger tendency toward seeing as the authentic and authenticating form of religious experience.

Religious traditions not only differ in how they organize the aural-oral mediation of religion; they interlock in various and changing ways with regionally and culturally specific hierarchies of perception, that is, of definitions of which sensory impressions provide the most reliable and authoritative knowledge about the sacred (Stolow 2005). As we will see below, in Muslim West Africa, text-based understandings of the central importance of hearing in conveying God's truth interlock with broader cultural appreciations of the voice as a central vehicle of mediating spiritual power and divine truth (e.g., Stoller 1984; Schulz 2003). However, the central importance of orally-aurally mediated religious experience has not precluded the emergence of visual forms of Muslim piety in some areas of West Africa. Followers of the Muride Sufi order in Senegal, for instance, engage in visual tokens and representations of their spiritual leaders and their divine blessing (*baraka*) in ways that disprove generalizing assumptions about the allegedly strong anti-iconic bent in Islam (Roberts and Nooter Roberts 2003). Because of these regionally divergent hierarchies of authentic spiritual perception and engagement, there sometimes exist fierce debates within particular religious traditions as to which mode of sensual and embodied mediation is the most truthful and effective one.

The relevance of soundscape to explorations of religious experience and its sensual mediation comes out most clearly in Feld's refined analysis of auditory space as a complex field of meanings that is closely related to spiritual and religious practices, to cosmology, and to a conceptual ordering of the world through material objects, practices, and social organization. Feld's study is highly important in yet another respect. To a greater extent than other explorations of the role of soundscape in mediating experiences of the transcendent (e.g. Beck 1993; Hirschkind 2006), he takes seriously the notion of scape (rather than simply focusing on sound as most other authors do) by positing the spatial as the starting place for our exploration of the role of bodily movement and sensual orientation in religious experience and mediation.

Drawing on these important insights, future anthropological investigations need to address more consistently the question of how the practices, conventions, technologies, and institutions that generate and inhabit a religious soundscape map onto divisions along power inequalities and gender and other forms of social and economic difference.

Another, highly important insight to be drawn from recent anthropological work on soundscape is the insistence on the contingent and dynamic nature of sensual ordering. In other words, rather than assuming and essentializing any fixed culturally specific hierarchy of the senses (e.g., Ong 1981; Burrows 1990; see Beck 2006: 11), studies of processes of religious mediation need to take into consideration the always open-ended, indeterminate nature of sensual perception and ordering. The particular relationship that emerges between perceiving subjects and objects and experience of the religious is not a function of the specific prescripts of a "culture" or "tradition." Rather, it is the outcome of a historically determinate yet open-ended process of "perceptual completion" that emerges from a plurality of modes of sensuous mediation and being in the world (Hirschkind 2006: 20f).

From this, a set of questions emerges. What particular, regionally specific forms does this process of perceptual completion take in a particular historical and social setting? How and to what extent are these modalities of perception influenced by locally dominant religious traditions, and how do they feed into, and are in turn shaped by, broader cultural regimes of ordering and authenticating religious experience, community, and authority?

Soundscape and religious mediation: authenticating authority and religious experience in Muslim West Africa

Central to the practice of spiritual and religious authority in West African Islam are conceptions of power that center on sound-touch sensation. Yet, the importance of sound and touch, of the tactile dimension of sound perception and mediation, have been largely overlooked in the conventional scholarship on Islam in West Africa. This is partly owing to the text-centered forms of analysis that have been predominant in scholarly discussions of Muslim authority and that tended to oppose two kinds of authority: one being based primarily on access to the written texts of Islam, Arabic literacy, and interpretive knowledge, and the second drawing on the special "charisma" or divine blessings (*baraka*) associated with Sufi leadership, which grant family members of "Sufi-related" clans, men and women, special powers to assume an intermediate position between God and human beings.

Disciples of a Sufi *shayk* but also non-initiated Muslims are convinced that the sheer physical presence of these leaders and haptic engagements with them and with objects that previously came in touch with them allow them to partake in the spiritual powers they are said to hold. Other people, too, are considered to carry God's special blessings and to pass them on through touch. Among them are those considered "friends of God" because they not only command special religious knowledge but are examples of pious conduct, compassion, and religious devotion. The tombs of these "saints" are often centers of pious attraction (*ziyara*; literally "visit") where believers flock to ask the *wali* for his or her spiritual intercession. Their devotional activities revolve on various haptic engagements, such as kneeling and touching the stone marking the tomb with one's forehead or touching other material tokens of the wali's pious excellence.

These practices illustrate that touch, as a synaesthetic mode of sensation and perception (e.g. Marks 2000; Verrips 2006), has conventionally played a pivotal role in local protocols of generating and experiencing authority, not only in interactions with leaders associated with mystical Islam but with Muslim scholars claiming spiritual excellence by reference to text-

and sharia-based appropriations of Islam. There thus exists an intricate connection between touch and aurality in local conventions of asserting and experiencing spiritual authority.

The centrality of sound-as-touch takes on a new significance in the case of religious leaders who embrace new recording and broadcasting technologies to disseminate their teachings to new constituencies. In other words, sound-touch, in its interlocking with other forms of sensual perception, plays a central role in the ways in which the "media preachers" assert and generate authority in the course of their broadcast sermonizing.

To understand how sound-touch operates as a continuum of sensual mediation in local regimes of authenticating religious experience and authority, it is necessary to situate it in the context of culturally specific conceptions of sound and of the affective and ethical powers of sound sensation. That is to say, an exploration of the status that sound, voice, the spoken word, and its touching effects enjoy in West African Muslim societies will help us to understand what forms of spiritual experience are at the basis of the authority that "disciples" and other acolytes attribute to religious leaders in this context. It also sheds light on the ways in which new technologies and materials intervene in, and possibly complicate, these processes of sensuous mediation and authentication of leadership.

Throughout West Africa, conceptions of spiritual and religious leadership, as they are articulated by the broad mass of Muslim believers, are not—or only to a very limited extent—informed by a text-based Islamic tradition. They are therefore at variance with practices and understandings of sound-mediated religious experience that exist in other areas of the Muslim world. Most notably, they contrast with Egypt, where a long tradition of text-based understandings of the ethical and religious merits of sermon and Qur'anic recitation audition exists (e.g. Nelson 2001; Hirschkind 2006). Yet, rather than taking this tenuous link between text-based religious understandings and West African Muslims' engagements with religious authority as a divergence from "orthodox" Islam, I propose another interpretation. West African Muslims' understandings of authority, in their appropriation of local conceptions of compelling speech and a genuine, "heart-felt" hearing experience, form an essential element of the symbolic and discursive parameters in which the practice of Islam is grounded in West Africa. In this sense, it should be conceptualized and recognized as a locally or regionally specific discursive tradition of Islam (see Asad 1986; Bowen 1993).

Many West African societies attribute a particular agentive capacity to both aural experience and the spoken word. In southern Mali, for instance, orality and aurality are said to bear a particular transformative potential, a capacity that tends to be conceived as a specific form of power (*se* in Bamanakan, the lingua franca of southern Mali) and is commonly associated with superhuman, divine powers. Whereas *fanga* denotes the capacity to affect and transform the world through the use of sheer force, *se* refers to the invisible powers mobilized in the course of turning (unspoken, sometimes written) words into voiced, forceful speech (*kuma*; e.g., Zahan 1963). Worldly domination, religious intellectual authority, and the power of speech thus refer to complementary, not always neatly divided, realms of knowledge/ power (e.g., Wright 1989; Schulz 2001). By virtue of its "touching" effects, voice (*kan*) mobilizes a listener's existential, sensual, cognitive, and ethical capacities by moving her or him from stillness and immobility to action and the performance of exemplary "deeds" (*kewale*).

In recognition of the powers of voice and speech, people's attitude toward the spoken word is highly ambivalent. Human speech is held to have an enormous potential to effect transformation by affecting the human senses. Because speech has such indeterminate effects, people who are associated with speech are treated with ambivalent feelings of distrust, reverence, and disdain because their act of transforming silence into speech releases the damaging forces of untruth, delusion, and human betrayal (e.g., Diawara 2003).

Among Muslims, the ambivalence toward the transformative potential of speech has been historically reflected in a "double-edged" appreciation of the moralizing activities of women, as opposed to that of male preachers. Those elite Muslim women, who were highly valued, convinced through pious comportment and the "truthfulness" of their moral lessons, a truthfulness assessed in terms of the capacity of their "warm," "piercing," and simultaneously "restrained" voice to affect their disciples' hearts. This moving capacity of their voice was contrasted to the "loud" and "shameless" speech of professional orators whose words could affect listeners against their will. Still, these female Muslim "educators" were urged not to circulate their moral lessons beyond the confines of the women-only educational settings. The sermons of male preachers, conversely, whose truthfulness was assessed primarily in terms of argument and oratorical skills, were expected to circulate in a wider, public setting and affect male and female listeners, even if in separate listening contexts. Conventional understandings of the "compelling" force of moral lessons offered by female teachers as opposed to male preachers thus revealed a gender-specific regime of authenticating "truthful" and proper speech.

How does this culturally specific conceptualization of the power of speech and of the moving qualities of voice reverberate in the ways in which religious authority is asserted and validated in the interaction between individual religious leaders and their followers? Do these modalities of mediating spiritual experience and of validating religious authority continue to be gender-specific? And how do audio reproduction technologies, as new technologies for the mediation of religious experience, authority, and community intervene in these dynamics?

People "sound out" the ethical quality and efficiency of speech according to its effects (i.e., by assessing its capacity to compel listeners into action). Their stress on the special, moving power of speech and voice resonates with the importance they attribute to aural perception: a person's sound sensation, her capacity to feel touched by sound, is considered a prerequisite for moral being and action. In situations wherein religious leaders assert authority through the medium of sermonizing and moral lessons, hearing and speaking thus pair up in validating a moral lesson. Feeling touched or, literally, "apprehended" by the sound of a voice is the principal marker of compelling speech. A truly "touching" experience thus shows itself in the effective blurring of hearing and heeding: whoever is genuinely touched by a voice and truthful moral lesson will immediately move into action.

The spontaneous reactions by believers to male preachers whose charismatic performances are broadcast in audio recordings and on local radio also reveal the widespread perception that audio recording technologies, as diverse as sermon tapes and radio broadcasts, allow this leader's special powers to become more palpable and effective. To listeners, engaging a radio preacher's "forceful speech" creates a new space for spiritual experience, one that is mediated through an at once haptic and sonic sensation. Pervasive in many accounts of personal "conversion" or of the decision to associate oneself with a particular religious leader was the mention of an overwhelming, almost cataclysmic sound experience: the experience of "feeling struck" by a leader's "poignant voice," the "forceful" nature of which convinced listeners of his "chosen" status as a mediator of God's undeniable truth. Spontaneous comments also reveal the perception of audio-broadcasting technologies' potential to render his presence immediate and heighten the spiritual aura of his voice. As these broadcasting technologies allow a leader's voice to come from everywhere and nowhere, they reinforce a totalizing, seemingly all-encompassing hearing experience that envelopes listeners in a soundscape of divine presence, moves them to tears and, as it is often described, purifies their hearts and minds from evil intentions.

Notions of the tactile and the kinesthetic are prominent in these culturally specific understandings of the touching, ethically moving dimensions of a soundscape generated through sermonizing and mass-mediated speech. These notions thus shed light on the larger cultural framework of sensual perception in which these protocols and conventions for authenticating religious experience and authority are embedded: a person's capacity to "touch" and "move" people indicates his or her special capacities to mediate between the here-and-now and an invisible world. Technologies that highlight a person's special emotive capacities play an instrumental role in the interactive generation of spiritual authority.

Believers' perception of the special powers of individual media also come out in the ways in which some of them, in an act of "technological transference," associate the technology's powers with its physical incarnation (i.e., with the technical apparatus). In the case of some charismatic leaders, this "transference" manifests itself in the ways in which acolytes engage with the physical manifestations of their leader's authority, such as various religious paraphernalia and memorabilia of the leader's spiritual career. Their engagement with his sermons relies on a range of multisensory practices that allow for and mediate the experience of the extraordinary and of transcendent immanence. Mediated through their sermons, these charismatic leaders' spiritual powers invade spaces of the mundane and give them, literally, a new touch.

Sound-as-touch is not the only synaesthetic modality through which spiritual leadership is rendered immanent and authenticated in West African Muslim contexts. Visuality constitutes another important form of synaesthetic mediation that draws on various materials and technologies, old and new, to generate "imagetexts" constitutive of (and circumscribing) particular forms of spiritual experience and worship (see Roberts and Nooter Roberts 2003: 55–9; Morgan 2005: 65–7). Visual representations of a leader's spiritual authority generate a dialectical movement between seeing and the experience of being seen (e.g. Mitchell 1994; Pinney 2004:8). Similar to the sensation of sound-as-touch, meeting the gaze of the leader's portrait or photograph involves, according to many followers, a (literally) striking haptic experience. Posters, stickers, other visual decorations, and video-taped sermon recordings, for instance, provide occasions for his followers to interact with him in socially sanctioned ways, such as touching his (photographed) hands with their foreheads or stroking the sleeves of his robe. For some female acolytes, donning a "veil" with an imprint of the leader's portrait means to inhabit a physically felt space in which the leader's spiritual powers touch and engulf them in a protective embrace. While emanating from entirely distinct technologies of mediation, visual representations of sainthood allow for various modes of tactile engagement and thus generate sometimes novel experiences of oneself *as* religious subject (Schulz 2004, ch. 9).

Similar multisensory forms of engagement and authentication are at work in the case of Muslim women who assert a position of moral or spiritual leadership. Yet, interactions between them and their (predominantly female) acolytes also point to substantial differences with respect to first, the particular form of charismatic authority that these female leaders are thought to hold and, second, the particular modality through which a leader's spiritual powers are passed on to followers. In contrast to male leaders, only few women in leadership positions can claim to possess the divine blessings associated with leading Sufi clans. Accordingly, haptic modes of mediating spiritual powers are subordinate to other forms of passing down charisma to make followers partake in it. Nevertheless, in their case too, the tactile and kinaesthetic dimensions of sound play a central role in captivating the moral imagination of listeners and in compelling them into action. Audio recording technologies reinforce listeners' perceptions of the tactile dimension of aurality that is of the "touching" experience of voice and of moral excellence conveyed through voice. These technologies thus enable female leaders to establish their authority as figures of ethical guidance yet simultaneously perpetuate distinct conventions of generating spiritual authority.

Conclusion

The various, often synaesthetic modes of sensation and their attendant practices and technologies, which are constitutive of the contemporary religious soundscape(s) in West Africa, illustrate how misleading it would be to conceive of soundscape exclusively in terms of aural-oral modalities of mediation. The sensual complexity of these religious soundscapes also helps to refute the still widespread assumption that modern society is characterized by the hegemony of vision over hearing and of forms of sensual perception. Both the continuities and the recent transformations in local understandings and techniques relating to the transmission of spiritual power through voice and word point to the continued and pervasive importance of aural-oral forms in mediating and authenticating experience, religious and otherwise.

Soundscape is particularly useful to think of the continued relevance and omnipresence of sound because it highlights the spatial and embodied dimensions of sound perception and the all-enveloping sensual experience it generates. Because soundscape is closely related to body movement and sensation and anchors religious experience in the here-and-now, it implies a notion of localized "scape" that differs from deterritorialized conceptualizations of "scape," such as reflected in Appadurai's famous "ethno"scape. That is to say, though certain materials and elements of a religious soundscape may travel across distances, such as in the case of the audio-recordings of Ayatollah Khomeini's sermons (Sreberny-Mohammadi and Mohammadi 1994), the particular experiences they generate are always inscribed in, and generative of, locally specific regimes of ethical practice and religious power-knowledge.

The central role of soundscape in fashioning, anchoring, orienting, and authenticating religious experience evolves and transforms over time, in a dialectical movement. Believers, practitioners, and religious authorities, by engaging in (and debating) particular forms of sound-mediated religious practice, make and reconstitute not only soundscapes but the particular religious traditions of which they are part. At the same time, these religious traditions, whether anchored in written or aural forms of transmission, are constitutive of particular religious subjects by legitimating particular forms of aural perception. They thereby (literally) "tune" the senses of the pious, venerating subject. In this sense, soundscapes constitute a scape in yet another respect: they form the backdrop for the making of historically and regionally-culturally determinate religious subjectivities.

14

Technology

Jeremy Stolow

Religion versus technology
Religion and technology
Religion as technology

The popular melodramatic comedy film, *The Gods Must Be Crazy*, recounts a series of adventures ensuing from the fateful encounter between a Kalahari Bushman, Xi, and an empty Coca-Cola bottle discarded from a passing airplane (Uys 1980). In the film, Xi and his fellow Bushmen are depicted as prelapsarian "noble savages," blissfully ignorant of the vast, technologically advanced world that lies beyond the Kalahari's borders, who marvel in their discovery of the bottle as a "gift from the gods." Over time, however, the presence of this strange foreign object foments unprecedented social problems for the Bushmen—envy, greed, and even violence—leading Xi to embark on a mission to take the bottle, now named "the evil thing," to "the end of the earth," where he plans to cast it back to the gods. In the course of his travels, Xi is exposed to an even wilder, and hitherto unimaginable, world of industrial cityscapes and mass-mediated consumer lifestyles, evincing a cosmic state of affairs for which the title of the film offers the most plausible explanation. Paternalistic and racially charged politics of representation notwithstanding, *The Gods Must Be Crazy* resonated deeply with international audiences (in the United States, for instance, it broke all existing records as the biggest foreign box-office hit). One reason for its success was that the film presented a powerful allegory about the place of technology within the religious imagination and also about the "cosmic destiny" of the technologically mediated modernity with which the film's audience was all too familiar. Indeed, how else ought one to characterize a universe replete with such things as genetically engineered "Frankenfoods," invasive computer surveillance systems, and industrial mega-projects that threaten the planetary ecosystem, if not as a world created by "crazy," if not merciless, impotent—or perhaps even now-deceased—gods?

Religion versus technology

The narrative of *The Gods Must Be Crazy* also presents a popular but ultimately specious way of thinking about technology and religion as two inherently distinct, even incommensurable, types of relationships between humans and the cosmic order. In the first case, technology typically refers to the order of things that are "supposed to work," and the failure of any given technology to do so is usually attributed to problems of misapplication or errors of design. Religion, for its part, is often defined as precisely that which is *not* supposed to work, at least to the extent that actions and perceptions falling under its rubric are assumed not to produce any objectively measurable effects within the natural order. So, returning to *The Gods Must Be Crazy*, one might locate the "real" Coca-Cola bottle on a spatiotemporal plenum regulated by the known laws of physics and also within its traceable, interconnected systems of production (such as sugar refineries and bottling plants), distribution, consumption, and disposal: even the haphazard act of disposal out the window of an airplane. The Coke bottle that was apprehended by the Kalahari Bushmen, conversely, would seem to be the product of a *quid pro quo*: a substitution of rational and empirically confirmable relationships for "enchanted" ones, transforming the once-mundane bottle into an object of wonder and veneration or a tool for the performance of ritual and magic. Of course, any serious examination of the iconography of Coca-Cola bottles, or their ritual uses among so-called non-primitives—such as in advertising, home decoration, or museum collections—would make it somewhat harder to see where the Bushmen's magico-religious worldview ends and the modern secular imagination begins.[1] This in turn invites us to reflect further on the taken-for-granted division between the natural and supernatural order of things and thereby to rethink our use of the term *technology* with respect to both religious and nonreligious regimes of thought and action.

Broadly speaking, technologies are pragmatic and productive forms of mediation between human subjects and their environments, including the constructed environments of social life and even the environment of our own bodies. As the anthropologist Alfred Gell reminds us, technology consists not only of the artifacts employed as tools but of the kinds of knowledge that make possible their invention, design, and use. In this sense, the term *technology* refers to all the material and social relationships "which make it socially necessary to produce, distribute and consume goods and services using 'technical' processes" (Gell 1988: 6). This would include what Gell calls *technologies of production* (by which we secure the "stuff" we think we need: food, shelter, clothing, communication networks, and other material manufactures), *technologies of reproduction* (such as kinship systems, bodily techniques, and other means whereby we domestic ourselves and all the other "animals" with whom we remain in traffic), and also *technologies of enchantment* (such as art, music, dance, rhetoric, gifts, and all the other 'technical' strategies used by human beings to exert control over the thoughts and actions of other human beings; Gell 1988: 6–7). However, *pace* Gell's imaginative taxonomy of technological forms, what is left to say here about the place of "religion"? There are two readily available answers. One approach involves tracking the actions and beliefs of particular social groups, distinguished by their religious commitments, affinities, and habits, who either use or refuse particular technologies in their efforts to achieve such goals as spiritual purification, missionary conquest, salvation, or the expiation of sin. So, for instance, we might want to know more about the theological grounds that lead the Amish to avoid zippers and automobiles, or Orthodox Jews not to use elevators on the Sabbath, or the reasons why Pentecostal preachers so heartily embrace microphones and electric guitars. This first approach, we should note, posits a narrowly instrumental relationship between religion and technology. The latter is conceived here as little more than a realm of mechanical devices and material objects that can be embraced, rejected, or avoided by otherwise integral communities of religious actors.

A second approach would focus not so much on the uses of individual technologies among particular religious groups but rather on the larger discursive framework within which one can locate and evaluate the entire realm of technology within the ethical and cosmic order: that is to say, to define the place of technology itself within the religious imagination. So, for instance, one might treat as "quasi-religious," if not explicitly theological, the popular forms of "faith" in technological progress, which see technology as the guarantor of convenience and abundance and of physiological and civic improvement. Pointing to the vast array of modern devices and technical procedures in industrial production, communication, medicine, or urban planning, technological prognosticators such as Bill Gates, Alvin Toffler, or Nicholas Negroponte can thus be likened to religious prophets, who invoke an imminent, salvific future free from toil, disease, forgetfulness, and other bodily catastrophes. Such progress narratives are structured by an even deeper faith in machines themselves: a faith that they can and will "do their job," so to speak. Others, however, see the progress narrative as little more than a blind, and dangerous, belief in technological transcendence (e.g., Noble 1997) or as the mark of humanity's defiance of a higher, "sacred" law or, even worse, as the work of the devil. One need look no further than the cautionary tales of fate visited on Icarus or Prometheus, or in a comparable Biblical narrative, the builders of the tower of Babel (Szerszynski 2005: 52). However, the most trenchant, and theologically the most important, critiques of the progress narrative are found in the works of Martin Heidegger (1977);

Horkheimer and Adorno (1973); Jacques Ellul (1964); Quentin Schultze (2002); Albert Borgmann (2003); and others who share an understanding of technology as a deep, systemic, and insidious mode of apprehending and dealing with the world.[2] In this narrative—no less indulgent in the language of cosmogony and prophecy—technology is disparaged for its privileging of the principle of efficiency over all other normative criteria, which compels us to regard all of nature as nothing more than an object of mastery and control or, to use Heidegger's term, to see the world as *Gestell* ("standing reserve"). This suspicion seems most readily confirmed by looking at the ways in which modern technologies develop: as they incorporate larger and more complicated functions, their operational properties become increasingly difficult to discern, increasingly unpredictable and unstable, and to those extents increasingly displaced from the willful intentions of their designers and users. Their apparent autonomy and self-determining functionality thus makes modern technologies appear inexorable, sublime, even imperious. To borrow the famously sinister salutation of The Borg, the rapacious and technologically omnivorous alien villain in the *Star Trek* television series, "resistance is futile." Or, as Heidegger himself put it, in a posthumously published interview, we have become so thoroughly entangled within the thickets of modern technology that "only a God can save us."[3]

Religion and technology

All these accounts also appear to share a common approach to religion as something set apart from technology: in other words, as a mode of thinking, feeling, and acting that can be layered on—and therefore also detached from—the objectively knowable arena of technical actions and effects. This way of dividing religion and technology rests on a deeply fraught history of cosmology, science, and popular imaginings of the relationship between humans and nonhumans, including transcendent, supernatural, or sacred things. Our commonsense definition of technology is in fact a modernist abstraction—what Bruno Latour (1993) calls a "purification"—of a messier and far more ambiguous set of historically sedimented representations of and interactions among human, nonhuman, and supernatural beings. In classical Greek philosophy, we might bear in mind, *techne*—a term that originally meant to put together, to weave, or connect things through art, artifice or craft—was generally understood to furnish an inferior form of knowledge about the cosmos in comparison to contemplation—*episteme*—which furnished universal and timeless truths.[4] The inherent flaws of technical knowledge were further underscored by the tendency to use the plural form, *technai*, which were conceived as separate crafts, not necessarily united by an overarching set of generalized principles. It is only in the modern period that we begin to see an erosion of the classical division between the base, "mechanical arts" and the lofty, contemplative powers of natural philosophy. And it was only in the nineteenth century that people began referring to technology in the singular, an abstraction that was furthered over the course of the twentieth century with the rise of large-scale, increasingly bureaucratized networks of scientists, engineers, planners, and managers working in trade, industry, and government (see Marx 1991; Mitcham 1994).

This "modern constitution" (Latour 1993) emerged in the shadow of an elaborate collusion between post-Reformation Christianity and natural philosophy, which, coupled with the history of colonial conquest and Western technological supremacy, had dramatic, global consequences. On the one hand, it consolidated the disenchantment of nature, rendering it an inert cosmos, existing apart from and subject to human inspection and calculated manipulation. On the other hand, it restricted the religious sphere to "matters of the heart," safely segregated from politics and public life and also from the performative, epistemological, and instrumental prerogatives of modern techno-scientific practice. One exemplary contribution to this effort was provided by Calvinist theology, which denied the intermediate power of bishops, kings, saints, angels, and even the Virgin Mary and, in so doing, radically distanced both human subjects and the natural order from their absolute, unknowable, sovereign creator. The founding fathers of modern European science and natural philosophy, such as Galileo, Descartes, Bacon, and Newton, likewise stood before what they perceived as a disenchanted natural order. By overturning the existing Thomist, neo-Platonic, and magical understandings of nature as a vast web of resemblances, sympathetic rapports, or final causes, these "secular theologians" transformed nature into "mere matter": a uniform entity, extended in space—and therefore amenable to precise measurement and controlled observation—and organized by universal principles of mechanical cause and effect, action and reaction (Funkenstein 1989). But as Bronislaw Szerszynski argues, the disenchantment of nature did not simply entail the "removal" of the sacred. Rather, it heralded a new way of ordering and conceptualizing the sacred sphere itself:

> the very constitution of the world as inert matter behaving according to mathematical laws in absolute space required a specific transformation of religious meanings, one that involved a newly literal approach not just to matter, but also to God. The melancholy of the modern world, the vast gulf between the sublime and the painful, lonely and finite world of humans, is thus the result not of the abandonment of the sacred, but of the adoption of a particular ordering of it.
>
> (Szerszynski 2005: 48–9)

By emphasizing how historically contingent is the modern, occidental division between a mundane, knowable world of technical action and an imperceptible, transcendent, numinous, or supernatural "other," Szerszynski reminds us that this is hardly a universal, let alone a self-evident, way of understanding the cosmos. Consider, as a counter-example, the animist cosmogony found throughout indigenous Amazonia, where humans, animals, and other natural and supernatural beings are seen to exist in a state of metaphysical continuity, based on a shared set of principles and forces emanating from all bodily organs (Viveiros de Castro 1998). A basic precept in the Christian tradition involves drawing a fundamental distinction between human bodies, which are said to possess souls (and therefore uniquely capable of salvation), and all the other living and inanimate bodies that do not. However, such a divide makes little sense in Amazonian terms. As Viveiros de Castro argues, rather than trying to distinguish between spiritual essences (which are authentic and real) and bodily appearances (which, as surfaces, only hide the truth), Amazonian indigenes confront an undifferentiated cosmic order wherein efficacious meanings slip backward and forward, between and among its various human and nonhuman inhabitants, and in and through the "equipment" that is used to connect such beings. Within this framework, a shaman engages with objects such as animal skins as *technologies*,

> endowed with the power metaphysically to transform the identities of those who wear them, if used in the appropriate ritual context. To put on mask-clothing is not so much to conceal a human essence beneath an animal appearance, but rather to activate the powers of a different body. The animal clothes that shamans use to travel the cosmos are not fantasies but instruments: they are akin to diving equipment, or space suits, and not to carnival masks. The intention when donning a wet suit is to be able to function like a fish, to breathe underwater, not to conceal oneself under a strange covering. In the same way, the "clothing" which, amongst animals, covers an internal "essence" of a human type, is not a mere disguise but their distinctive equipment, endowed with the affects and capacities which define each animal.
>
> (Viveiros de Castro 1998: 482)

Lest we be tempted here to indulge in the sort of romantic primitivism that we have already seen used to relegate Kalahari Bushmen to the far side of Western modernity, we might further note that Amazonian shamans are not the only "technologists" who, in their efforts to gain such things as power, knowledge, health, or release from suffering recognize no fixed or impermeable boundaries between humans and nonhumans, the visible and the invisible, or the immanent and the transcendent. A quintessentially "Western" and "modern" corollary is found in the writings of the nineteenth-century geologist and Spiritualist psychometrist, William Denton. For Denton, the natural world consisted of a vast moral apparatus of radiant forces inscribed into all things, from rocks and fossils in the ground, to the leaves on a tree, to the birds perched on its branches, to the human eye that beholds such a scene, to the daguerreotype camera, which—like the disciplined techniques of psychometry—possesses the power to catalogue the broad canopy of eternal things and which, by the beautiful "chemistry" of intermingling of material and spiritual fluids, impresses these essential properties onto our conscious minds (Denton 1888; see also Cox 2003: 109–10, 225–7).

Denton was only one of many adherents to Spiritualism, the popular religious movement that spread across and beyond the Atlantic world over the course of the nineteenth and early twentieth centuries, from the United States to Britain, France, Germany, Brazil, and further-flung locales. Spiritualists were marked by considerable differences of social location, political orientation, and degrees of accommodation to prevailing religious orthodoxies (such as mainline Protestantism, Anglicanism, or the Roman Catholic Church), but for the most part they were united in their commitment to a cosmology of sympathetically interconnected and eternal intelligences, in the form of spirits that survived corporeal life and that served as the animating force behind all things. Often, the rapport of spirits with the material world was explained in terms of a "universal fluid," analogous to the flow of electricity—another mysterious power that in the nineteenth century was propelling dramatic, new technological advancements in the form of telegraph cables, telephones, light bulbs, and dynamo engines. By thus proposing to ground the moral, social, and physical order in a "naturalist" account of universal spirit forces, Spiritualists sought to overcome what many nineteenth-century witnesses perceived as the increasingly shaky foundations of Christian scripture and at the same time to win scientific credibility from skeptical detractors and curious onlookers. Not unlike the animist shaman who "activates the powers of a different body," Spiritualists turned to their own material culture of writing instruments, metal wires and cables, magnets, pressure gauges, clocks, and cameras in their efforts to communicate with the dead. In so doing, they dissolved the distinctions between the material and the immaterial and between "this world" and "the next," just as, all around them, modern subjects were dissolving once-fixed notions of past and present, or proximate and distant, through the transmission of a telegraph message across the ocean, the recording of one's voice on a phonograph, or the photographic preservation of one's image after death (see Connor 1999; Noakes 2002; Stolow 2007).

Indigenous animists and Spiritualist "pseudo-scientists" are not the only ones who have such trouble distinguishing religion and technology. Here we might also invoke a growing body of historical and ethnographic scholarship that only adds to our difficulty in holding on to the popular narrative of modern techno-science as a mundane, "disenchanted" realm of mechanical interactions. Indeed, given their imponderable complexities and their dramatic abilities to compress time, erase distance, store memory, or reproduce identical copies, many modern technologies are said to elicit from their users affective dispositions and modes of conduct that are phenomenologically comparable with prayer, ritual, and magic.[5] Likewise, the performance of modern techno-science—in laboratories, workshops, conferences, schools, and other places—is said to resemble a system of magical or religious action, to the extent that it partakes in a pragmatic engagement with the world through skilled techniques and disciplined perceptions, through the power of spectacle, and through the institutional organization of faith regarding the true workings of nature.[6] The latest advances in the arenas of bioengineering, computer modeling, or nanotechnology have even further eroded once-confident distinctions between humans and other bodies, giving way to a variety of fantastic creations and half-human, half-machine hybrid "monsters" (Balsamo 1999; Graham 2002; Haraway 1991). Through these increasingly dizzying interpenetrations of humans and nonhumans and of spirits and machines, a significant challenge has been mounted to the longstanding authority of Linnaean taxonomy, wherein the world of the living is supposed to be divided into stable categories of plant and animal, vertebrate and invertebrate, or male and female. In its wake, we find a cosmos that far more resembles the one perceived "primitively" as a relatively undifferentiated order of humans, gods, animals, and the diverse forms of equipment that tie them together. All of this suggests that the distinction between religion and technology is far more invidious than the aforementioned popular narratives might have us believe. Indeed, the more one looks, the more difficult it becomes to determine where, or even how, to draw the line separating "religious" and "technological" things.

Religion as technology

So, when posing the question of how "technology" would most fruitfully serve as a key word in the study of religion and media, one might wish to try the following thought experiment: imagine any form of religious experience, practice, or knowledge and see what you have left "without technology." No instruments, tools, or devices; no architecture or clothing; no paint, musical instruments, incense, or written documents; not even the disciplined practices of bodily control—such as learned and performed methods of breathing, sitting, or gesturing with one's hands—for these too are technical practices. Even thoughts and images seem to vanish with the removal of the representational technologies of language and iconography. The inescapable conclusion to be drawn from this exercise is that "religion," however we choose to define it, is inherently and necessarily technological. Rather than searching for an interior experience or feeling of divine presence, of the numinous, or the sacred that can somehow be shorn of all outward trappings, we are more amply rewarded by examining the myriad ways in which religious experiences are materialized, rendered tangible and palpable, communicated publicly, recorded, and reproduced—in short, *mediated*—in and through its given range of technological manifestations and techniques.

Mediation, Bruno Latour reminds us, means the creation of a link that did not exist before, and to that degree it entails a modification of the originally unconnected elements. Within a given network of action, mediation thus refers to the process of redistribution and exchange of properties, functions, competencies, and goals among associated actors or, more precisely stated, the *delegation* of action programs from one actor (e.g., a human) to another (e.g., a machine), as in the case of a lock that translates and replaces the actions of a human guard, who no longer needs to stand by a door to keep it shut (Latour 1999). From this perspective, the term *technology* refers to the mediation of skills that have been extended from humans to nonhumans: a translation that produces new forms of "congealed labour." However, as Latour is also at pains to show, as nonhuman actors, technologies are never simply the means to ends that have been defined and circumscribed by humans. On the contrary, technologies in turn shape human experience by actively participating in—and thereby transforming—networks of action. Put otherwise, when we exchange properties with nonhumans through technical delegation, we at the same time allow artifacts to enter into the stream of human relations as mediators, not simply intermediaries, that is to say, as actors in their own right:

> "Of course," one might say, "a piece of technology must be seized and activated by a human subject, a purposeful agent." But...what is true of the "object" is still truer of the "subject." There is no sense in which humans may be said to exist as humans without entering into commerce with what authorizes and enables them to exist (that is, to act).
>
> (Latour 1999: 192; cf 1993: 79–82)

For the purposes of this discussion, it is important to bear in mind that the category of the "nonhuman" includes such things as staircases, chimes, ink, flowers, hair, animal blood, video-recorders, and mobile telephones, but it also encompasses gods, angels, jinns, demons, bodhisattvas, saints, and other "supernatural" creatures. These diverse figures define the horizons of human action at the same time that we humans define ourselves and our "others." Put otherwise, technological devices, such as gods, must ultimately be placed in a single continuum, in relation to which humans enact, confirm, transform, or even deny our own humanity in the ceaseless traffic with other actors that populate our cosmos. Of course, this insight is already well rooted in most religious traditions, where one can easily find a vast repertoire of deified engagements with humans and their ever-evolving technological appurtenances. In Hinduism, for instance, there is Lord Vishvakarma, the Divine Architect of the Universe, designer of the gods' palaces, chariots, and sacred weapons, and also the popular deity among modern-day engineers, factory workers, craftsmen, and artists, who every September 17, the day of Vishvakarma Puja, bring out the tools of their trades and seek the deity's blessings. For Roman Catholics, there is St. Clare of Assisi, traditionally the Patron Saint of eye diseases and embroidery (hence her popularity among needle and gold workers), but who, in the twentieth century, came to include television within her sphere of influence. For his part, God's messenger, the Archangel Gabriel, has established his patronage over all the modern telecommunication and transmission industries, including postal services, radio and television broadcast, and e-mail. One significant challenge for scholars of religion and media is to find comparable divinities and sacred powers in less obvious places—perhaps even in our relationship with such mundane nonhuman actors as discarded Coke bottles.

Notes

1 For an analysis of the fetishistic dimensions of Coca-Cola, see Chidester (1996). For a broader discussion of the deep entanglement of magic and modernity, see Meyer and Pels (2003).

2 Of course, this summary risks caricaturing the complexities of these writers, and the reader should not infer here any suggestion that their positions with respect to technology are interchangeable. The primary goal of this discussion is to bring to light the popular narratives that absorbed these philosophical discussions and rendered them "commonsensical."

3 Interview with Heidegger for *Der Spiegel*, conducted on September 23, 1966 and published posthumously on May 31, 1976. English translation in Wolin (1992: 91ff).

4 Interestingly, the classical definition of *techne* compares favorably with the idea of magic, which is etymologically rooted in the Proto-Indo-European *magh*: to make, or to have the power to do things.

5 See, e.g., Davis (1998); Hankins and Silverman (1995); Sconce (2000); Stivers (2001); Styers (2004)

6   See, *inter alia*, During (2002); Lotfalian (2004); Meyer and Pels (2003); Morus (1998); Nadis (2005); Nye (1996); Serres (1999); Tambiah (1990); Taussig (1997). Such discussions of modern science, religion, and magic are built on a large literature devoted to the importance of mystical thought, millenarian speculation, and ecclesiastical allegiance for the workings of power, patronage, and gentlemanly civility that helped to construct scientific credibility, from the European Renaissance to Victorian society to the contemporary period. This is exemplified by studies of the religious sensibilities and ambitions of European natural philosophers, doctors, inventors, and engineers (Boyle the Puritan, Newton the alchemist, Edison the Theosophist, etc.), or the overlaps between an expanding scientific culture of exhibition and display and the public spectacles of religious ceremony. See, e.g., Funkenstein (1989), Merton (1957), Webster (1982).

15

Text

Isabel Hofmeyr

Transnational textual circulation
Translation
Can religious texts be translated?
The Pilgrim's Progress
The Pilgrim's Progress in Africa

In the religious sphere, texts are tasked with onerous responsibilities. Whether prayers, hymns, or incantations, all must cross the forbidding barrier separating the living and the dead in an attempt to beguile the gods and ancestors to whom they are addressed. Texts traveling in the reverse direction must likewise convince believers that they are sacred messages.

Religious texts hence pose in extreme form the key methodological issues that confront any form of textual analysis. How do texts create meaning? How do they manage to address their audiences? What happens to texts as they cross time and space?

Indeed, communication theorists maintain that religious texts provide the model for mass media that address those who are not present: "all communication via media of transmission or recording…is ultimately undistinguishable from communication with the dead" (Peters 1999: 176).

However, what do we mean by text? In the field of media studies, text is a cornerstone concept, particularly of the culturalist wing of the discipline. Understood as a configuration of signs on which the viewer, hearer, or auditor confers significance, text has become a flexible concept that can as well be applied to a newspaper story as a shopping mall (Hanks 1989). In this sense, a religious text would be multidimensional involving all aspects of a spiritual event like its architecture, choreography, clothing, use of voice, song, sacrifices, and the like.

Other definitions of text are narrower and single out the element of print or writing. David Morgan provides one definition: "A text is something written, published, stored, read silently or aloud, purchased and shared, traded, displayed. It is cited, edited, rewritten, compared with other texts, and taught" (2005: 89). For the purposes of this chapter, we use this definition but extend it to include spoken language. A text would hence be a configuration of verbal signs recognized as having coherence and addressivity by its users.

With regard to the analysis of texts, the scholarly study of both religion and media has prompted a dazzling array of literary and textual methodologies. Scriptural hermeneutics constitutes one of the oldest Western traditions of textual scholarship. English literary studies as a discipline emerged in the mid-nineteenth century and since then has been formulating methods for how best to interpret texts. Over the last half-century, media, cultural, and literary studies have prompted and formed part of the linguistic turn of the humanities and social sciences, which has sought to analyze the multivalent nature of discourse and textuality. In Barthes's memorable phrasing, texts are objects of "shimmering depth," "vast cultural spaces through which our person...is only one passage." Texts are filled with the elusive "rustle of language" (1989: 31).

These rich legacies of textual analysis are well known and have produced evermore ingenious ways of interpreting oral or written texts (or both). Yet, some of these approaches tend to assume that a text is self-evident. They seldom ask the prior question of how a text comes to be defined as such. Addressing this question requires an engagement with questions of readership, reception, audiences, and publics.

This is a crowded field. Media studies has a long tradition of studying audiences. Earlier models of the "silver bullet" text piercing the consciousness of the passive viewer-reader have given way to ideas of the active reader-viewer wherein consumption of a text is simultaneously its production. Put differently, any reading of a text generates a new text. An allied body of scholarship on the public sphere has asked broader questions about the notions of social solidarity that may emerge from the shared consumption of particular texts and discourses (Warner 2002).

The anthropology of religion is also relevant. This body of scholarship asks questions about how words and objects must be aligned in religious ceremonies for these words to acquire spiritual significance (Keane 2007; Engelke 2007). As Webb Keane demonstrates, in Sumba, Indonesia, for the ancestors to pay attention to an intercessory ritual, a sacrifice of a particular animal must be accompanied by a recognized set of rhetorical forms uttered by a particular person. Likewise, a Catholic communion minimally requires a consecrated host to be accompanied by certain verbal formulas pronounced by a priest.

Histories and ethnographies of reading have equally illuminated questions of religious textual community and how, through endless repetition, religious texts come to assume authority and canonicity. Whether Bible reading groups among South Africa's black poor (West 1999) or a yeshiva in

Lower East Side, New York (Boyarin 1992), these studies explore different dimensions of the mutually constitutive relationship of readers and texts and what kinds of social practice such textual events (or multi-literacies [Street 1993]) constitute.

Allied to this work have been traditions of scholarship that seek to engage self-consciously with the materiality of the text and what role this plays in interpretation.

As Lynn Schofield Clark asks, what difference does it make to read the Bible in a leather-bound, gilt-edged edition or in the format of the new teenage magazine Bibles that mimic publications such as *Cosmo Girl*, *Seventeen*, and *Teen People* (2007a: 1–33)? To purloin the subtitle of George Bornstein's *Material Modernism* (2001), "What is the politics of the page?" Book history as a field of enquiry has sought to answer this question. In the words of Roger Chartier, we need to understand "the text itself, the object that conveys the text, and the act that grasps it" (1989: 161).

The remainder of this chapter seeks to explore these themes of text, textual community, and social practice. The examples on which the chapter relies are mainly drawn from nineteenth-century mission Protestantism. Apart from this being my area of specialization, this topic provides us with a unique purchase on questions of transnationalism. As the world globalizes apace, the academy has to grapple with ways to address these emerging realities. One key issue is how transnational subjects come into being. What are the genres, modes of address, and forms of reading that must be formulated for readers to imagine themselves in transnational terms? All too often, this process is assumed to be self-evident. As mission Christianity is always transnational, it provides a good point from which to consider this question methodologically.

A focus on nineteenth-century textual transnationalism can act as a supplement to the growing body of work on religion and media. Much of this work tends to be on the reception and use of media within a defined national territory. Whether examining Pentecostal films in Ghana (Meyer 2006) or Christian bookstores in the United States (Borden 2007), the emphasis is on the consumption of these media in a defined national space rather than asking what happens between these spaces.

This chapter explores these questions under two rubrics: transnational textual circulation and translation.

Transnational textual circulation

The Protestant evangelical mission movement can usefully be considered as a pioneer of transnational print mass media. Driven by urgent evangelical imperatives, Protestant mission organizations were responsible for pumping out billions of printed texts to all corners of the globe. In the words of one of its historians, the movement was "the greatest single medium of mass communication in the nineteenth century" (Bradley 1976: 41).

Seen theologically, this activity is not surprising. Evangelicals held that Christ's "great commission" to spread the gospel formed the core of Christianity. There was an urgent imperative to disseminate Christian ideas to as many people as possible.

Unsurprisingly, one prevalent theme in mission media was that of conspicuous circulation. Mission exhibitions invariably included displays of religious material that had been translated into foreign languages. This translation dramatized the fact that these texts had circulated far and wide. Likewise figures such as the colporteur or Bible woman enacted mission texts in motion. Transport was a trope in mission narratives with ships forming a common thread in mission publicity. Most large mission societies owned sea-going vessels to ferry their personnel about. Such ships provided publicity opportunities in terms of funding drives, stories, pictures, hymns, and poems. The ship became a metaphor of the word itself, sailing out to all corners of the globe.

In the early years of the Protestant mission movement, this belief in conspicuous circulation expressed itself in the widespread notion that the Bible, unaided by human hands, would magically circulate, converting all those it encountered. The early propaganda of the British and Foreign Bible Society (BFBS), founded in 1804, portrayed Bibles rather like mini-missionaries (Canton 1904: 317). In these parables, texts are invested with extraordinary powers of possession and enchantment.

This theory of enchanted reading is particularly clear in relation to a key evangelical genre, the tract. Handbooks on tract distribution and reading portrayed these "noiseless messengers" (USCL 1948: title) as mesmerizing objects. In one account, a man is given a tract that he tears up in a rage and throws down on the carpet, expecting that the servant will sweep it away. The next day, the torn scraps remain. The man summons the servant. She explains that she saw the word *eternal* on one of the pieces of paper and felt afraid to sweep it away. The man sticks the pieces of torn paper together, reads the tract and is converted (Watts 1934: 8).

On the face of it, this view of textuality may appear unremarkable. Across all religions, sacred texts are assumed to have magical properties: they fall from heaven, they are acquired in dreams, they are dictated by angels. This example would constitute an evangelical Protestant instance of this phenomenon, driven as such ventures were by urgency and fervor.

However, this miraculous circulation also has to be read in terms of technological development on which it depended and at times stimulated. As Lesley Howsam's history of the BFBS demonstrates, the modernization of the bookbinding industry was precipitated by the BFBS-created demand for Bibles (1991). The BFBS were ever on the lookout for new forms of technology that could provide sturdily bound Bibles in the numbers required. By the early nineteenth century, bookbinding was still organized as a small craft industry. Before the 1820s, books were not bound as a matter of course and instead, it was common practice to buy unbound sheets and have them bound to the customer's specifications (Howsam 1991: 123).

The book as we know it today, namely as a modern commodity, identically produced in edition bindings, did not fully exist. The organization that helped to bring this practice into being was the BFBS, which required large numbers of books whose bindings could withstand the distances they had to travel. Under the pressure of BFBS production schedules, bookbinding was forcibly shifted from a pre-modern craft to a modern mass-production industry.

A consideration of religious texts in the Protestant mission domain, then, leads us into the heart of modernity itself. One part of this relationship hinges on the ways in which the production and management of Protestant texts acted as a force for modernist innovation. David Nord's work on the American Bible Society demonstrates how the exigencies of distributing texts across vast distances brought into being modern management practices such as detailed record keeping and statistics (2007: 37–66).

A second aspect of Protestant textual production and modernity is less direct and pertains to the oft-noted way in which modernity, an apparently austere and secular process, in fact feeds off ideas of magic and enchantment. By its own account, modernity is meant to be a universal force of rationality, secularism, and disenchantment. However, as much recent work indicates, this universal rationality is something of an optical illusion. On the one hand, this mirage depends on the trick of passing off a particular European historical experience as universal (Chakrabarty 2000). On the other, modern institutions and their audiences conspire to imbue modernity with magical abilities as a way of making these new institutions intelligible (Murdock 1997). The widely studied phenomena of viewers believing that televisual media are haunted forms part of this process (Sconce 2000). Televisual media portray people who are not there. Rather than mastering the boring mechanical details of this phenomenon, popular cultural beliefs gloss this process in terms of ghosts and spirits.

The mass production and circulation of Bibles captures these processes of enchantment admirably. This development depended on a combination of magical evangelical belief and cutting-edge technology through which identical commodities poured out of bookbinding factories. BFBS publicity insisted this circulation was divinely inspired and at times sought to suppress its mechanical aspects, in one case removing the phrase "printed by machinery" from a BFBS edition (Howsam 1991: 95). More speculatively, we might also ask how Protestant ideas of magical circulation create an environment in which the idea of transnational circulation itself can start to make sense.

Yet, what of the reception of these circulating texts? What did readers in various parts of the world make of Protestant Bibles? To address this issue, we turn to themes of translation.

Translation

The idea that "the Bible" existed in the early Protestant mission empire is something of a misnomer. Biblical translation was time consuming. Getting agreement on how to translate key terms such as baptism, spirit, and resurrection was arduous. Most mission societies worked through the Bible Society, which generally demanded that all Protestant missions in one language area collaborate on the translation. Diversity of denominational opinion further delayed the process. In some cases, it took half a century before both testaments were translated and published as one volume. "The Bible" could hence exist as a handful of separate booklets that were indistinguishable from other pamphlets (Hofmeyr 2004: 77–9).

Complicating this picture was the way in which the Bible (or parts of it) was changed as it entered new spiritual traditions. In the case of Africa, with some 1,000 languages and as many ethnic groups, the Bible came to be reinterpreted in diverse ways. This "reformation" was possible since Christianity in Africa was spread by Africans. Missionaries were few and far between and were generally culturally remote from the people they proselytized. The work of brokering the gospel fell to the African foot soldiers of Christianity, the catechists, evangelists, and Bible women who knew how best to present new ideas to their audiences.

African Christianity produced distinctive theologies. These included an African Christology (Christ as intermediary rather than son of God), a stress on healing, and an emphasis on the gifts of the Holy Spirit. In other cases, African Christians "re-biblicized" the Bible, playing up Old Testament themes of prophecy and polygamy that the missionaries sought to downplay (Hastings 1994).

Orality and literacy provided another site for both re- and (in some instances) de-biblicization. Christian sacred texts pivot on a metaphorical conjunction of the oral and the written. God's oral voice is mediated in print (or manuscript): "The ritual of reading recapitulates the primal experience of speaking and hearing the word of God" (Stock 1990: 149). These themes assumed an added edge when introduced into sub-Saharan societies that were oral or paraliterate. Here ideas of divine orality and literacy were fused in novel ways. In some cases, literacy was believed to come directly from God (rather than via the tainted agency of the missionaries) and was conferred miraculously on believers by angels in dreams and visions (Hofmeyr 2006). In a very different instance, the Friday Masowe Church in Zimbabwe refuses to use the Bible because they receive the Word "live and direct" as they say from the Holy Spirit (Engelke 2007).

Can religious texts be translated?

These transformations form part of a much longer history of translation within Christianity that has spurred extensive controversy. Can sacred texts be translated? Can a divine language be translated into a human one? Does translation assist or impede the spread of religions?

This debate has produced a continuum of positions stretching from an insistence that the divine cannot be translated to an equally enthusiastic assertion that it can. The first position is associated with Islam wherein Arabic, the language in which an angel dictated the Koran, is deemed to be the most superior version in which to encounter the sacred text. Translations are not disallowed but are seen as lesser than the Arabic. The position of the Catholic Church (until 1962), which held that the Bible was best read in Latin, represents a not dissimilar position.

By contrast, Protestants, particularly those of an evangelical stripe, have been ardent translators (Sanneh 1991). These evangelical versions of translation generally go hand in hand with the idea of translation as revelation. In this view, translation becomes possible as God will ensure that his meaning infuses the new version. A second Protestant view is more modest and holds that translation is a human activity prone to error and dependent on human decisions and interpretations (Engelke 2007: 22–3).

Questions of translation enrich the methodological field of religious textual inquiry. One focus is obviously on the source and the target text to see what orders of understanding the linguistic and stylistic choices of the translation do or do not enable. Outside the text, we need to ask how translation is actually done and what ideas about translation the participants hold. Finally as translation studies indicate, we need to consider broader political questions to ask how ideas of equivalence or non-equivalence come into being. Whether texts are seen as faithful renditions of one another depends not only on the quality of the translation but on a broader political willingness to believe in the commensurability of people, ideas, and cultures (Liu 1999).

To see how these issues worked in practice, we turn to the translation of John Bunyan's *The Pilgrim's Progress*, a key text of evangelical Protestantism often considered a second Bible by Nonconformists and widely translated by missionaries drawn from their ranks.

The Pilgrim's Progress

The Pilgrim's Progress was published in two parts in 1678 and 1684 in the wake of the English revolution. The first part of the book tells the story of the hero Christian making his way from earth to heaven. The second tells of his wife Christiana and family who follow in his footsteps to join him in heaven.

The book very rapidly became an evangelical classic and traveled beyond England, making its way to Protestant Europe and the New World. Its next major migration came courtesy of the nineteenth-century Protestant mission movement. Drawn largely from Low Church evangelicals to whom *The Pilgrim's Progress* was a most beloved book, the movement propagated the text in most parts of the globe, resulting in some 200 versions worldwide.

To understand what fuelled this translation activity, we need to grasp the seminal role of Bunyan's book in the lives of Protestant evangelicals, most of whom grew up with the book, hearing it in Sabbath day readings, poring over the illustrations, and acting out scenes to entertain themselves. As adults, they read Bunyan on a daily basis, and encountered the story in choir services, pageants, dramas, tableaux, magic lantern slides, postcards, and posters. One fan even landscaped his garden as a *Pilgrim's Progress* theme park. As a book that was woven into the emotional fabric of everyday life and was featured in conversion narratives, *The Pilgrim's Progress* was seen as a user-friendly Bible that summarized the core verities of the Protestant message.

Once these evangelicals became missionaries, they hastened to translate the text. Back home, Nonconformist mission supporters assiduously publicized these translations not only as a way of raising the profile of overseas mission, but to add value to their most beloved writer, who was still regarded as vulgar and theologically suspect by the Anglican establishment. At fundraising meetings, magic lantern slides showed illustrations from foreign editions. Mission periodicals reported on translations and how they were received. In one instance, a mission exhibition showed a live tableau of a missionary translating *The Pilgrim's Progress*. Cumulatively, these reports created the idea that the text had miraculous powers of circulation and acted like a mini-Bible in converting those it encountered (Hofmeyr 2004: 56–75).

The Pilgrim's Progress in Africa

Africa was host to eighty translations of Bunyan's book and so provides a useful site to examine how the book was changed as it traveled into new spiritual communities.

One response to *The Pilgrim's Progress* was conditioned by African appropriations of Protestantism more generally. One tenet of Protestant theology that never proved portable was the idea of original sin. Concepts of social sin certainly existed, but the idea that, whether one liked it or did not, one was sinful never caught on among African readers, translators, or missionaries. Those aspects of the text that discussed these ideas were generally edited out, a feature that depended on the material practices of mission translation. Translation was generally pursued in teams made up of second-language missionaries and first-language converts. Missionaries were also inveterate experimenters having to try out bits and pieces with their new audiences to see what would work. Between the African translators and the pressure of popular taste, the sections of the text expounding ideas of original sin were edited out. Where these could not be removed, the meaning of original sin was changed. The most famous image of Bunyan's story, namely, the burden on Christian's back, stood for original sin. In many Africa editions, this meaning was erased, and instead the burden came to stand for colonial rule itself (Hofmeyr 2004: 76–97).

One further theme that African translations highlighted pertained to themes of orality and literacy. In the paraliterate world in which Bunyan's story unfolds, documents are not everyday objects, and they tend to stand out either as items of great religious significance or as agents of state oppression, like the pass that Christian, a masterless man, must carry. This ambivalence around documents resonated with the experience of many African Christians seeking religious advancement but kept back on the one hand by the colonial state with its network of documentary control and on the other, by the white-controlled structures of the mission churches. In the final scene of Part I of the book, Christian arrives at the gates of heaven but first has to produce his certificate to get in. Ignorance, who is next in the queue, has no certificate and is unceremoniously pitched down into hell. This scene of difficult and select entry into the portals of power proved popular with African Christians and made its way into illustrations, novels, hymns and songs (Hofmeyr 2004: 137–50).

Important is that African Christians used *The Pilgrim's Progress* to project their concerns into a broader international arena. By using the internationally recognized story of *The Pilgrim's Progress*, which came to acquire African illustrations and hence African characters, African Christians could project themselves into an international arena, often seeking to go over the heads of their various oppressors—the colonial state, white settlers or royal chiefly lineages who persecuted commoner converts—to appeal to an international public.

However, what were the limits of the text's circulation? When did the text cease to be itself? In some cases, the text disappeared as part of a political decision to eschew the white-dominated world of mission and colonial state. In one case, Simon Kimbangu, who broke away from the Baptists in the central Congo region, probably picked up some symbols from the book, in all likelihood from illustrations. One of them shows Christian emerging dripping from the Slough of Despond. In his hand is a Bible that is dry. Kimbangu traditionalized this image of fetching a book from the next world, a process that involved passing through a body of water. Kimbangu "poached" from the text but disavowed the source (Hofmeyr 2004: 28–9).

In other cases, the text disappears not because of difference but because of similarity. Here the story evaporates into African oral traditions that share many similarities with Bunyan's storytelling techniques that emerge from a paraliterate world, Bunyan himself being a first-generation literate. Both *The Pilgrim's Progress* and African oral narrative traditions share folktale motifs such as the use of dramatic dialogue, two characters to a scene, proverbs, riddles, formulaic phrasings, and onomastic strategies. Particles of Bunyan's story could hence be elided into African literary traditions. In these circumstances, texts disintegrate, not through political resistance but rather under systems unaware of, or indifferent to, their supposedly "correct" and "original" meaning (Hofmeyr 2004: 30).

Conclusion

We began by asking what a text is. We conclude with some speculation on what a religious text might be. What confers spiritual power on texts? The answers lie both outside and inside a text. Texts need to be institutionalized, endlessly taught and interpreted within religious textual communities for them to gain spiritual authority and canonicity. Such textual communities provide forums of apprenticeship in which believers learn to allow themselves to be addressed by the generic conventions of texts and to experience such address as sacred.

Central to this process of address is the idea of circulation. One feature of a religious text is that it comes from somewhere else. In part, religious ritual that collapses time and space seeks to erase this distance so that most believers never ponder in great detail as to whether or how religious texts have been translated. Yet, as nineteenth-century Protestantism became more globalized, this fact of circulation became increasingly important for sustaining the idea of a transnational religious community. Readers then had to undertake interpretive apprenticeships that involved reading for circulation.

Further research in this area would be important and may reveal how such apprenticeships played a role in sustaining a secular idea of transnational circulation.

One route that this research could follow would be to examine ideas of copyright, which seeks to limit a text's circulation. Most contemporary understandings of text today hinge at some level on copyright, intellectual property law, and the figure of the author as a legal function. Understandings of how such ideas interact with older notions of circulation, particularly between heaven and earth, will prove a fruitful route to pursue. Could one ever imagine copyright in heaven?

Works cited

Abu-Lughod, Lila (2004) *Dramas of Nationhood: The Politics of Television in Egypt*, Chicago: University of Chicago Press.

Adams, Nicholas (2006) *Habermas and Theology*, Cambridge: Cambridge University Press.

Adorno, Theodor (2001), J. M. Bernstein (ed.) *The Culture Industry*, London: Routledge.

Agger, Ben (1992) *Cultural Studies as Critical Theory*, London: The Falmer Press.

Al Jazeera (2006) November 9, 2006: last update, *Al Jazeera English—About US Corporate Profile* Homepage of aljazeera.net. Online. Available: HTTP://english. aljazeera.net/NR/exeres/DE03467F-C15A-4FF9-BAB0-1B0E6B59EC8F.htm (accessed September 30, 2007).

Alexander, Bobby C. (1994) *Televangelism Reconsidered: Ritual in the Search for Human Community*, Atlanta, GA: Scholars Press.

Anderson, Benedict (1991) *Imagined Communities: Reflections on the Origin and Spread of Nationalism*, rev. ed., London: Verso.

Anon. (1861) "Poor Dead Horse," *The Well-Spring* 18 (7): 27.

Anon. (1861a) "The Well-Spring Caught Napping," *The Well-Spring* 18 (15): 60.

Anon. (1861b) "The Well-Spring Pictures," *The Well-Spring* 18 (22): 86.

Anon. (1863) *My Picture-Book*, New York: American Tract Society.

Appadurai, Arjun (1997) *Modernity at Large: Cultural Dimensions of Globalization*, Minneapolis, MN: University of Minnesota Press.

Armbrust, Walter (ed.) (2000) *Mass Mediations: New Approaches to Popular Culture in the Middle East and Beyond*, Berkeley, CA: University of California Press.

Armbrust, Walter (2006) "Synchronizing Watches: The State, the Consumer, and Sacred Time in Ramadan Television," in Birgit Meyer and Annelies Moors (eds.) *Religion, Media, and the Public Sphere*, Bloomington, IN: Indiana University Press, pp. 207–26.

Arthur, Chris (ed.) (1993) *Religion and the Media: An Introductory Reader*, Cardiff: University of Wales Press.

Arweck, Elizabeth and Keenan, William (eds.) (2006) *Materializing Religion: Expression, Performance and Ritual*, Aldershot: Ashgate Publishing.

Asad, Talal (1983) "Anthropological Conceptions of Religion: Reflections on Geertz," *Man* n.s. 18 (2): 237–59.

—— (1986) "The Idea of an Anthropology of Islam," Georgetown University, Center for Contemporary Arab Studies Occasional Papers Series.

—— (1993) *Genealogies of Religion: Discipline and Reasons of Power in Christianity and Islam*, Baltimore, MD: Johns Hopkins University Press.

Asamoah-Gyadu, Kwabena (2005) *African Charismatics: Independent Indigenous Pentecostalism in Ghana*, Leiden: E.J. Brill.

—— (2005a) "Of Faith and Visual Alertness: The Message of "Mediatized" Religion in an African Pentecostal Context, *Material Religion* 1 (3): 336–56.

Associated Press, The (2004) January 7, 2004: last update, "Russia marks Christmas with religious, secular celebrations," Homepage of beliefnet, Online. Available: HTTP://www.beliefnet.com/story/138/story138271.html (accessed October 1, 2007).

Attali, Jean (1977) *Bruits: Essai sur l'economie politique de la musique*, Paris: Presses Universitaires de France.

Babb, Lawrence A. and Susan S.Wadley (eds.) (1995). *Media and the Transformation of Religion in South Asia*, Philadelphia, PA: University of Pennsylvania Press.

Balsamo, Ann (1999) *Technologies of the Gendered Body: Reading Cyborg Women*, Durham, NC: Duke University Press.

Bantug, Ascuncion Lopez-Rizal, with Sylvia Mendez Ventura (1997) *Indio Bravo: The Story of José Rizal*, Makati City, Manila: Tahanan.

Barrett, Xian (2005) "Racial Pro-File." Online. Available. HTTP://yellowcontent.blogspot.com/2005/10/greys-anatomy.html.

Barthes, Roland (1981) *Camera Lucida: Reflections on Photography*, trans. Richard Howard, Berkeley, CA: University of California Press.

—— (1989) *The Rustle of Language*, trans. Richard Howard, Berkeley, CA: University of California Press.

—— (1989a) *The Semiotic Challenge,* trans. Richard Howard, New York: Hill and Wang.

Bataille, Georges (1985) "The Notion of Expenditure," in Bataille, *Visions of Excess: Selected Writings, 1927–1939*, Allan Stoekl (ed.) and trans. Allan Stoekl, Carl R. Lovitt and Donald M. Leslie, Jr., Minneapolis, MN: University of Minnesota Press.

—— (1991) *The Accursed Share: An Essay on General Economy*, 2 vols, trans. Robert Hurley, New York: Zone Books.

Baudrillard, Jean (1981) *For a Critique of the Political Economy of the Sign*, trans. Charles Levin, St. Louis, MO: Telos.

—— (1994) *Simulacra and Simulation*, trans. Sheila Faria Glaser, Ann Arbor, MI: University of Michigan Press.

—— (2001) "Simulacra and Simulations," in Mark Poster (ed.) *Selected Writings*, 2nd rev. ed., Stanford, CA: Stanford University Press, pp. 169–87.

Bauman, Zygmunt (2004) "Liquid Sociality," in Nicholas Gane (ed.) *The Future of Social Theory*, London and New York: Continuum.

Baumgarten, Alexander (1936 [1735]) *Aesthetica*, Barii: J. Laterza et filios.

Beal, Timothy K. (2005) *Roadside Religion*, Boston, MA: Beacon Press.

Beaujon, Andrew (2006) *Body Piercing Saved My Life: Inside the Phenomenon of Christian Rock*, Cambridge, MA: Da Capo Press.

Beck, Guy (1993) *Sonic Theology*, Columbia, SC: University of South Carolina Press.

—— (2006) "Hinduism and Music," in Guy Beck (ed.) *Sacred Sound. Experiencing Music in World Religions*, Waterloo, Ontario: Wilfried Laurier University Press, pp. 113–40.

Bediako, Kwame (1985) *Christianity in Africa: The Renewal of a Non-Western Religion*, Edinburgh: Edinburgh University Press.

Bell, Catherine (1992) *Ritual Theory, Ritual Practice*, New York: Oxford University Press.

Bender, Courtney (2003) *Heaven's Kitchen: Living Religion at God's Love We Deliver*, Chicago, IL: University of Chicago Press.

Benedict, Ruth (1959 [1934]) *Patterns of Culture*, Boston, MA: Houghton Mifflin.

Benjamin, Walter (1972–89), Rolf Tiedemann and Hermann Schweppenhäuser (eds.) *Gesammelte Schriften*, 7 vols, Frankfurt: Suhrkamp.

—— (1977) "Das Kunstwerk im Zeitalter seiner technischen Reproduzierbarkeit," in Walter Benjamin, *Illuminationen. Ausgewählte Schriften*, Frankfurt am Main: Suhrkamp, pp. 136–69.

—— (1996) "Capitalism as Religion," in Marcus Bullock and Michael W. Jennings (eds.) *Walter Benjamin: Selected Writings, Volume 1, 1913–1926*, Cambridge, MA: Harvard University Press.

—— (1999) "Reflections on Radio," in *Walter Benjamin: Selected Writings*, vol. 2, 1927–1934, Cambridge, MA: Harvard University Press, pp. 543–4.

Berger, Helen and Douglas Ezzy (2007) *Teenage Witches: Magical Youth and the Search for Self*, New Brunswick, NJ: Rutgers University Press.

Berger, John (1972) *Ways of Seeing*, London: Penguin Books.

Berger, Peter L. (1969) *The Sacred Canopy: Elements of a Sociological Theory of Religion*, Garden City, NY: Anchor Books.

Bloch, Ernst, Theodore W. Adorno and Georg Lukacs (1977) *Aesthetics and Politics*, Ronald Taylor (trans. and ed.), London: NLB.

Boltanski, Luc (1999) *Distant Suffering*, Cambridge: Cambridge University Press.

Bonnet, James (1999) *Stealing Fire from the Gods: A Dynamic New Story Model for Writers and Filmmakers*, Studio City, CA: Michael Wiese Productions.

Boorstin, Daniel J. (1992) *The Image: A Guide to Pseudo-Events in America*, New York: Vintage Books.

Borden, Anne L. (2007) "Making Money, Saving Souls: Christian bookstores and the commodification of Christianity," in Lynn Schofield Clark (ed.) *Religion, Media and the Marketplace*, New Brunswick, NJ: Rutgers University Press, pp. 67–89.

Bordwell, David (1985) *Narration in the Fiction Film*, Madison, WI: University of Wisconsin Press.

Borgmann, Albert (2003) *Power Failure: Christianity in the Culture of Technology*, Grand Rapids, MI: Brazos Press.

Bornstein, George (2001) *Material Modernism: The Politics of the Page*, Cambridge: Cambridge University Press.

Bourdieu, Pierre (1977) *Outline of a Theory of Practice*, trans. Richard Nice, Cambridge: Cambridge University Press.

—— (1984) *Distinction: A Social Critique of the Judgement of Taste*, trans. Richard Nice, Cambridge, MA: Harvard University Press.

—— (1990) *In Other Words: Essays toward a Reflexive Sociology*, Stanford, CA: Stanford University Press.

—— (1990a) *The Logic of Practice*, Cambridge: Polity Press.

—— (1993) *The Field of Cultural Production: Essays on Art and Literature*, New York: Columbia University Press.

Bowen, John R. (1993) *Muslims through Discourse: Religion and Ritual in Gayo Society*, Princeton, NJ: Princeton University Press.

—— (2007) *Why the French don't like Headscarves: Islam, the State, and Public Space*, Princeton, NJ: Princeton University Press.

Bowker, John (2005) *Oxford Concise Dictionary of World Religions*, Oxford: Oxford University Press.

Boyarin, Jonathan (1992) "Voices Around the Text: The Ethnography of Reading at Mesivta Tifereth Jerusalem," in Jonathan Boyarin (ed.) *The Ethnography of Reading*, Berkeley: University of California Press, pp. 212–37.

Bradley, Ian (1976) *The Call to Seriousness: The Evangelical Impact of the Victorians*, London: Jonathan Cape.

Bragg, Melvyn (2006) "The Media and the Church," in M.W. Brierley (ed.) *Public Life and the Place of the Church: Reflections to Honour the Bishop of Oxford*, Burlington, VT and Aldershot: Ashgate Publishing Company, pp. 57–63.

Brasher, Brenda (2004) *Give Me that On-Line Religion*, Brunswick, NJ: Rutgers University Press.

Brennan, Teresa and Martin Jay (eds.) (1996) *Vision in Context. Historical and Contemporary Perspectives on Sight*, New York and London: Routledge.

Brown, Candy Gunther (2004) *The Word in the World: Evangelical Writing, Publishing, and Reading in America, 1789–1880*, Chapel Hill, NC: University of North Carolina Press.

Bryson, Norman (1983) *Vision and Painting: The Logic of the Gaze*, London: Macmillan.

Buck-Morss, Susan (1992) "Aesthetics and Anaesthetics: Walter Benjamin's Art Works Essay Reconsidered," *October* 62: 3–41.

Bull, Michael, and Les Back (eds.) (2003) *The Auditory Culture Reader*, Oxford and New York: Berg.

Bullard, Asa (1866) "A Book for All the Children," *The Well-Spring* 23 (49), December 7: 196.

Burke, Kenneth (1961) *Attitudes Toward History*, Boston, MA: Beacon Press.

Burke, Peter (2001) *Eyewitnessing: The Uses of Images as Historical Evidence*, Ithaca, NY: Cornell University Press.

Burrows, David (1990) *Sound, Speech, Music*, Amherst, MA: University of Massachusetts Press.

Butler, Judith (1993) *Bodies that Matter: On the Discursive Limits of Sex*, New York: Routledge.

Calvin, John (1989) *Institutes of the Christian Religion*, trans. Henry Beveridge, Grand Rapids, MI: Eerdmans.

Campbell, Colin (1987) *The Romantic Ethic and the Spirit of Modern Consumerism*, Oxford: Blackwell.

Campbell, Heidi (2005) "Considering Spiritual Dimensions within Computer-mediated Communication Studies," *New Media and Society* 7 (1): 111–35.

Canton, William (1904) *A History of the British and Foreign Bible Society*, vol. 1, London: John Murray.

Carey, James W. (1975) "A Cultural Approach to Communication," *Communication* 2 (2): 1–25.

—— (1975a) "Communication and Culture," *Communication Research* 2 (2): 173–91.

—— (1989) *Communication as Culture: Essays on Media and Society*, Boston, MA: Unwin Hyman.

Carpenter, Edmund (1960) "Acoustic Space," in Edmund Carpenter and Marshall McLuhan (eds.) *Explorations in Communications,* Boston, MA: Beacon Press, pp. 65–70.

Casey, Edward (1987 [1976]) *Remembering. A Phenomenological Case Study*, Bloomington, IN: Indiana University Press.

Castells, Manuel (2000) *The Rise of Network Society*, Oxford: Blackwell Publishing.

Catholic Church (1999) *Catechism of the Catholic Church*, rev. ed., Ottawa: Publications Service, Canadian Conference of Catholic Bishops.

CBC News (2007) February 8: last update, *Indo-Canadian Mother killed in Surrey*, Homepage of cbc.ca. Online. Available: HTTP://www.cbc.ca/canada/british-columbia/story/2007/02/08/bc-murder.html?ref=rss (accessed October 1, 2007).

Chakrabarty, Dipesh (2000) *Provincializing Europe: Postcolonial Thought and Historical Difference*, Princeton, NJ: Princeton University Press.

Chartier, Roger (1989) "Texts, Printings, Readings," in Lynn Hunt (ed.) *The New Cultural History*, Berkeley, CA: University of California Press, pp. 154–75.

Chen, Chiung H. (2007) "Building the Pure Land on Earth: Ciji's Media Cultural Discourse," *Journal of Media and Religion* 6 (3): 181–99.

Chidester, David (1996) "The Church of Baseball, the Fetish of Coca-Cola, and the Potlatch of Rock 'n' Roll: Theoretical Models for the Study of Religion in American Popular Culture," *Journal of the American Academy of Religion* 64 (4): 743–65.

—— (2000) *Christianity: A Global History*, London: Penguin.

—— (2002) *Patterns of Transcendence: Religion, Death, and Dying*, 2nd ed., Belmont, CA: Wadsworth.

—— (2005) *Authentic Fakes: Religion and American Popular Culture*, Berkeley, CA: University of California Press.

Chouliaraki, Lilie (2006) *The Spectatorship of Suffering*, London and Thousand Oaks, CA: Sage.

Chow, May (2004) "Long Weekend Rites Fuel Demand for Hmong Funeral Homes: Sacred burial customs cause tension between Hmong and neighbors", AsianWeek.com, (accessed July 9).

Clark, Lynn Schofield (2003) *From Angels to Aliens: Teenagers, the Media, and the Supernatural*, New York: Oxford University Press.
—— (2007a) "Identity, Belonging, and Religious Lifestyle Branding (Fashion Bibles, Bhangra Parties, and Muslim Pop)," in Lynn Schofield Clark (ed.) *Religion, Media and the Marketplace*, New Brunswick, NJ: Rutgers University Press, pp. 1–33.
—— (ed.) (2007b) *Religion, Media and the Marketplace*, New Brunswick, NJ: Rutgers University Press.
Classen, Constance (1993) *Worlds of Sense: Exploring the Senses in History and across Cultures*, New York: Routledge.
Coakley, Sarah (ed.) (1997) *Religion and the Body*, New York: Cambridge University Press.
Coleman, Simon (2006) "Materializing the Self: Words and Gifts in the Construction of Evangelical Identity," in Fenella Cannell (ed.) *The Anthropology of Christianity*, Durham, NC: Duke University Press, pp. 163–84.
Collingwood, R.G. (Robin George) (2005) "Art and the Machine," in David Boucher, Wendy James, and Philip Smallwood (eds.) *The Philosophy of Enchantment: Studies in Folktale, Cultural Criticism, and Anthropology*, Oxford: Clarendon Press, pp. 291–304.
Comaroff, Jean and John L. Comaroff (1999) "Occult Economies and the Violence of Abstraction: Notes from the South African Postcolony," *American Ethnologist* 26 (3): 279–301.
—— (2000) "Millennial Capitalism: First Thoughts on a Second Coming," *Public Culture* 12 (2): 291–343.
Conner, Steven (1999) "The Machine in the Ghost: Spiritualism, Technology and the 'Direct Voice,'" in Peter Buse and Andrew Stott (eds.) *Ghosts: Deconstruction, Psychoanalysis, History*, London: Macmillan Press, pp. 203–25.
Corbin, Alain (1998) *Village Bells. Sound and Meaning in the 19th-century French Countryside*, New York: Columbia University Press.
Couldry, Nick (2003) *Media Rituals: A Critical Approach*, London: Routledge.
—— (2004) "Theorising Media as Practice," *Social Semiotics* 14 (2): 115–32.
—— (2008) "Form and Power in an Age of Continuous Spectacle," in David Hesmondhalgh and Jason Toynbee (eds.) *Media and Social Theory*, London: Open University Press, 2008.
Cox, Robert S (2003) *Body and Soul: A Sympathetic History of American Spiritualism*, Charlottesville, VA: University of Virginia Press.
Crary, Jonathan (2001) *Attention, Spectacle, and Modern Culture*, Boston, MA: MIT Press.
Cressy, David (1986) "Books as Totems in Seventeenth-Century England and New England," *Journal of Library History* 21: 92–106.
Danius, Sara (2002) *The Senses of Modernism: Technology, Perception, and Aesthetics*, Ithaca, NY: Cornell University Press.
Danner, Mark (2004) *Torture and Truth: America, Abu Ghraib, and the War on Terror*, New York: The New York Review of Books.
Dasa, Rasaraja (2007) "Declarations on a Grave." Online. Available. HTTP://www.weare108.com.

Davis, Erik (1995) "Technopagans: May the Astral Plane Be Reborn in Cyberspace." Online. Available. HTTP://www.techgnosis.com/technopagans.html.

—— (1998) *Techgnosis: Myth, Magic, and Mysticism in the Age of Information*, New York: Harmony Books.

Dayan, Daniel (2006) *La terreur spectacle. Terrorisme et télévision*, Brussels: De Boek.

Dayan, Daniel and Elihu Katz (1994) "Defining Media Events: High Holidays of Mass Communication," in Horace Newcomb (ed.) *Television: The Critical View*, 5th ed., New York: Oxford University Press, pp. 332–51.

De Abreu, Maria José (2005) "Breathing into the Heart of the Matter: Why Padre Marcelo Needs No Wings," *Postscripts* 1 (2/3): 325–49.

De Certeau, Michel (1984) *The Practice of Everyday Life*, trans. Steven Rendall, Berkeley, CA: University of California Press.

Denton, William (1888) *The Soul of Things: Or, Psychometric Researches and Discoveries*, 8th ed., Wellesley, MA: Denton Publishing Company.

Deocampo, Nick (2007) *Cine: Spanish Influences on Early Cinema in the Philippines*, Manila: Anvil.

De Vries, Hent (2001) "In Media Res: Global Religion, Public Spheres, and the Task of Contemporary Religious Studies," in Hent de Vries and Samuel Weber (eds.) *Religion and Media*, Stanford, CA: Stanford University Press, pp. 4–42.

De Vries, Hent (ed.) (2007) *Religion, Beyond the Concept*, New York: Fordham University Press.

De Vries, Hent and Samuel Webe (eds.) (2001) *Religion and Media*, Stanford, CA: Stanford University Press.

De Witte, Marleen (2003) "Altar Media's *Living Word:* Televised Charismatic Christianity in Ghana," *Journal of Religion in Africa* 33 (2): 172–202.

—— (2005) "The Spectacular and the Spirits: Charismatics and Neo-Traditionalists on Ghanaian Television," *Material Religion* 1 (3): 314–35.

Diawara, Mamadou (2003) *L'Empire du verbe et l'eloquence du silence*, Cologne: Ruediger Koeppe Verlag.

Dickey, Sara (1997) "Anthropology and its Contributions to the Study of Mass Media," *International Social Science Journal* 153: 413–427.

Doniger, Wendy (2000) "Post-modern and -colonial -structural Comparisons," in Kimberley C. Patton and Benjamin C. Ray (eds.) *A Magic Still Dwells: Comparative Religion in the Postmodern Age*, Berkeley, CA: University of California Press, pp. 63–74.

Doss, Erika (2006) "Spontaneous Memorials and Contemporary Modes of Mourning in America," *Material Religion* 2 (3): 294–319.

Douglas, Mary (2002[1966]) *Purity and Danger: An Analysis of Concepts of Pollution and Taboo*, New York: Routledge.

Dufrenne, Mikel (1973) *The Phenomenology of Aesthetic Experience*, Evanston, IL: Northwestern University Press.

During, Simon (2002) *Modern Enchantments: The Cultural and Secular Power of Magic*, Cambridge, MA: Harvard University Press.

Durkheim, Emile (1995) *The Elementary Forms of Religious Life*, trans. Karen E. Fields, New York: Free Press.

Economist, The (2007) September 27, "Burma's Saffron Revolution."

Edwards, Jonathan (1959) *A Treatise on the Religious Affections*, ed. John E. Smith, vol. 2 of *The Works of Jonathan Edwards*, New Haven, CT: Yale University Press.

Edwards, Mark. U. Jr. (1994) *Printing, Propaganda and Martin Luther*, Berkeley, CA: University of California Press.

Eickelman, Dale F. and Jon W. Anderson (eds.) (1999) *New Media in the Muslim World: The Emerging Public Sphere*, Bloomington, IN: Indiana University Press.

Eickelman, Dale F. and Jon W. Anderson (2003) *New Media in the Muslim World: The Emerging Public Sphere*, 2nd edn, Bloomington, IN: Indiana University Press.

Eisenstein, Elizabeth (1979) *The Printing Press as an Agent of Change: Communications and Cultural Transformations in Early Modern Europe*, 2 vols, Cambridge: Cambridge University Press.

Elkins, James (1996) *The Object Stares Back: On the Nature of Seeing*, San Diego, CA: Harcourt.

Elkins, James and David Morgan (eds.) (2008) *Re-Enchantment*, New York: Routledge.

Ellens, J. Harold (1974) *Models of Religious Broadcasting*, Grand Rapids, MI: Eerdmans.

Ellul, Jacques (1964) *The Technological Society*, New York: Vintage Books.

Engelke, Matthew (2007) *A Problem of Presence: Beyond Scripture in an African Church*, Berkeley, CA: University of California Press.

Fabian, Johannes (1983) *Time and the Other: How Anthropology Makes Its Object*, New York: Columbia University Press.

Fadiman, Anne (1997) *The Spirit Catches You and You Fall Down: A Hmong Child, Her American Doctors, and the Collision of Two Cultures*, New York: Farrar, Straus and Giroux.

Feher, Michel, with Ramona Naddaff and Nadia Tazi (eds.) (1989) *Fragments for a History of the Human Body*, New York: Zone; Cambridge, MA: MIT Press.

Feld, Steven (1991) "Sound as a Symbolic System: The Kaluli Drum," in David Howes (ed.) *The Varieties of Sensory Experience*, Toronto: University of Toronto Press, pp. 79–99.

—— (1996) "Waterfalls of Song: An Acoustemology of Place Resounding in Bosavi, Papua Guinea," in Steven Feld and Keith Basso (eds.) *Senses of Place*, Santa Fe, NM: School of American Research Press, pp. 91–135.

Fiske, John (1987) *Television Culture*, London: Routledge.

Foltz, Richard (2007) "'The Religion of the Market': Reflections on a Decade of Discussions," *Worldviews* 11: 135–54.

Fore, William F. (1987) *Television and Religion: The Shaping of Faith, Values, and Culture*, Minneapolis, MN: Augsburg.

Fossum, John E. and Philip Schlesinger (2007) *The European Union and the Public Sphere: A Communicative Space in the Making?* London: Routledge.

Foucault, Michel (1986) "Of Other Spaces," *Diacritics* 16 (1): 22–7.

Foxtrot (2000) www.nettoilet.com/users/memorial (accessed November 13, 2000).

Frankenberry, Nancy K. and Hans H. Penner (1999) "Clifford Geertz's Long-Lasting Moods, Motivations, and Metaphysical Conceptions," *Journal of Religion* 79 (4): 617–40.

Frankl, Razelle (1987) *Televangelism: The Marketing of Popular Religion*, Carbondale, IL: Southern Illinois University Press.

Fraser, Nancy (2005) "Rethinking Recognition," in Pepi Leistyna (ed.) *Cultural Studies from Theory to Action*, Oxford: Blackwell Publishing.

Freedberg, David (1989) *The Power of Images: Studies in the History and Theory of Response*, Chicago, IL: University of Chicago Press.

Funkenstein, Amos (1989) *Theology and the Scientific Imagination from the Middle Ages to the Seventeenth Century*, Princeton, NJ: Princeton University Press.

Gamble, H.Y. (1995) *Books and Readers in the Early Church: A History of Early Christian Texts*, New Haven, CT: Yale University Press.

Geertz, Clifford (1973) *The Interpretation of Cultures*, New York: Basic Books.

Gell, Alfred (1988) "Technology and Magic," *Anthropology Today* 4 (2): 6–9.

Giddens, Anthony (1991) *Modernity and Self-Identity: Self and Society in the Late Modern Age*, Stanford, CA: Stanford University Press.

Ginsburg, Carlo (1980) *The Cheese and the Worms: The Cosmos of a Sixteenth-Century Miller*, trans. Ann and John Tedeschi, New York: Penguin.

Ginsburg, Faye (1999) "Shooting Back: From Ethnographic Film to Indigenous Production/ethnography of Media," in Toby Miller and Robert Stam (eds.) *A Companion to Film Theory*, New York: Blackwell, pp. 295–322.

—— (2002) "Mediating Culture: Indigenous Media, Ethnographic Film, and the Production of Identity," in Kelly Askew and Richard R. Wilk (eds.) *The Anthropology of Media: A Reader*, Oxford: Blackwell, pp. 210–35

—— (2005) "Re-thinking the 'Voice of God' in Indigenous Australia: Secrecy, Exposure and the Efficacy of Media," in Birgit Meyer and Annelies Moors (eds.) *Religion, Media, and the Public Sphere*, Bloomington, IN: Indiana University Press, pp. 188–204.

Ginsburg, Faye, Lila Abu-Lughod and Brian Larkin (eds.) (2002) *Media Worlds: Anthropology on New Terrain*, Berkeley, CA: University of California Press.

Gitelman, Lisa (1999) *Scripts, Grooves, and Writing Machines: Representing Technology in the Edison Era*, Stanford, CA: Stanford University Press.

—— (2006) *Always Already New: Media, History, and the Data of Culture*, Boston, MA: MIT Press.

Gitelman, Lisa and Geoffrey B. Pingree (2003) *New Media, 1740–1915*, Cambridge, MA: MIT Press.

Goethals, Gregor T. (1981) *The TV Ritual: Worship at the Video Altar*, Boston, MA: Beacon Press.

—— (1990) *The Electronic Golden Calf: Images, Religion, and the Making of Meaning*, Cambridge, MA: Cowley.

Goody, Jack (2000) *The Power of the Written Tradition*, Washington, DC: Smithsonian Institution.

Gouk, Penelope (1991) "Some English Theories of Hearing in the Seventeenth Century: Before and After Descartes," in Charles Burnett, Michael Fend and

Penelope Gouk (eds.) *The Second Sense*, London: The Warburg Institute, University of London, pp. 95–113.

Goux, Jean-Joseph (1990) *Symbolic Economies: After Marx and Freud*, Ithaca, NY: Cornell University Press.

Graham, Elaine (2002) *Representations of the Post/Human: Monsters, Aliens and Others in Popular Culture*, Manchester: Manchester University Press.

Greenfield, Liah and Michel Martin (eds.) (1988) *Center: Ideas and Institutions*, Chicago, IL: University of Chicago Press.

Gregory, C.A. (1982) *Gifts and Commodities*, London: Academic Press.

Griffith, R. Marie (1997) *God's Daughters: Evangelical Women and the Power of Submission*, Berkeley, CA: University of California Press.

Grimes, Ronald. L. (1995) *Beginnings in Ritual Studies*, rev. edn, Columbia, SC: University of South Carolina Press.

Guthrie, Stewart Elliott (1993) *Faces in the Clouds: A New Theory of Religion*, New York: Oxford University Press.

Gutjahr, Paul (2001) "Sacred Texts in the United States: The State of the Discipline," *Book History* 4: 335–70.

Habermas, Jürgen (1991) *The Structural Transformation of the Public Sphere: An Inquiry into a Category of Bourgeois Society*, Cambridge, MA: MIT Press.

Hackett, Rosalind I.J. (1998) "Charismatic/Pentecostal Appropriation of Media Technologies in Nigeria and Ghana," *Journal of Religion in Africa* 28 (3): 1–19.

—— (2000) "Religious Freedom and Religious Conflict in Africa," in Mark Silk (ed.) *Religion on the International News Agenda*, Hartford, CT: The Leonard E. Greenberg Center for the Study of Religion in Public Life, pp. 102–14.

—— (2006) "Mediated Religion in South Africa: Balancing Airtime and Rights Claims," in Birgit Meyer and Annelies Moors (eds.) *Religion, Media and the Public Sphere*, Bloomington, IN: Indiana University Press, pp. 166–87.

Hadden, Jeffrey K. and Charles E. Swan (1981) *Prime Time Preachers*, Reading, MA: Addison-Wesley.

Hall, David (1989) *Worlds of Wonder, Days of Judgment: Popular Religious Belief in Early New England*, New York: Alfred Knopf.

—— (1997) *Lived Religion in America: Toward a History of Practice*, Princeton, NJ: Princeton University Press.

Hall, Stuart (1980) "Cultural Studies: Two Paradigms," *Media, Culture & Society* 6: 57–72.

—— (1980a) "Encoding/Decoding," in Stuart Hall *et al.* (eds.) *Culture, Media, and Language: Working Papers in Cultural Studies, 1972–1979*, London: Hutchinson, pp. 128–38.

—— (1981) "Notes on Deconstructing 'the Popular,'" in Raphael Samuel (ed.) *People's History and Socialist Theory*, London: Routledge.

—— (1985) "Signification, Representation, Ideology: Althusser and the Post-structuralist Debates," *Critical Studies in Mass Communication* 2: 91–114.

Hammond, Phillip (1999) "Can Religion be Religious in Public?" in William H. Swatos and James K. Wellman (eds.) *The Power of Religious Publics: Staking Claims in American Society*, Westport, CT: Praeger Publishers, pp. 19–31.

Hangen, Tona J. (2002) *Redeeming the Dial: Radio, Religion, and Popular Culture in America*, Chapel Hill, NC: University of North Carolina Press.

Hankins, Thomas and Robert Silverman (1995) *Instruments and the Imagination*, Princeton, NJ: Princeton University Press.

Hanks, W. F. (1989) "Text and Textuality," *Annual Review of Anthropology* 18: 95–127.

Hansen, Miriam (1993) "Of Mice and Ducks: Benjamin and Adorno on Disney," *The South Atlantic Quarterly* 92 (1): 27–61.

Haraway, Donna (1991) *Simians, Cyborgs and Women: The Reinvention of Nature*, New York: Routledge.

Hastings, Adrian (1994) *The Church in Africa 1450–1930*, Oxford: Clarendon.

Hatch, Nathan O. (1983) "Elias Smith and the Rise of Religious Journalism in the Early Republic," in William L. Joyce *et al.* (eds.) *Printing and Society in Early America*, Worcester, MA: American Antiquarian Society, pp. 250–77.

Hawley, John S. (1995) "The Saints Subdued: Domestic Virtue and National Integration in *Amar Chitra Katha*," in Lawrence A. Babb and Susan S. Wadley (eds.) *Media and the Transformation of Religion in South Asia*, Philadelphia, PA: University of Pennsylvania Press, pp. 107–34.

Hayes, David P. (2007) *The Production Code of the Motion Picture Industry*. Available: HTTP://prodcode.dhwritings.com/index.php (accessed October 1, 2007).

Heidegger, Martin (1977) *The Question Concerning Technology, and Other Essays*, New York: Harper.

Hendershot, Heather (2004) *Shaking the World for Jesus: Media and Conservative Evangelical Culture*, Chicago, IL: University of Chicago Press.

Henríquez, Juan Carlos (ed.) (2007) *Medios y Creencias: Perspectivas Culturales del Cristianismo en el Entorno Mediático*, Mexico: Universidad Iberoamericana and Madrid: Plaza y Valdés, S.A. de C.V.

Herman, David (ed.) (2007) *The Cambridge Companion to Narrative*, Cambridge: Cambridge University Press.

Hertenstein, M. (2006) "Days of the Dead: A Report from Imaginarium 2006." Online. Available. HTTP://www.cornerstonefestival.com/imaginarium.

Hertz, Todd (2003) "Jesus' Woodstock," *Christianity Today*, July 1. Online. Available. HTTP://www.christianitytoday.com/ct/2003/july/5.46.html.

Hilmes, Michelle (1997) *Radio Voices: American Broadcasting, 1922–1952*, Minneapolis, MN: University of Minnesota Press.

Hirsch, Paul (1978) "The Relevance of Humanistic Models to Communication Research," *Communication Research* 5 (3): 235–9.

Hirschkind, Charles (2006) *The Ethical Soundscape: Cassette Sermons and Islamic Counterpublics*, New York: Columbia University Press.

Hofmeyr, Isabel (2004) *The Portable Bunyan: A Transnational History of The Pilgrim's Progress*, Princeton, NJ: Princeton University Press.

—— (2006) "Books in Heaven: Dreams, Texts and Conspicuous Circulation," *Current Writing* 18 (2): 136–49.

Hoover, Stewart M. (1988) *Mass Media Religion: The Social Sources of the Electronic Church*, Newbury Park, CA: Sage.

—— (2003) "Religion, Media and Identity: Theory and Method in Audience Research," in Jolyon Mitchell and Sophia Marriage (eds.) *Mediating Religion: Conversations in Media, Religion and Culture*, London: T&T Clark, pp. 9–19.

—— (2006) *Religion in the Media Age*, London: Routledge.

Hoover, Stewart M. and Knut Lundby (eds.) (1997) *Rethinking Media, Religion, and Culture*, Thousand Oaks, CA: Sage.

Hoover, Stewart M. and Lynn Schofield Clark (eds.) (2002) *Practicing Religion in the Age of the Media: Explorations in Media, Religion, and Culture*, New York: Columbia University Press.

Hoover, Stewart M., Lynn Schofield Clark and Diane F. Alters (2004) *Media, Home, and Family*, New York: Routledge.

"Hope for the Rejected" (2007). Online. Available. HTTP://www.hopefortherejected.org.

Horkheimer, Max and Theodor W. Adorno (1973) *The Dialectic of Enlightenment*, trans. John Cumming, London: Verso.

Horsfield, Peter G. (1984) *Religious Television: The American Experience*, New York: Longman.

Horsfield, Peter, Mary E. Hess and Adán M. Medrano (eds.) (2004) *Belief in Media: Cultural Perspectives on Media and Christianity*, Aldershot: Ashgate.

Howes, David (1991) "Introduction. 'To Summon all the Senses,'" in David Howes (ed.) *The Varieties of Sensory Experience. A Sourcebook in the Anthropology of the Senses*, Toronto: University of Toronto Press, pp. 3–21.

—— (2004) "Sound Thinking," in Jim Drobnick (ed.) *Aural Cultures*, Toronto: YYZ Books, pp. 240–51.

Howsam, Lesley (1991) *Cheap Bibles: Nineteenth-Century Publishing and the British and Foreign Bible Society*, Cambridge: Cambridge University Press.

Huesmann, L. Rowell, Jessica Moise-Titus, Cheryl-Lynn Podolski and Leonard D. Eron (2003) "Longitudinal Relations between Children's Exposure to TV Violence and Their Aggressive and Violent Behavior in Young Adulthood: 1977–1992," *Developmental Psychology* 39 (2): 201–21.

Idhe, Don (1976) *Listening and Voice: A Phenomenology of Listening*, Athens, OH: Ohio University Press.

Innis, Harold A. (1950) *Empire and Communications*, Toronto: University of Toronto Press.

—— (1951) *The Bias of Communication*, Toronto: University of Toronto Press.

Jain, Kajri (2007) *Gods in the Bazaar: The Economies of Indian Calendar Art*, Durham, NC: Duke University Press.

James, Liz (2004) "Senses and Sensibility in Byzantium," *Art History* 27 (4): 523–37.

Jay, Martin (1988) "Scopic Regimes of Modernity," in Hal Foster (ed.) *Vision and Visuality*, Seattle, WA: Bay Press, pp. 3–28.

Jenkins, Henry (1992) *Textual Poachers: Television Fans and Participatory Culture*, London: Routledge.

Jensen, Klaus Bruhn (1987) "Qualitative Audience Research: Toward an Integrative Approach to Reception," *Critical Studies in Mass Communication* 4: 21–36.

Johns, Adrian (1996) "The Physiology of Reading and the Anatomy of Enthusiasm," in Ole Peter Grell and Andrew Cunningham (eds.) *Religio Medici: Medicine and Religion in Seventeenth Century England*, Aldershot: Scolar, pp. 136–70.

Johnson, Pauline (2006) *Habermas: Rescuing the Public Sphere*, London: Routledge.

Kant, Immanuel (1951) *Critique of Judgment*, trans. J.H. Bernard, New York: Hafner Publishing Company.

—— (2001 [1790]) *Kritik der Urteilskraft*, Heiner F. Klemme (ed.), Hamburg: Felix Meiner Verlag.

Keane, John (1995) "Structural Transformations of the Public Sphere," *The Communication Review* 1 (1): 1–22.

Keane, Webb (2007) *Christian Moderns: Freedom and Fetish in the Mission Encounter*, Berkeley, CA: University of California Press.

Kelly, James R. (1999) "Conserving Religious Identity While Doing Public Theology: On Public Churches and Common Ground," in William H. Swatos and James K. Wellman (eds.) *The Power of Religious Publics: Staking Claims in American Society*, Westport, CT: Praeger Publishers, pp. 115–29.

Kellner, Douglas (2007) "The Time of the Spectacle," in Matteo Stocchetti and Johanna Sumiala-Seppanen (eds.) *Images and Communities: The Visual Construction of the Social*, Helsinki: Gaudemus, Helsinki University Press, pp. 27–51,

Klassen, Pamela (2006) "Textual Healing: Mainstream Protestants and the Therapeutic Text, 1900–1925," *Church History* 75 (4): 809–48.

—— (2007) "Radio Mind: Christian Experimentalists on the Frontiers of Healing," *Journal of the American Academy of Religion* 75 (3): 651–83.

Knight, Michael Muhammad (2007) *The Five Percenters: Islam, Hip-Hop and the God of New York*, Oxford: Oneworld Publications.

Kreiling, Albert (1978) "Toward a Cultural Studies Approach for the Sociology of Popular Culture," *Communication Research* 5 (3): 240–63.

Kuhns, William (1969) *The Electronic Gospel: Religion and Media*, New York: Herder and Herder.

LaFleur, William (1998) "Body," in Mark C. Taylor (ed.) *Critical Terms for Religious Studies*, Chicago, IL: University of Chicago Press, pp. 36–54.

Lange, Yvonne (1974) "Lithography, an Agent of Technological Change in Religious Folk Art: A Thesis," *Western Folklore* 33 (1): 51–64.

Laplanche, Jean and Jean-Bertrand Pontalis (2006 [1973]) *The Language of Psychoanalysis*, London: Karnac Books.

Larkin, Brian (2001) "Notes on Media and the Materiality of Qur'an Recitation," paper presented at the Media, Religion, and the Public Sphere Conference, Amsterdam.

—— (2007) *Signal and Noise: Technology, Infrastructure, and Culture in Northern Nigeria*, Durham, NC: Duke University Press.

Lash, Scott and John Urry (1994) *Economies of Signs and Space*, London: Sage.

Latour, Bruno (1987) *Science in Action: How to follow Scientists and Engineers through Society*, Milton Keynes: Open University Press.

—— (1988) *The Pasteurization of France*, Cambridge MA: Harvard University Press.

—— (1993) *We Have Never Been Modern*, Cambridge, MA: Harvard University Press.

—— (1997) "Where Are the Missing Masses? The Sociology of a Few Mundane Artifacts," in Wiebe Bijker and John Law (eds.) *Shaping Technology/Building Society: Studies in Sociotechnical Change*, Cambridge, MA: MIT Press, pp. 225–58.

—— (1999) *Pandora's Hope: Essays on the Reality of Science Studies*, Cambridge, MA: Harvard University Press.

—— (2005) *Reassembling the Social. An Introduction to Actor-Network-Theory*, Oxford: Oxford University Press.

—— (2007) *Beware, Your Imagination Leaves Digital Traces*. On-line. Available. HTTP://bruno.latour.name

Latour, Bruno and Peter Weibel (eds.) (2002) *Iconoclash: Beyond the Image Wars in Science, Religion, and Art*, Karlsruhe: Center for Art and Media; Cambridge, MA: The MIT Press.

Lears, T. J. Jackson (1994) *Fables of Abundance: A Cultural History of Advertising in America*, New York: Basic Books.

Lefebvre, Henri (1966) *Sociologie de Marx*, Paris: Presses Universitaires de France.

—— (2002) *Critique of Everyday Life*, vol. 2, New York: Verso.

Lehikoinen, Taisto (2003). *Religious Media Theory: Understanding Mediated Faith and Christian Applications to Modern Media*, Jyvaskyla: Jyvaskyla University Press.

Lewis, J. (2005) *Language Wars: The Role of Media and Culture in Global and Political Violence*, London: Pluto Press.

Lincoln, Bruce (2000) "Culture," in Willi Braun and Russell T. McCutcheon (eds.) *Guide to the Study of Religion*, London and New York: Cassell, pp. 409–22.

Lippmann, Walter (1922) *Public Opinion*, New York: Harcourt, Brace.

Lister, Martin *et al.* (eds.) (2003) *New Media: A Critical Introduction*, London and New York: Routledge.

Litz, Dwayna (2006) "Lighting the Way Worldwide." Online. Available. HTTP://lightingtheway.blogspot.com/2006/07/days-of-dead-at-cornerstone-christian.html.

Liu, Lydia (1999) "The Question of Meaning-Value in the Political Economy of the Sign," in Lydia Liu (ed.) *Tokens of Exchange: The Problem of Translation in Global Circulations*, Durham, NC: Duke University Press, pp. 13–42.

Lopez, Donald S. Jr. (1998) "Belief," in Mark C. Taylor (ed.) *Critical Terms for Religious Studies*, Chicago, IL: University of Chicago Press, pp. 21–35.

—— (1999) *Asian Religions in Practice*, Princeton, NJ: Princeton University Press.

Lotfalian, Mazyar (2004) *Islam, Technoscientific Identities and the Culture of Curiosity*, Lanham, MD: University Press of America.

Lövheim, Mia (2006) "A Space Set Apart? Young People Exploring the Sacred on the Internet" in Johanna Sumiala-Seppänen, Knut Lundby, and Raimo Salokangas (eds.) *Implications of the Sacred in (Post)Modern Media*, Sweden: Nordicom, pp. 255–72.

Loy, David (1997) "The Religion of the Market," *Journal of the American Academy of Religion* 65 (2): 275–90.

Lundquist, Kathleen (2006) "My Summer Vacation and Its Aftermath." Online. Available. HTTP://kathleenlundquist.blogspot.com/20060701archive.html.

Lury, Celia (1998) *Prosthetic Culture. Photography, Memory and Identity*, London and New York: Routledge.

Luther, Martin (1958) *Against the Heavenly Prophets in the Matter of Images and Sacraments* (1525), in *Luther's Works*, Philadelphia, PA: Muhlenberg Press, vol. 40.

Lynch, Gordon (ed.) (2007) *Between Sacred and Profane: Researching Religion and Popular Culture*, London: I.B. Tauris.

Lyotard, Jean François (1993) *The Libidinal Economy*, trans. Iain Hamilton Grant, Bloomington, IN: Indiana University Press.

McCartney, Andra (2004) "Soundscape Works, Listening, and the Touch of Sound," in Jim Drobnick (ed.) *Aural Cultures*, Toronto, Ontario: YYZ Books, pp. 179–89.

McClintock, Anne (1995) *Imperial Leather: Race, Gender and Sexuality in the Colonial Contest*, New York: Routledge.

McCracken, Grant (1988) *Culture and Consumption: New Approaches to the Symbolic Character of Consumer Goods and Activities*, Bloomington, IN: Indiana University Press.

McDannell, Colleen (ed.) (2001) *Religions of the United States in Practice*, vol. 2., Princeton, NJ: Princeton University Press.

MacDougall, David (2006) *The Corporeal Image: Film, Ethnography, and the Senses*, Princeton, NJ: Princeton University Press.

McLellan, David (1977) *Karl Marx: Selected Writings*, New York: Oxford University Press.

McLuhan, Marshall (1964) *Understanding Media: The Extensions of Man*, New York: Signet.

McNally, Michael D. (2000) *Ojibwe Singers: Hymns, Grief, and a Native Culture in Motion*, Oxford: Oxford University Press.

McQuail, Denis (1994) *Mass Communication Theory: An Introduction*, 3rd edn, London: Sage.

Macherey, Pierre ([1966] 1978) *A Theory of Literary Production*, New York: Routledge.

Mack, Beverly and Jean Boyd (2004) *One Woman's Jihad. Nana Asma'u, Scholar and Scribe*, Bloomington, IN: Indiana University Press.

Maffesoli, Michel (1996) *The Contemplation of the World. Figures of Community Style*, Minneapolis, MN and London: University of Minnesota Press.

Maffly-Kipp, Laurie F., Leigh E. Schmidt and Mark Valeri (eds.) (2006) *Practicing Protestants: Histories of Christian Life in America, 1630–1965*, Baltimore, MD: Johns Hopkins University Press.

Mahar, Cheleen, Richard Harker and Chris Wilkes (1990) "The Basic Theoretical Position," in Richard Harker, Cheleen Mahar and Chris Wilkes (eds.) *An Introduction to the Work of Pierre Bourdieu: The Theory of Practice*, London: Macmillan.

Maria, Felice Prudente Sta. (1996) *In Excelsis*, Manila: Studio Five Designs.

Marks, Laura (2000) *The Skin of Film: Intercultural Cinema, Embodiment and the Senses*, Durham, NC: Duke University Press.

Martín-Barbero, Jesús (1987/1993) *De los medios a las mediaciones: Comunicación, cultura y hegemonía*, Barcelona and Mexico City: Ediciones G. Gili. Translation: *Communication, Culture, and Hegemony: From the Media to Mediations*, trans. Elizabeth Fox and Robert A. White, London: Sage, 1993.

—— (1997) "Mass Media as a Site of Resacralization of Contemporary Cultures," in Stewart M. Hoover and Knut Lundby (eds.) *Rethinking Media, Religon, and Culture*, pp. 102–16.

Marty, Martin E. (1961) *The Improper Opinion: Mass Media and the Christian Faith*, Philadelphia, PA: Westminster.

—— (1999) "The *the* Public and the Public's Publics," in William H. Swatos and James K. Wellman (eds.) *The Power of Religious Publics: Staking Claims in American Society*, Westport, CT: Praeger Publishers, pp. 1–18.

Marx, Karl (1954 [1867]) *Capital*, 2 vols, trans. Samuel Moore and Edward Aveling, Moscow: Progress.

—— (1970 [1859]) *A Contribution to the Critique of Political Economy*, in Karl Marx and Friedrich Engels, *Selected Works*, Moscow: Progress.

Marx, Leo (1991) "The Idea of Technology and Postmodern Pessimism," in Merritt Roe Smith and Leo Marx (eds.) *Does Technology Drive History? The Dilemma of Technological Determinism*, Cambridge, MA: MIT Press, pp. 237–57.

Masuzawa, Tomoko (1998) "Culture," in Mark C. Taylor (ed.) *Critical Terms for Religious Studies*, Chicago, IL: University of Chicago Press, pp. 70–93.

Mathewes, Charles T. (2006) "Religion and Secrecy," *Journal of the American Academy of Religion* 74 (2): 273–482.

Mauss, Marcel (1969) *The Gift: Forms and Functions of Exchange in Archaic Societies*, trans. Ian Cunnison, London: Cohen & West.

May, Meredith (2004) "R.I.P. Shirts Become an Urban Tradition," *San Francisco Chronicle*, October 24, p. A1.

Mazzarella, William (2004) "Culture, Globalization, Mediation," *Annual Review of Anthropology* 33: 345–67.

Mendieta, Eduardo (2006) "Introduction," *The Frankfurt School on Religion: Key Writings by the Major Thinkers*, New York: Routledge, pp. 1–17.

Merleau-Ponty, Maurice (1945) *Phénoménologie de la perception*, Paris: Gallimard.

—— (2002 [1948]) *Causeries*, Stéphanie Ménasé (ed.), Paris: Seuil.

Merton, Robert (1957) "Studies in the Sociology of Science," in Robert Merton (ed.) *Social Theory and Social Structure*, rev. edn, New York: The Free Press, pp. 531–627.

Meyer, Birgit (1999) *Translating the Devil: Religion and Modernity among the Ewe in Ghana*, Edinburgh: University of Edinburgh Press.

—— (2003) "Impossible Representations: Pentecostalism, Vision and Video Technology in Ghana," in *Working Papers*, number 25, Institut für Ethnologie und Afrikastudien, Johannes Gutenburg Universität, Mainz.

—— (2004) " 'Praise the Lord...': Popular Cinema and Pentecostalite Style in Ghana's New Public Sphere," *American Ethnologist* 31 (1): 92–110.

—— (2005) "Religious Remediations: Pentecostal Views in Ghanaian Video-Movies," *Postscripts* 1 (2/3): 155–81.

—— (2006) "Religious Revelation, Secrecy, and the Limits of Visual Representation," *Anthropological Theory* 6 (4): 431–53.

—— (2006a) *Religious Sensations: Why Media, Aesthetics, and Power Matter in the Study of Contemporary Religion*, Professorial Inaugural Address, Amsterdam: Faculty of Social Sciences, Free University.

Meyer, Birgit and Annelies Moors (eds.) (2006) *Religion, Media, and the Public Sphere*, Bloomington, IN: Indiana University Press.

Meyer, Birgit and Peter Pels (eds.) (2003) *Magic and Modernity: Interfaces of Revelation and Concealment*, Stanford, CA: Stanford University Press.

Meyer, Richard (ed.) (2003) *Representing the Passions. Histories, Bodies, Visions*, Los Angeles, CA: The Getty Research Institute.

Meyrowitz, Jerome (1994) "Medium Theory," in David Crowley and David Mitchell (eds.) *Communication Theory Today*, Cambridge: Polity Press.

Michael [no surname] (2000). Online. Available. HTTP://www.nettoilet.com/users/memorial.

Miller, Daniel and Don Slater (2000) *The Internet: An Ethnographic Approach*, Oxford and New York: Berg.

Milspaw, Yvonne J. (1986) "Protestant Home Shrines: Icon and Image," *New York Folklore* 12 (3–4): 119–36.

Mirzoeff, Nicholas (1999) *An Introduction to Visual Culture*, London: Routledge.

Mitcham, Carl (1994) *Thinking through Technology: The Path between Engineering and Philosophy*, Chicago, IL: University of Chicago Press.

Mitchell, Jolyon (1999) *Visually Speaking: Radio and the Renaissance of Preaching*, Edinburgh: T&T Clark.

—— (ed.) (2005) "Christianity and Television," special issue of *Studies in World Christianity* 11 (1): 1–8.

—— (2006) "Posting Images on the Web: The Creative Viewer and Non-violent Resistance against Terrorism," *Material Religion* 2 (2): 146–73.

—— (2007) *Media Violence and Christian Ethics*, Cambridge: Cambridge University Press.

Mitchell, Jolyon and Sophia Marriage (eds.) (2003) *Mediating Religion: Conversations in Media, Religion and Culture*, London: T&T Clark.

Mitchell, W. J. T. (1994) *Picture Theory: Essays on Verbal and Visual Representation*, Chicago, IL: University of Chicago Press.

—— (2005) "There are No Visual Media," *Journal of Visual Culture* 4 (2): 257–66.

—— (2005a) *What Do Pictures Want? The Lives and Loves of Images*, Chicago, IL: University of Chicago Press.

Moore, Lawrence (1994) *Selling God: American Religion in the Marketplace of Culture*, New York: Oxford University Press.

Morgan, David (1998) *Visual Piety: A History and Theory of Popular Religious Images*, Berkeley, CA: University of California Press.

—— (1998a) "Notes on Meaning and Medium in the Aesthetics of Visual Piety," unpublished paper.

—— (1999) *Protestants and Pictures: Religion, Visual Culture, and the Age of American Mass Production*, New York: Oxford University Press.

—— (2005) *The Sacred Gaze: Religious Visual Culture in Theory and Practice*, Berkeley, CA: University of California Press.

—— (2007) *The Lure of Images: A History of Religion and Visual Media in America*, London: Routledge.

—— (2007a) "The Visual Construction of the Sacred," in Matteo Stocchetti and Johanna Sumiala-Seppänen (eds.) *Images and Communities: The Visual Construction of the Social*, Helsinki: Gaudeamus, Helsinki University Press.

Morgan, David and Sally M. Promey (eds.) (2001) *The Visual Culture of American Religions*, Berkeley, CA: University of California Press.

Morgan, John H. (1977) "Religion and Culture as Meaning Systems: A Dialogue between Geerts and Tillich," *The Journal of Religion* 57 (4): 363–75.

Morris, Rosalind C. (2000) *In the Place of Origins: Modernity and Its Mediums in Northern Thailand*, Durham, NC: Duke University Press.

Morus, Iwan Rhys (1998) *Frankenstein's Children: Electricity, Exhibition and Experiment in Early Nineteenth-Century London*, Princeton, NJ: Princeton University Press.

Mràzek, Rudolf (1997) "Let Us Become Radio Mechanics: Technology and National Identity in Late-Colonial Netherlands East Indies," *Comparative Studies in Society and History* 39: 3–33.

Murdock, Graham (1997) "The Re-Enchantment of the World: Religion and the Transformation of Modernity," in Stewart M. Hoover and Knut Lundby (eds.) *Rethinking Media, Religion, and Culture*, Thousand Oaks, CA: Sage, pp. 85–101.

Nadis, Fred (2005) *Wonder Shows: Performing Science, Magic, and Religion in America*, New Brunswick, NJ: Rutgers University Press.

NCC (1993) "Violence in Electronic Media and Film," a policy statement approved by the General Board of the National Council of Churches in the USA, November 11, 1993; document 2, "The Church and Media: An NCC Policy Guide." On-line. Available. HTTP:// at www.ncccusa.organ/about/comcompolicies.html.

Nelson, Kristina (1993) "The Sound of the Divine in Daily Life," in Donna Lee Bowen and Evelyin Early (eds.) *Everyday Life in the Muslim Middle East*, Bloomington, IN: Indiana University Press, pp. 257–61.

—— ([1985] 2001) *The Art of Reciting of the Qur'an*, Cairo and New York: The American University in Cairo Press.

Noakes, Richard J. (2002) "'Instruments to Lay Hold of Spirits': Technologizing the Bodies of Victorian Spiritualism," in Iwan Rhys Morus (ed.) *Bodies/Machines*, Oxford: Berg, pp. 125–63.

Noble, David F. (1997) *The Religion of Technology: The Divinity of Man and the Spirit of Invention*, New York: Albert A. Knopf.

Nord, David Paul (1984) *The Evangelical Origins of Mass Media in America, 1815–1835*. Journalism Monographs, no. 88, Columbia, SC: Association for Education in Journalism and Mass Communication.

—— (2004) *Faith in Reading: Religious Publishing and the Birth of Mass Media in America*, Oxford: Oxford University Press.

—— (2007) "Free Grace, Free Books, Free Riders: The Economics of Religious Publishing in Early Nineteenth-century America," in Lynn Schofield Clarke (ed.) *Religion, Media and the Marketplace*, New Brunswick, NJ: Rutgers University Press, pp. 37–66.

Nye, David (1996) *American Technological Sublime*, Cambridge, MA: MIT Press.

Ollman, Bertel (1976) *Alienation: Marx's Conception of Man in Capitalist Society*, Cambridge: Cambridge University Press.

Ong, Walter J. 1981 [1967] *The Presence of the Word: Some Prolegomena for Cultural and Religious History*, Minneapolis, MN: University of Minnesota Press.

—— (1982) *Orality and Literacy: The Technologizing of the Word*, London: Methuen.

Oosterbaan, Martijn (2005) "Mass Mediating the Spiritual Battle: Pentecostal Appropriations of Mass Mediated Violence in Rio de Janeiro," *Material Religion* 1 (3): 358–85.

Orsi, Robert A. (2005) *Between Heaven and Earth: the Religious Worlds People Make and the Scholars Who Study Them*, Princeton, NJ: Princeton University Press.

Ortner, Sherry B. (1994) "Theory in Anthropology since the Sixties," in Nicholas B. Dirks, G. Eley and S.B. Ortner (eds.) *Culture/Power/History: A Reader in Contemporary Social Theory*, Princeton, NJ: Princeton University Press, pp. 372–411.

Parker, Everett C., David W. Barry and Dallas W. Smythe (1955) *The Television-Radio Audience and Religion*, New York: Harper & Brothers.

Parsons, Talcott (1966) *Societies: Evolutionary and Comparative Perspectives*, Englewood Cliffs, NJ: Prentice Hall.

Peters, John Durham (1999) *Speaking into the Air: A History of the Idea of Communication*, Chicago, IL: University of Chicago Press.

Peterson, Richard A. and N. Anand, (2004) "The Production of Culture Perspective," *Annual Review of Sociology* 30: 311–34.

Pietz, William (1985) "The Problem of the Fetish, I," *Res: Anthropology and Aesthetics* 9: 5–17.

Pike, Sarah M. (2001) *Earthly Bodies, Magical Selves: Contemporary Pagans and the Search for Community*, Berkeley, CA: University of California Press.

—— (2004) *New Age and Neopagan Religions in America*, New York: Columbia University Press.

—— (2005) "No Novenas for the Dead: Ritual Action and Communal Memory at the Temple of Tears," in *Afterburn: Reflections on Burning Man*, Albuquerque, NM: University of New Mexico Press.

Pinney, Christopher (2004) *"Photos of the Gods": The Printed Image and Political Struggle in India*, London: Reaktion.

Plate, S. Brent (2003) "Introduction: Film Making, Mythmaking, Culture Making," in Brent Plate (ed.) *Representing Religion in World Cinema: Film Making, Mythmaking, Culture Making*, New York: Palgrave, pp. 1–18.

—— (2005) *Walter Benjamin, Religion, and Aesthetics. Rethinking Religion through the Arts*, New York: Routledge.

Plato (1992) *Republic*, trans. G.M.A. Grube, revised by C.D.C. Reeve, Indianapolis, IN: Hackett Publishing Company.

Pritchett, Frances W. (1995) "The World of *Amar Chitra Katha*," in Lawrence A. Babb and Susan S. Wadley (eds.) *Media and the Transformation of Religion in South Asia*, Philadelphia, PA: University of Pennsylvania Press, pp. 76–106.

Propp, Vladimir (1928 [1968]) *Morphology of the Folktale*, 2nd edn trans. Lawrence Scott, Austin: University of Texas Press.

Pylyshyn, W. Zenon (2006) *Seeing and Visualizing. It's Not What You Think*, Cambridge, MA: The MIT Press.

Qureshi, Regula (2006) "Islam and Music," in Guy Beck (ed.) *Sacred Sound: Experiencing Music in World Religions*, Waterloo, Ontario: Wilfried Laurier University Press, pp. 89–112.

Radway, Janice A. (1984) *Reading the Romance: Women, Patriarchy, and Popular Literature*, Chapel Hill, NC: University of North Carolina Press.

Rajagopal, Arvind (2001) *Politics after Television: Hindu Nationalism and the Reshaping of the Public in India*, Cambridge: Cambridge University Press.

Real, Michael R. (1977) *Mass-Mediated Culture*, Englewood Cliffs, NJ: Prentice-Hall.

Reinders, Eric (1997) "The Iconoclasm of Obeisance: Protestant Images of Chinese Religion and the Catholic Church," *Numen* 44 (3): 296–322.

Roberts, Allen F. and Mary Nooter Roberts (2003) *A Saint in the City: Sufi Arts of Urban Senegal*, Los Angeles, CA: UCLA Fowler Museum of Cultural History.

Roof, Wade Clark (1999) *Spiritual Marketplace: Baby Boomers and the Remaking of American Religion*, Princeton, NJ: Princeton University Press.

Rosenthal, Michele (2007) *American Protestants and TV in the 1950s: Responses to a New Medium*, New York: Palgrave Macmillan.

Rothenbuhler, Eric W. (1998) *Ritual Communication: From Everyday Conversation to Mediated Ceremony*, Thousand Oaks, CA: Sage.

Rountree, Kathryn (2006) "Materializing Magical Power: Imagination, Agency and Intent in Feminist Witches' Rituals," in Elizabeth Arweck and William Keenan (eds.) *Materializing Religion: Expression, Performance and Ritual*, Aldershot: Ashgate Publishing, pp. 190–201.

Rushdie, Salman (1991 [1990]) *Haroun and the Sea of Stories*, London: Penguin.

Russolo, Luigi (1986) *The Art of Noises*, New York: Pendragon Press.

Sanchez, Rafael (2001) "Channel-Surfing: Media, Mediumship, and State Authority in the María Lionza Possession Cult (Venezuela)," in Hent de Vries and Samuel Weber (eds.) *Religion and Media*, Stanford, CA: Stanford University Press, pp. 388–434.

Sanders, Hannah E. (2005) "*Buffy* and Beyond: Language and Resistance in Contemporary Teenage Witchcraft," in *The Journal for the Study of Magic* 3: 25–60.

Sandler, Lauren (2006) *Righteous: Dispatches from the Evangelical Youth Movement*, New York: Viking.

Sanneh, Lamin (1991) *Translating the Message: The Missionary Impact on Culture*, Maryknoll, NY: Orbis Books.

Santino, Jack (ed.) (2006) *Spontaneous Shrines and the Public Memorialization of Death*, New York: Palgrave Macmillan.

Schafer, Murray R. (1977) *Our Sonic Environment and the Soundscape: The Tuning of the World*, Rochester, VT: Destiny Books.

—— (1985) "Acoustic Space," in David Seamon and Robert Mugerauer (eds.) *Dwelling, Place and Environment*, Dordrecht: M. Nijhoff, pp. 87–98.

Schatzki, Theodore R., Karin Knorr Cetina and Eike von Savigny (eds.) (2001) *The Practice Turn in Contemporary Theory*, London: Routledge.

Schmidt, Leigh E. (2000) *Hearing Things: Religion, Illusion, and the American Enlightenment*, Cambridge, MA: Harvard University Press.

Schultze, Quentin J. (2002) *Habits of the High-Tech Heart: Living Virtuously in the Information Age*, Grand Rapids, MI: Baker Academic.

—— (ed.) (1990) *American Evangelicals and the Mass Media*, Grand Rapids, MI: Zondervan.

Schulz, Dorothea (2001) *Perpetuating the Politics of Praise. Jeli Singers, Radios, and the Politics of Tradition in Mali*, Cologne: Ruediger Koeppe Verlag.

—— (2003) "Charisma and Brotherhood Revisited. Mass-mediated Forms of Spirituality in Urban Mali," *Journal of Religion in Africa* 33 (2): 146–71.

—— (2004) "Islamic Revival, Mass-mediated Religiosity, and the Moral Negotiation of Gender Relations in Urban Mali," Habilitation thesis, Free University, Berlin.

—— (2006) "Promises of (Im)mediate Salvation. Islam, Broadcast Media, and the Remaking of Religious Experience in Mali," *American Ethnologist* 33 (2): 210–29.

—— (2007) "Evoking Moral Community, Fragmenting Muslim Discourse. Sermon Audio-Recordings and the Reconfiguration of Public Debate in Mali," *Journal for Islamic Studies* 26: 39–71.

Schweizer, Hans Rudolf (1973) *Ästhetik als Philosophie der sinnlichen Erkenntnis. Eine Interpretation der Aesthetica A. G. Baumgartens mit teilweiser Wiedergabe des lateinischen Textes und deutscher Übersetzung*, Basel and Stuttgart: Schwabe & Co. Verlag.

Sconce, Jeffrey (2000) *Haunted Media: Electronic Presence from Telegraphy to Television*, Durham, NC: Duke University Press.

Scudder, John (1853) *Dr. Scudder's Tales for Little Readers, About the Heathen*, New York: American Tract Society.

Seaton, Jean (2005) *Carnage and the Media. The Making and Breaking of News about Violence*, London: Allen Lane, Penguin Books.

Sekula, Allan (1986) "The Body and the Archive," *October* 39: 3–65.

Senate Committee on the Judiciary (1999) "Children, Violence, and the Media: A Report for Parents and Policy Makers," Senate Committee on the Judiciary, Senator Orrin G. Hatch, Utah, Chairman, September 14, 1999.

Seppänen, Janne (2005) *The Power of the Gaze*, New York: Peter Lang.

Serres, Michel (1999) *La légende des anges*, Paris: Flammarion.

Shepherd, Gregory J. and Eric W. Rothenbuhler (eds.) (2001) *Communication and Community*, Mahwah, NJ: Lawrence Erlbaum Associates.

Shils, Edward (1975) "Center and Periphery," in Edward Shils, *Center and Periphery: Essays in Macrosociology*, Chicago, IL: University of Chicago Press, pp. 3–16.

Shusterman, Richard (2002) "Wittgenstein's Somaesthetics: Body Feeling in Philosophy of Mind, Art, and Ethics," *Revue internationale de philosophie* 219: 91–108.

Siefert, Marsha (1994) "The Audience at Home: Sound Recording and the Marketing of Musical Taste in the Early Twentieth Century," in D. Chuck Whitney and James S. Ettema (eds.) *Audiencemaking: Media Audiences as Industrial Process*, Beverly Hills, CA: Sage, pp. 186–214.

Silverstone, Roger (1981) *The Message of Television: Myth and Narrative in Contemporary Culture*, London: Heinemann.

Singh, Pashaura (2006) "Sikhism and Music," in Guy Beck (ed.) *Sacred Sound: Experiencing Music in World Religions*, Waterloo, Ontario: Wilfried Laurier University Press, pp. 141–68.

Smith, Adam (1776) *An Inquiry into the Nature and Causes of the Wealth of Nations*, London: W. Strahan and T. Cadell.

Smith, Bruce (1999) *The Acoustic World of Early Modern England*, Chicago, IL: University of Chicago Press.

Smith, Jonathan Z. (2004) *Relating Religion: Essays in the Study of Religion*, Chicago, IL: University of Chicago Press.

Smulyan, Susan (1994) *Selling Radio: The Commercialization of American Broadcasting, 1920–34*, Washington, D.C.: Smithsonian Institution Press.

Sobchack, Vivian (2004) *Carnal Thoughts: Embodiment and Moving Image Culture*, Berkeley, CA: University of California Press.

Sontag, Susan (2001) *Where the Stress Falls*, New York: Farrar, Strauss and Giroux.

—— (2003) *Regarding the Pain of Others*, New York: Farrar, Straus and Giroux.

—— (2004) "Regarding the Torture of Others," *The New York Times*, May 23, 2004.

Spigel, Lynn (1992) *Make Room for TV: Television and the Family Ideal in Postwar America*, Chicago, IL: University of Chicago Press.

Spitulnick, Deborah (1993) "Anthropology and the Mass Media," *Annual Review of Anthropology* 22: 293–315.

Spyer, Patricia (2006) "Media and Violence in an Age of Transparency: Journalistic Writing on War-Torn Maluku," in Birgit Meyer and Annelies Moors (eds.) *Religion, Media and the Public Sphere*, Bloomington, IN: Indiana University Press, pp. 152–65.

Sreberny-Mohammadi, Annabelle and Ali Mohammadi (1994) *Small Media, Big Revolution: Communication, Culture, and the Iranian Revolution*, Minneapolis, MN: University of Minnesota Press.

Steel, Ronald (1980) *Walter Lippmann and the American Century*, Boston, MA: Little, Brown and Co.

Stevenson, Nick (1995) *Understanding Media Cultures: Social Theory and Mass Communication*, London: Sage.

Stivers, Richard (2001) *Technology as Magic: The Triumph of the Irrational*, New York: Continuum Books.

Stock, Brian (1990) *Listening for the Text: On the Uses of the Past*, Philadelphia, PA: University of Pennsylvania Press.

Stolow, Jeremy (2005) "Religion and/as Media," *Theory, Culture & Society* 22 (4): 119–45.

—— (2006) "Communicating Authority, Consuming Tradition: Jewish Orthodox Outreach Literature and Its Reading Public," in Birgit Meyer and Annelies Moors (eds.) *Religion, Media, and the Public Sphere*, Bloomington, IN: Indiana University Press, pp. 73–90.

—— (2007) "Salvation by Electricity," in Hent de Vries (ed.) *Religion—Beyond a Concept*, New York: Fordham University Press, pp. 668–86.

—— (2007a) "Holy Pleather: Materializing Authority in Contemporary Orthodox Jewish Publishing," *Material Religion* 3 (3): 314–35.

Stout, Daniel A. and Buddenbaum, Judith M. (eds.) (1996) *Religion and Mass Media: Audiences and Adaptations*, Thousand Oaks, CA: Sage.

Stout, Harry S. (1977) "Religion, Communication, and the Ideological Origins of the American Revolution," *William and Mary Quarterly* 34: 519–41.

Street, Brian (1993) *Cross-cultural Approaches to Literacy*, Cambridge: Cambridge University Press.

Sturken, Marita and Lisa Cartwright (2005) *Practices of Looking: An Introduction to Visual Culture*, Oxford: Oxford University Press.

Styers, Randall (2004) *Making Magic: Religion, Magic, and Science in the Modern World*, Oxford and New York: Oxford University Press.

Sumiala-Seppänen, Johanna and Matteo Stocchetti (2005) "Mediated Sacralization and the Construction of Postmodern *Communio Sanctorum*: The Case of the Swedish Foreign Minister Anna Lindh," *Material Religion* 1 (2): 228–48.

—— (2007) "Rethinking the Visual Dimension of the Social," in Matteo Stocchetti and Johanna Sumiala-Seppänen (eds.) *Images and Communities: The Visual Construction of the Social*, Helsinki: Gaudeamus, Helsinki University Press.

Sumiala-Seppänen, Johanna, Knut Lundby and Raimo Salokangas (eds.) (2006) *Implications of the Sacred in (Post)Modern Media*, Göteborg: Nordicom.

Sutherland, John (1948) *Make Mine Freedom*, New York: Sutherland Productions, HTTP://www.archive.org/details/MakeMine1948 (accessed October 8, 2007).

Sutherland, John (1956) *Destination Earth*, New York: Sutherland Productions. HTTP://www.archive.org/details/Destinat1956 (accessed October 8, 2007).

Sweet, Leonard I. (ed.) (1993) *Communication & Change in American Religious History*, Grand Rapids, MI: Wm. B. Eerdmans.

Swidler, Ann (2001) "What Anchors Cultural Practices?" in Theodore R. Schatzki, Karin Knorr Cetina and Eike von Savigny (eds.) *The Practice Turn in Contemporary Theory*, New York: Routledge, pp. 74–92.

Szerszynski, Bronislaw (2005) *Nature, Technology and the Sacred*, Oxford: Blackwell.

Tambiah, Stanley Jeyaraja (1990) *Magic, Science, Religion, and the Scope of Rationality*, Cambridge: Cambridge University Press.

Taussig, Michael (1997) *The Magic of the State*, New York: Routledge.

Taylor, Charles (2002) *Varieties of Religion Today. William James Revisited*, Cambridge, MA: Harvard University Press.

Tayob, Abdulkader (1999) *Islam in South Africa: Mosques, Imams, and Sermons*, Gainesville, FL: University Press of Florida.

Ter Haar, Gerrie (1998) *Halfway to Paradise: African Churches in Europe*, Cardiff: Wales University Press.

Thomas, Pradip (2005) "Christian Fundamentalism and Media," *Media Development: Journal of the World Association for Christian Communication* 2: 3–8.

Thompson, Richard F. and Stephen A. Madigan (2005) *Memory: The Key to Consciousness*, Washington, DC: Joseph Henry Press.

Tim [no surname] (2007) "Tim's Cornerstone blog." Online. Available. HTTP:// cstone.blogspot.com/20060701archive.html.

Trott, Jon (2006) "Cornerstone Festival 2006 and the Fundamentalists." Online. Available.   HTTP://bluechristian.blogspot.com/2006/07/cornerstone-festival-2006-and.html.

Turner, Bryan S. (2007) "Religious Authority and the New Media," *Theory, Culture and Society* 24 (2): 117–34, 238.

Tweed, Thomas A. (2006) *Crossing and Dwelling: A Theory of Religion*, Cambridge, MA: Harvard University Press.

Tylor, Edward B. (1874) *Primitive Culture: Researches into the Development of Mythology, Philosophy, Religion, Art, and Custom*, 2 vols, Boston, MA: Estes & Lauriat.

Udesky, Laurie (2006) "A Matter of Respect: Training Hmong Shaman in the Ways of Western Medicine is Saving Lives in Merced," *The San Francisco Chronicle Magazine*, June 4: 8–11.

Ukah, Asonzeh, F-K. (2003) "Advertising God: Nigerian Christian Video-Films and the Power of Cosumer Culture," *Journal of Religion in Africa* 33 (2): 203–31.

Urban, Hugh B. (2003) "Sacred Capital: Pierre Bourdieu and the Study of Religion," *Method and Theory in the Study of Religion* 15 (4): 354–89.

USCL (United Society for Christian Literature) (1948) *One-hundred-and-forty-ninth Annual Report*, London: USCL.

Uys, Jamie, director (1980) *The Gods Must Be Crazy*, South Africa/Botswana: CAT Films, US release, 1984, distributed by Twentieth Century Fox.

Van de Port, Mattijs (2005) "Circling Around the *Really Real*: Spirit Possession Ceremonies and the Search for Authenticity in Bahian Candomblé," *Ethos* 33 (2): 149–79.

—— (2006) "Visualizing the Sacred: Video Technology, 'Televisual' Style and the Religious Imagination in Bahian Candomblé," *American Ethnologist* 33 (3): 444–62.

Van Dijk, Jan (1999) *The Network Society: Social Aspects of New Media*, Thousand Oaks, CA: Sage.

Van Loon, Joost (2005) "Medium-Force: Exploring the Efficacy of Combining McLuhan and Latour in Theorizing Digital Connectivity," unpublished paper in ECCR Panel "New Media Technologies," The first European Communication Conference in Amsterdam, November 2005.

Verrips, Jojada (2006) "Aisthesis & An-aesthesia," in Orvar Löfgren and Richard Wilk (eds.) *Off the Edge. Experiments in Cultural Analysis*, Copenhagen: Museum Tusculanum Press, pp. 29–37.

—— (2008) "Offending Art and The Sense of Touch," *Material Religion* 4 (2): forthcoming.

Viveiros de Castro, Eduardo (1998) "Cosmological Deixis and Amerindian Perspectivism," *Journal of the Royal Anthropological Institute* 4 (3): 469–88.

Waggoner, Matt (2004) "Reflections from a Damaged Discipline: Adorno, Religious Radio, and the Critique of Historical Reason," *Culture and Religion* 5 (1): 23–40.

Warner, Michael (2002) "Publics and Counterpublics," *Public Culture* 14 (1): 49–90.

Warner, R. Stephen (1993) "Work in Progress toward a New Paradigm for the Sociological Study of Religion in the United States," *American Journal of Sociology* 98 (5): 1044–93.

Watts, Newman (1934) *The Romance of Tract Distribution*, London: Religious Tract Society.

Weber, Max (1958) *The Protestant Ethic and the Spirit of Capitalism*, trans. Talcott Parsons, New York: Scribner's.

Webster, Charles (1982) *From Paracelsus to Newton: Magic and the Making of Modern Science*, Cambridge: Cambridge University Press.

West, Gerald (1999) *The Academy of the Poor: Toward a Dialogical Reading of the Bible*, Sheffield: Sheffield Academic Press.

White, Robert (1981) "Television's Influence on Cultures," *Communication Research Trends* 2 (3): 1–8.

—— (1983) "Mass Communication and Culture: Transition to a New Paradigm," *Journal of Communication* 33 (3): 279–97, 300–1.

—— (1994) "Audience 'Interpretation' of Media: Emerging Perspectives," *Communication Research Trends* 14 (3): 5–29.

—— (2003) "The Emerging 'Communitarian' Ethics of Public Communication," in Jolyon Mitchell and Sophia Marriage (eds.) *Mediating Religion: Conversations in Media, Religion and Culture*, London: T&T Clark, pp. 285–92.

Whitehouse, Harvey (2000) *Arguments and Icons: Divergent Modes of Religiosity*, Oxford: Oxford University Press.

Wiegele, Katharine L. (2005) *Investing in Miracles. El Shaddai and the Transformation of Popular Catholicism*, Honolulu, HI: University of Hawai'i Press.

Williams, Peter W. (1980) *Popular Religion in America: Symbolic Change and the Modernization Process in Historical Perspective*, Englewood Cliffs, NJ: Prentice-Hall.

Williams, Raymond (1985 [1976]) *Keywords: A Vocabulary of Culture and Society*, New York: Oxford University Press.

—— (1995 [1981]) *The Sociology of Culture*, Chicago, IL: University of Chicago Press.

Williams, Rhys H. (2007) "The Languages of the Public Sphere: Religious Pluralism, Institutional Logics, and Civil Society," *The Annals of the American Academy of Political and Social Science* 612 (1): 42–61.

Winston, Diane (1999) *Red-Hot and Righteous: The Urban Religion of the Salvation Army*, Cambridge, MA: Harvard University Press.

Wittgenstein, Ludwig (1958) *Philosophical Investigations*, Oxford: Blackwell.

Wolin, Richard (ed.) (1992) *The Heidegger Controversy: A Critical Reader*, Cambridge, MA: MIT Press.

Wright, Bonnie (1989) "The Power of Articulation," in W. Arens and Ivan Karp (eds.) *Creativity of Power: Cosmology and Action in African Societies*, Washington, DC and London: Smithsonian Institution Press, pp. 39–58.

Wuthnow, Robert (2003) *All in Sync: How Music and the Arts are Revitalizing American Religion*, Berkeley, CA: University of California Press.

Young, Alison (2005) *Judging the Image. Art, Value, Law*, London: Routledge.

Young, Tara (2004) "The Art of the Funeral: Memorial T-shirts Are Fast Becoming Funeral Folk Art," *The Times-Picayune*, February 15. Online. Available. HTTP://www.nola.com/speced/cycleofdeath/index.ssf?/speced/cycleofdeath/artoffuneral.html.

Zahan, Dominique (1963) *La dialectique du verbe chez les Bambara*, Paris: Mouton.

Zuckerkand, Victor (1956) *Sound and Symbol: Music and the External World*, Princeton, NJ: Princeton University Press.

Zito, Angela (2007) "Can Television Mediate Religious Experience? The Theology of Joan of Arcadia," in Hent de Vries (ed.) *Religion: Beyond the Concept*, New York: Fordham University Press, pp. 724–38.

—— (2008) "Religion as Media(tion)," in Bradford Verter and Johannes Wolfart (eds.) *Rethinking Religion 101: Critical Issues in Religious Studies*, New York: Cambridge University Press.

Zoba, Wendy (2000) *Days of Reckoning: Columbine and the Search for America's Soul*, Grand Rapids, MI: Brazos Press.

Index